Unlocking the Profits of the New Swing Chart Method

Unlocking the Profits

of the

New Swing Chart Method

Jeff Cooper
&
David Reif, CMT

Marketplace Books
Columbia, Maryland

This book, along with other books, is available at discounts that make it realistic to provide them as gifts to your customers, clients, and staff. For more information on these long lasting, cost effective premiums, please call us at 800-272-2855 or e-mail us at sales@traderslibrary.com.

ISBN 1-59280-291-5

Printed in the United States of America.

1 2 3 4 5 6 7 8 9 0

Table of Contents

About the Presenters

Jeff Cooper began his trading career in 1981 at Drexel Burnham working for his father, a hedge fund manager. Jeff left Drexel Burnham in 1986, choosing to trade exclusively for himself. After establishing a successful career as a private trader, he went on to write two best selling books on the subject: *Hit & Run I* and *Hit & Run II*.

In addition to his books, Jeff has also released a video course, *Jeff Cooper on Dominating the Day Trading Market*, where he teaches viewers exactly what it takes to trade full time for a living.

Today, Jeff still trades for himself from his home overlooking the Pacific Ocean in Malibu California.

David C. Reif, CMT, founder of Mutual MoneyFlow Management, graduated from the U.S Naval Academy in 1963. Mr. Reif began his investment career with Merrill Lynch in Tulsa, Oklahoma in late 1973. He also passed the Certified Financial Planner test, becoming one of the first one thousand applicants to receive the CFP designation.

In 1993, he received the Chartered Market Technician designation (CMT) from the Market Technicians Association, becoming one of the first one hundred applicants to receive this designation in the world and the first in the state of Oklahoma. Mr. Reif is fluent in almost every discipline of technical analysis from A waves to the Zig Zag, but favors W.D. Gann's work more than any other discipline. His studies in this area led to the creation of the Reif Swing Chart Method of technical analysis.

Introduction

We are pleased that you have joined us in this informative and entertaining course presentation on the seemingly complex principles of the True Swing Chart Method. See how the presenters, Jeff Cooper and Dave Reif, took the work of W.D. Gann a critical step further…adding new dimension to his body of work that makes for a more reliable and accurate trading tool for twenty first century investors. In this edited and polished version of a live course sponsored by Marketplace Books and Traders Library, witness the emergence of clear and predictable market patterns from what may have earlier been considered random, or even chaotic, market activity.

See the complex become simple, and use it for your trading advantage!

Before you view the very substantive material in this course, it will help to understand some of the premises upon which it is based. Dave Reif and Jeff Cooper have thoroughly researched W.D. Gann's age-old strategies and have found some unique ways to apply them…particularly with the concepts of True Swing Chart Trading. Although many traders refer to swing trading, the True Swing Chart Method is a unified market theory that relates swings in both price and time.

Traditional Gann Swing Charts show highs and lows, but have no reference to time. They are constructed with vertical lines that track the range of the swing and horizontal lines that show the high and low of the swing… yet they have limitations. The visibility of a trend using this method is highly respected, however, it is impossible to determine the velocity of the trend as it does not show if the trend has been in place for a day, a week, or a month. Using this new, unprecedented, and multi-dimensional approach described by Reif and Cooper, you can now see the clarity the swing charts provide with the entry and exit power of the time value of these trends.

The charts you will see reflect the "wheels" of price moving through time. As you will see in the many examples in this course, these wheels will act like gears in a machine, with many smaller gears or wheels turning the larger wheels. The wheels will appear as:

- the daily, represented by each candle,
- the weekly, shown as the first box around the candle,
- the monthly, the next box moving outward encompassing 4 weekly "wheels",
- the quarterly which encloses 3 monthly "wheels",

Throughout the presentation, Reif and Cooper will refer to the wheels in a number of ways. We have put together some simple definitions for a few of the key terms they use, to help make the information more accessible, and also realize that these definitions, as well as the overall course, is not a "quick study". *The key terms:*

Inside bar: A period where the lowest low is higher than the low of the previous period, and the highest high is lower than the high of the previous period. Essentially the range of the previous period is greater than that of this period.

Outside bar: A period where the highest high is higher than that of the previous period and the lowest low is lower than that of the previous period.

Inside down day: This occurs when a down inside bar, for example a weekly bar, has turned and has taken out the prior day's low and the next week is inside the range of the previous bar.

Up inside day: The wheel, or weekly bar, for example, has turned up and the next week, or wheel, trades inside that range.

NR7: The narrowest range in a series of seven. It could be a daily, weekly, or monthly pattern. Searching groups of seven has proven to be the most successful in the research conducted by the presenters.

Real Accumulation Day or RAD: The 50 day average volatility on the Reif AVX tells you what the average daily range from the prior days close is over the last 50 days. That then tells you what number the price has to go up or down from. If it goes up and the volume is greater than the 50 day volume average, it is a RAD, or real accumulation day.

Real Distribution Day or RDD: If on the other hand, the price is down and greater than the 50 average volatility, the change in the close is greater than the 50 day average volatility and the volume is greater than the 50 day average volume… you get a RDD, or a real distribution day.

Tops & Bottoms: The trend line indicator only changes direction when we have an opposite day to the trend. That is on a down day in an uptrend or on an up day during a down trend. This doesn't necessarily mean we've made a top or bottom. A top or bottom is not declared until the reversal takes out the previous opposite swing peak.

Trends: Swing charts clearly identify trends in the market, removing noise that might normally hide them. A trend is determined by progressive swings in the same direction.

Entry Points: If the trend is up (signalled by consecutive swing points progressively higher), a buy signal is generated when a new high is made following a swing bottom.

Sell Signal: Conversely, a sell signal is made during a down-trend when a new low is made immediately after a swing top. New sell signals are made when we have a reversal followed by a new low. The sell signal is made as we see the new low

During the course you will also hear many references to various principles, including…Fractals, Squares, Reflexivity, and Tests. *The principles:*

Fractals - Patterns on the same time frame or another time frame will repeat or mirror image themselves.

Squares - Rather than a linear method, it is a way to chart stocks on a square root progression.

Reflexivity - When a wheel turns up you frequently get a quick turn back, or the reflex of the market.

Tests - The market almost always gives a graceful exit, whether at a top to get out… or a bottom to get in. Highs and lows are almost always tested and breakout points often see a knee jerk pullback

In addition to these key terms and principles, there is a full explanation of the approach outlined in Appendix A at the end of this book. To make sure you get the most out of this course, you are encouraged to review all of this material before beginning with the first DVD.

It is also useful to review the Swing Chart Plotting Rules included in that appendix, which is used for these examples. Understanding the exact guidelines used for creating these examples will make it much easier for you to apply these same strategies to other products and markets

The course begins with an introduction to the True Swing Chart Method and examples of its predictive power over a backdrop of the markets during the last century. By using the Dow Jones Industrial Average, S&P 500, as well as individual stocks, Reif and Cooper will show you how the True Swing Chart Method signals are discovered, and how to best exploit the set ups they precede.

Now, have this book available as reference, as you join us in this invaluable DVD course presentation. We trust you will benefit from the course, and will find immeasurable value in the practical and reliable guidelines, definitions, principles, and strategies offered.

Unlocking the Profits of the New Swing Chart Method has been developed by Dave Reif and Jeff Cooper, and sponsored and published by Marketplace books, in conjunction with Traders Library. Visit us on the web at www.traderslibrary. com , and feel free to contact us.

(DJ-30) Dow Jones Indust-Daily 05/06/2005 C=10345.400 +5.020 +0.05% O=10377.550 H=10454.400 L=10300.700 V=22891 -1 Quarterly Synthet(12,0)

This Chart Shows the Weekly, Monthly and Quarterly Wheels of Price moving through time. It is very important to know where you are on all of these wheels BEFORE you enter a trade.

The plot of the action is important but the most important information is learned by observing the BEHAVIOR of price when the plots of the individual wheels turn up or down.

In addition, the patterns formed by the plotted action provide clues on what to expect prices to do in future periods.

Created with TradeStation 2000i by Omega Research © 1999

PAGE 4

Unlocking the Profits of the New Swing Chart Method

CHART 1

This is the first chart that you have ever seen that demonstrates what we call True Swing Charts. There is a big difference between what many traders refer to as swing charts and True Swing Charts. One has to do with absolute prices while True Swing Charts revolve around highs and lows made within daily, weekly, monthly, quarterly, and yearly time frames.

Notice what happens in the line consolidation prior to the top in 1929. There is what we call rapid flipping of the weekly chart as it turns up and down. Such action often precedes a momentum move one way or the other—sometimes ultimately in both directions as was the outcome here eventually.

(A) The week before label A gave an outside week to the downside and one would have expected follow-through to the downside. Instead, as label A shows, the weekly plotted marginally lower and turned back up immediately leaving an outside week up. This is called a Slingshot. Fast moves come from failed moves and in this case the failed downside move leads to the 'whoop 'em up' into the Sept. '29 high

(B) Label B shows an outside week down—a large range outside week down—after the fast run suggesting a pull back. After a +1,-2 pattern you'd expect a turn-up in the weekly chart...especially after a down inside week. The market is always talking and the failure to turn back up on the heels of a fast run is a bearish warning.

(C) Consequently, the next wheel of time turns down—the monthly wheel. The monthly turns down with the quarterly chart turning down days later. There are two principals to note here, the concept that many of the turns on the big wheels of time occur at the beginning of the month and the concept of Reflexivity, which means that after a big wheel of time turns there is most often a reflex bounce.

(D) Note how the weekly chart turns up but dies and rolls over. This is classic bearish behavior. It is not the turn up in and of itself that indicates bearish behavior to follow but rather the behavior after the turn-up that counts which confirms a bearish bias. Bearishly the weekly chart turns immediately back down while trading back through the level where the quarterly chart turned down at C, which is the "Sign of the Bear" suggesting potentially significantly lower price. It is important to also point out the concept that many times, but not always, the market gives a graceful exit. The turn-up of the weekly chart to the scene of the crime where the bodies were buried at D is an example of this behavior.

(E) The Dow traced out a down inside month and we have learned that most down inside months lead to a turn up in the monthly chart and that is what occurs. Here again the end and beginning of the month, quarter and the year are high probability times for turn-ups and turn-downs.

NOTES

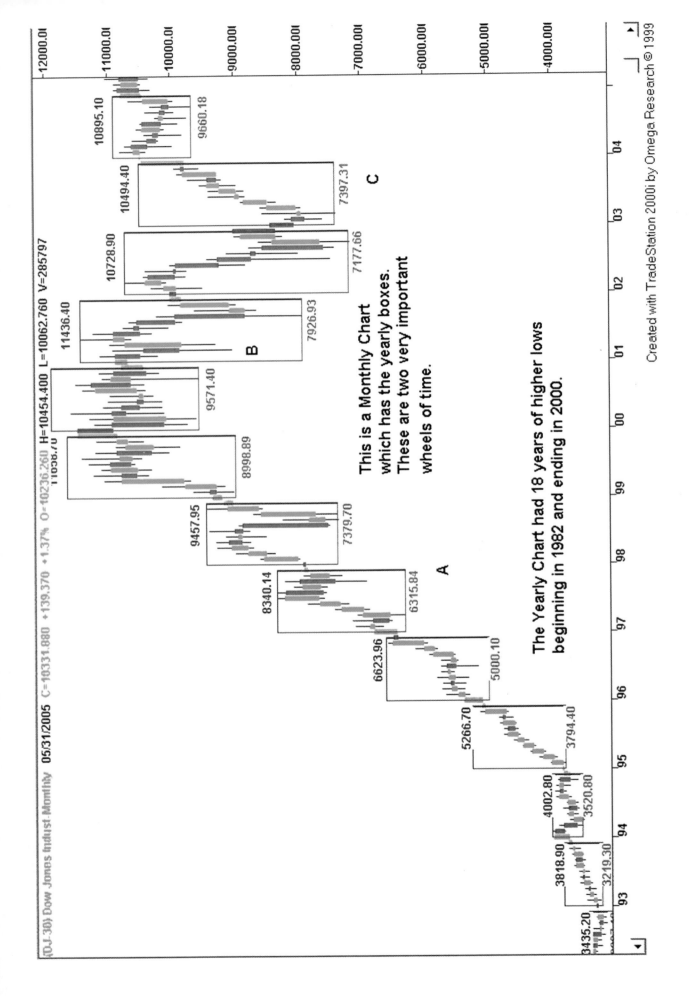

(DJ-30) Dow Jones Indust-Monthly   05/31/2005   C=10331.880 +139.370 +1.37% O=10236.260   H=10454.400   L=10062.760   V=285797

This is a Monthly Chart which has the yearly boxes. These are two very important wheels of time.

The Yearly Chart had 18 years of higher lows beginning in 1982 and ending in 2000.

Created with TradeStation 2000i by Omega Research © 1999

Unlocking the Profits of the New Swing Chart Method   PAGE 6

CHART 1A

(A) Label A demonstrates that the yearly chart can plot higher for many years in a row. There is a propensity for price movement in the markets to play out over threes and sevens. Note after the expansion of range in 1995 that the Dow continued to make higher highs and higher lows on the yearly chart only to reverse on the 7th year up.

(B) Note when the monthly chart turned down in 2001, the reflex action gave a -1 +2 signal.

(C) Label C shows 1-2-3 year pullback which is a +1 -2 on the yearly chart indicating a turn-up in the yearly chart is a good bet which occurs in January '04. 2003 is also a down inside year which gives us another reason to expect the yearly chart to turn up. Note the first pullback on the monthly chart is approximately 7 bars as the pullback finds low near the bottom of the range of the high of the December long range bar. That approximately 7 month Pullback after the yearly chart turned up offered a 'graceful' or "second mouse" entry.

NOTES

TradeStation Chart - (DJ-30) Dow Jones Indust-Daily

(DJ-30) Dow Jones Indust-Daily 12/30/1932 C=60.300 +1.200 +2.03% O=59.100 H=60.800 L=58.800 V=105

Weekly Wheel

390.000
380.000
370.000
360.000
350.000
340.000
330.000
320.000

Created with TradeStation 2000i by Omega Research © 1999

Unlocking the Profits of the New Swing Chart Method   PAGE 8

CHART 2

(A) The weekly was going down and then 2-plotted up. Then it 2-plotted back down. Then the weekly chart once again turned up. This is a good example of what happens when the market does not do what you expect it to do. The expectation when the weekly 2-plotted back down leaving a sling shot sell pattern was for a decline. However, the immediate plot back up leaving 5 plots in 3 bars was a double sling shot and led to the blow-off of the 1920's bull market, a move of 14.8% in one month. This was a classic 'whoop-um-up' pattern.

(B) Note the outside down day and the outside down week at the top. Also note the -1 + 2 sell set up on the dailies. When the weekly chart takes out the breakout bar from the line formation prior to the top a Boomerang sell signal is triggered. Note the failure of the daily sell boomerang in the line formation to generate downside traction led to the blow-off top...a mirror image fractal of the sell boomerang weekly pattern that led to the crash of '29.

NOTES

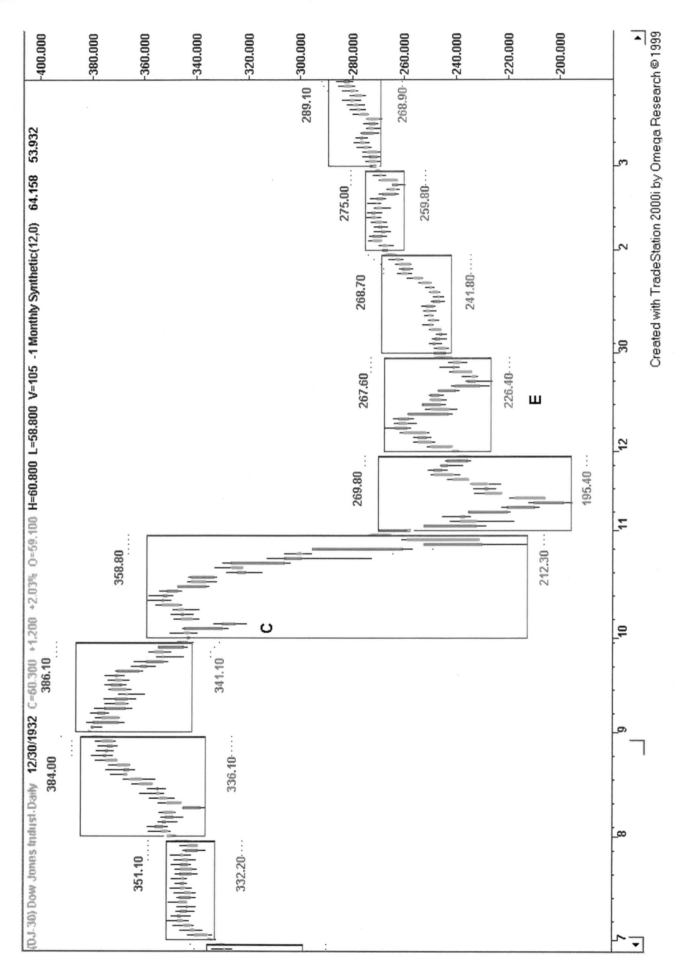

(DJ-30) Dow Jones Indust.Daily 12/30/1932 C=60.300 +1.200 +2.03% O=59.100 H=60.800 L=58.800 V=105 -1 Monthly Synthetic(12,0) 64.158 53.932

Created with TradeStation 2000i by Omega Research©1999

384.00
386.10
351.10
358.80
341.10
336.10
332.20

C

269.80
267.60
268.70
275.00
289.10

212.30
195.40
226.40
241.80
259.80
268.90

E

CHART 3

Chart # 3 is a picture of daily bars defined by monthly boxes.

(C) Label (C) shows the monthly turn down and how the Dow found, as would be expected, a low within a few days. The important thing to note is that all that occurs is a reflex bounce with a roll over on the 7th day. The market has a memory: look how the Dow breaks below the low made after the monthly turn down on a gap. That should put you on your heels: a defensive posture must be adopted at this juncture. Remember that one might expect just a reflex bounce rather than a continuation of the up-trend when the monthly chart turned down because of the outside down large range reversal week at the September high. When the daily turns up, into the gap down (in Oct.), and the market rolls over immediately the nail is in the coffin.

(E) December is a down inside month and this leads to an up move into April 1930.

NOTES

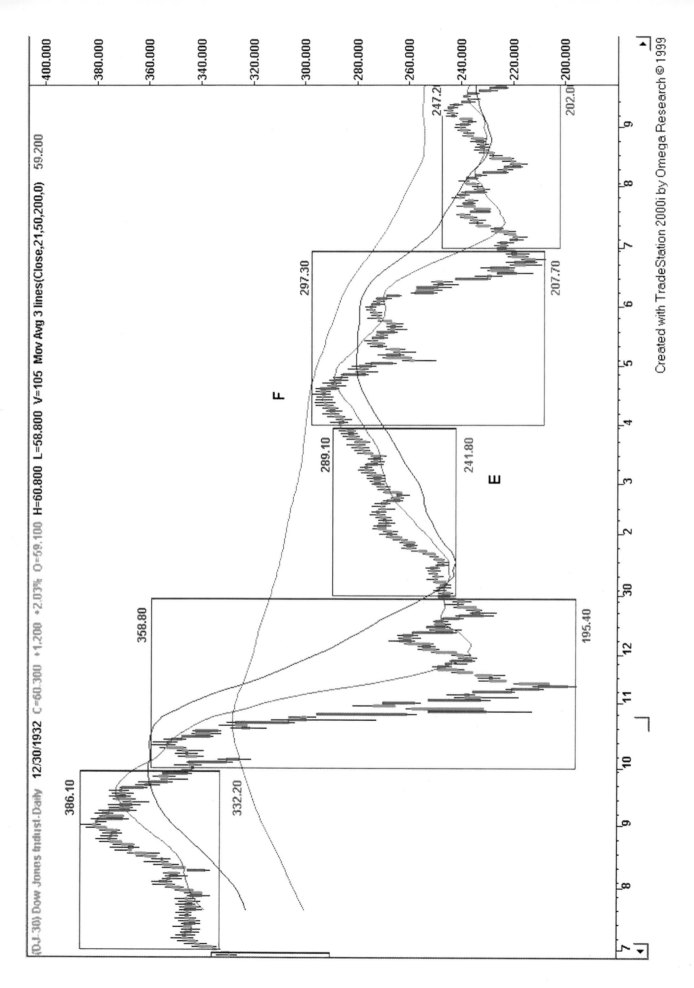

(DJ-30) Dow Jones Indust-Daily   12/30/1932   C=60.300   +1.200 +2.03%   O=59.100   H=60.800   L=58.800   V=105   Mov Avg 3 lines(Close,21,50,200,0)   59.200

Created with TradeStation 2000i by Omega Research © 1999

—— Unlocking the Profits of the New Swing Chart Method   ——   **PAGE 12**

CHART 4

This chart is a daily chart with quarterly boxes.

(E) Shows a down inside quarter. The expectation would be for a turn up on the quarterly and that is what occurs early in the next quarter at F.

(F) However, momentum dies and the price action begins to roll over. Note the bearish behavior and the sharp angle of attack to the downside on the dailies. Note now the Dow died at its 200 day moving average before rolling over. The other moving averages are the 50 DMA and the 21 DMA. Note how the Dow rolled over after approaching its 50 DMA in June 1930. Note that the rest of the 1929 low occurred at the end of the year tracing out a Sherlock's Pipe Pattern. Putting the pieces together, moving averages and the behavior of True Swing Charts will help determine the trend and define a trading edge. Note how the first bounce off the low is contained by the 50DMA.

NOTES

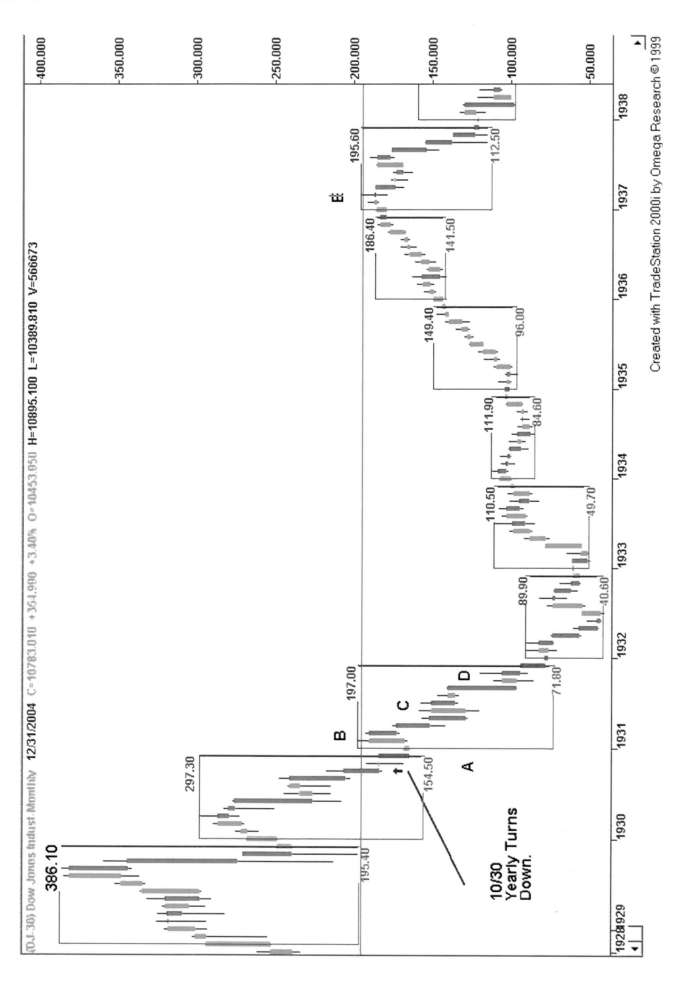

(DJ-30) Dow Jones Indust-Monthly 12/31/2004 C=10783.010 +354.990 +3.40% O=10453.050 H=10895.100 L=10389.810 V=566673

386.10

297.30

195.40

154.50

197.00

B

C

D

A

10/30
Yearly Turns
Down.

71.80

89.90

40.60

110.50

49.70

111.90

84.60

149.40

96.00

186.40

141.50

E

195.60

112.50

1928 1929 1930 1931 1932 1933 1934 1935 1936 1937 1938

400.000
350.000
300.000
250.000
200.000
150.000
100.000
50.000

Created with TradeStation 2000i by Omega Research © 1999

Unlocking the Profits of the New Swing Chart Method   PAGE 14

CHART 5

This chart shows monthly bars in yearly boxes.

(A) Label (A) shows that in Oct.1930 the yearly chart turns down and plots lower for two more months. The subsequent action shows a reflex bounce back to the 1929 lows over the next two months.

(B) Label (B) represents the turn up in the monthly chart. The important thing to understand is the behavior after the monthly chart turned up: the Dow was unable to advance higher than that turn up bar and the price action was contained by the level where the yearly chart turned down which is represented by the horizontal red line across the chart. Moreover, an up inside month is traced out and the expectation is for it to turn down.

(C) Label (C) marks another monthly turn up and an up inside month that defines continued bearish behavior. When the trend is bearish on whatever time scale, the market, or stock, will stall out and be unable to make much progress on the Turn Up in True Swing Chart Theory. The opposite of course, also applies: when the trend is bullish turndowns in the various time frames will typically define buying opportunities. At label (C) the market was talking when it didn't follow thru to the upside as the monthly turned up.

(D) Label (D) shows the result when the market fails to gain traction on the previous turn up: the Dow comes down in spades. From the 1929 high to the 1932 low The True Monthly Swing Chart shows 5 Turn ups each which fail to generate a meaningful advance...each which simply define a breathing point or pause in the persistent downtrend. This behavior is similar to the Bear trend after the 2000 blow-off top and the persistent decline through 2001 and 2002.

(E) Label (E) represents a 2-plot year down signaling that the rally was over. The second half of the Bear Market was about to ensue. Note that the level of the 1937 top is in the vicinity of the level where the Yearly Chart turned down in 1930. The market has a memory. Note also how this same level represents approximately 50% of the level of the 1929 high.

1933 shows a turn up in the yearly chart and the ability of the market and the chart to plot higher is constructive action signaling stocks are in rally mode. Note how the Dow pulls back in 1934 to give a second chance. Note how well the decline is contained.

NOTES

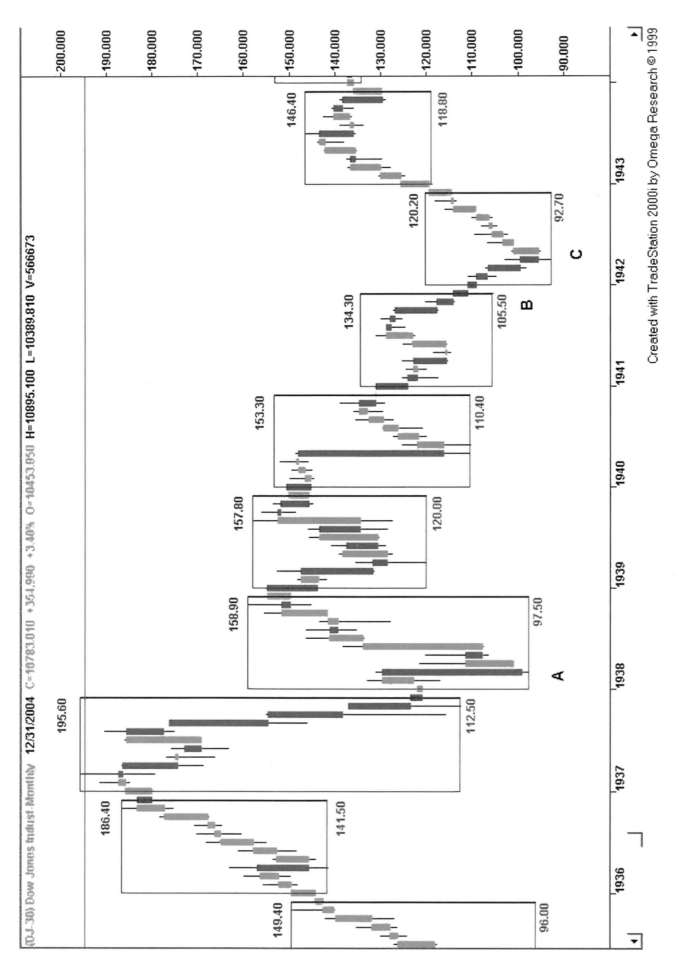

(DJ-30) Dow Jones Indust-Monthly 12/31/2004 C=10783.010 +354.990 +3.40% O=10453.050 H=10895.100 L=10389.810 V=566673

Created with TradeStation 2000i by Omega Research © 1999

Unlocking the Profits of the New Swing Chart Method   PAGE 16

CHART 6

Chart # 6 is another monthly chart with yearly boxes.

(A) Label (A) shows two years down after the 1937 top. It's always a good idea to look for a buy set up after two lower lows on the yearly chart. This set up presents itself as the Dow carves out two inside months putting in "time on the side." Down inside monthlies turn up most of the time and that is what occurs here as the Dow continues higher for seven months from the turn-up. Importantly the big yearly wheel of time does NOT turn up---close but no cigar. It is amazing how many times turn ups or turn downs miss occurring marginally and how many times turn downs and turn ups occur on the big wheels that define highs or lows within a few points or within a few days. This is very important behavior to observe. This behavior underscores that the market has its own internal clock and that the action of the Wheels of Time are not happenstance.

(B) Label (B) shows that the yearly chart has not plotted for almost 4 years.

(C) Note how when the yearly chart plots lower in 1942 than point A, that a low is scored within two months. The Dow 'soups' or undercuts briefly the low at point A and then goes inside for one month tracing out a potentially bullish down inside set up. This big monthly swing undercut puts the final low in for the Bear market, time wise, from the 1929 top. It was a very important period of 14 years (7X2). It is also interesting to note that from point A to point C represents 49 (7 squared) months indicating a possible turning point and change in trend. 1942 was also the first higher ringed low on the yearly swing chart.

NOTES

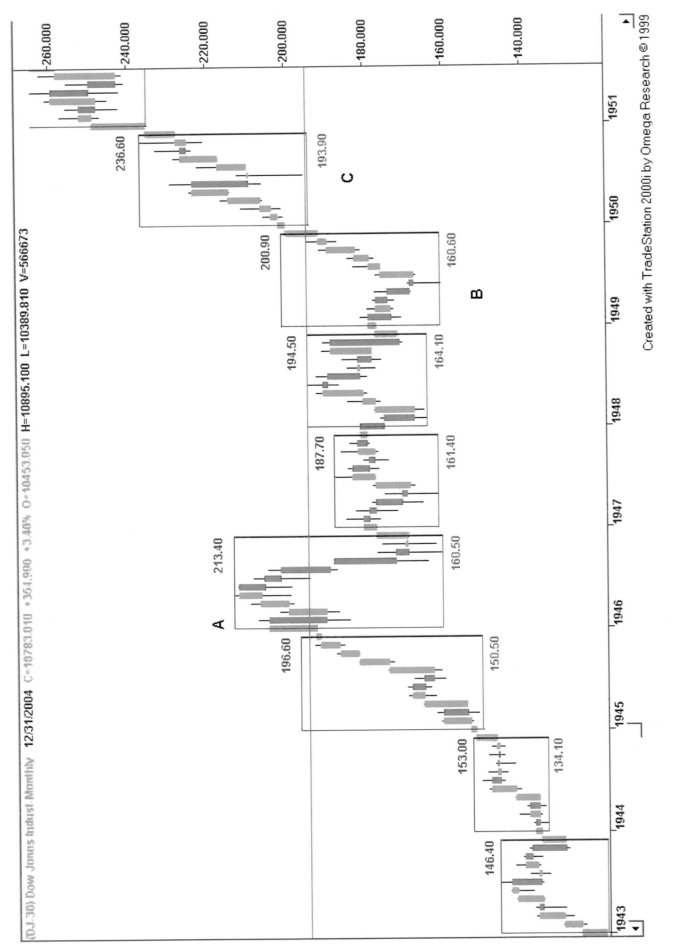

(DJ-30) Dow Jones Indust Monthly   12/31/2004   C=10783.010   +354.990   +3.40%   O=10453.050   H=10895.100   L=10389.810   V=566673

Created with TradeStation 2000i by Omega Research © 1999

— Unlocking the Profits of the New Swing Chart Method |

CHART 7

The important thing to understand about Chart #7 is that a long period of advance--4 years-- followed the yearly turn up in 1943. The clue to the 77% rally over 4 years was the turn up that HELD and plotted higher. The long period of not plotting higher on the yearly chart was followed by a long period of advance. Note that there was no immediate reflex pullback on the monthly chart after the 1943 yearly turn up but that the first pullback that did occur later in the year was a buying opportunity defined by a down inside month. Note the end of year turning point.

(A) Label (A) shows how the N/R (narrow range) 7 month in Nov. 1944, indicating the coming volatility move in 1945. Label (A) also demonstrates how the outside down month in Feb. which signaled the expectation for lower prices first saw a 3 month 'squeeze play' into the May top. The outside down month was a caution flag and the subsequent rally offered a graceful exit. Note how this graceful exit occurred at the 50% level off the 1929 high. Note how when the Dow traded back below the outside down 'signal bar' it stayed down for 3 years. Why is the move up in 1948 not a turn-up in the yearly chart? This is key to understanding the whole concept. The answer is because the yearly chart was up inside. It had never turned DOWN.

(B) Label (B) shows where the yearly chart actually does turn down and interestingly enough, a low is made immediately. Note the 'tail' month in June. We've seen this pattern before. June undercuts the prior price lows marginally but sees no downside follow thru. This yearly turndown in 1949 is a successful test of the sharp waterfall decline in 1946 and is a good example of how The Principle of Tests plays out. Label (B) also reflects the outside up year in 1949. Again note how the turn up occurs at the end of the year. The curve ball is that price did not make a new 'swing low' from the last high bar to below the 'swing low' of 1946 in terms of how most people look at swings and swing charts. However, in terms of True Swing Chart Theory and how we look at the True Trendline or a True Swing Chart, a low was generated on the turn down in the yearly chart even though the swing down held the 1946 low by 10 cents. This helps define the whole concept of True Swing Chart Theory. You would expect a low to be confirmed by the outside up year and you get it. Note, the behavior of the price action as it plots higher. A second chance, a graceful entry, comes as the red line denoting the 50% level off the 1929 all time high is tagged testing the highs of the prior three years in the process. The market has its own DNA, its own internal time and price clock.

(C) Label (C) shows this test of the red line after the outside down month of June 1950 which also leaves a bullish + 1 - 2 set up.

NOTES

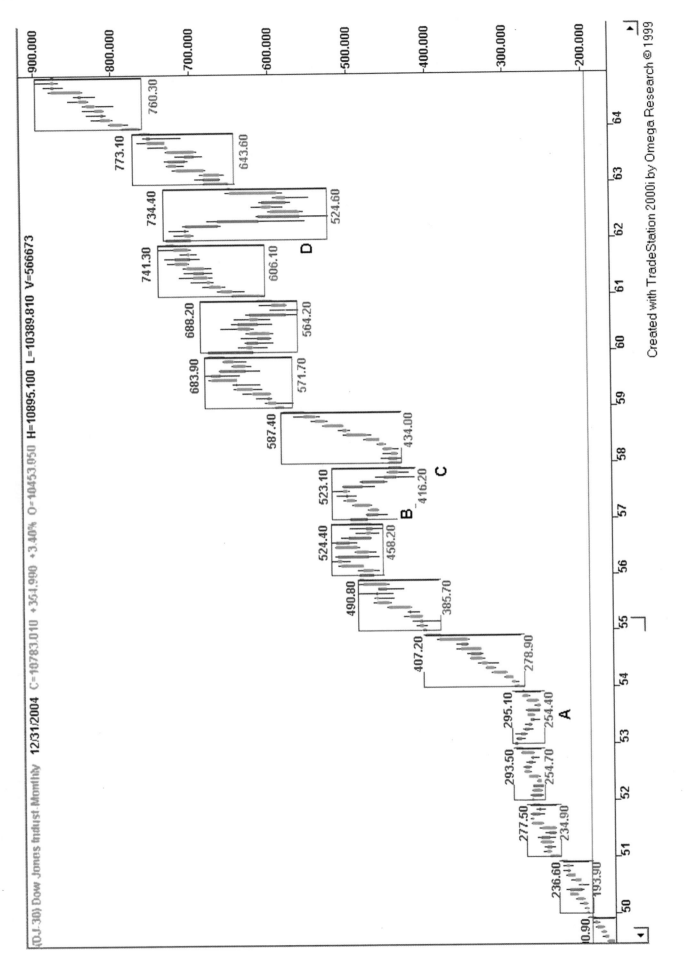

(DJ-30) Dow Jones Indust-Monthly 12/31/2004 C=10783.010 +354.990 +3.40% O=10453.050 H=10895.100 L=10389.810 V=566673

Created with TradeStation 2000i by Omega Research © 1999

PAGE 20

Unlocking the Profits of the New Swing Chart Method

CHART 8

Chart # 8 is another monthly chart with yearly boxes.

(A) Label (A) shows the outside down year in 1953. Note how the low after the turndown was made by only 30 cents. The outside down year does not generate a decline. Consequently, when the yearly chart turns back up the Dow accelerates. This is a "Y" up or Sling Shot pattern. (3 plots in 2 bars)

(B) Label (B) shows a turndown in the yearly which makes low immediately. A down inside month is traced out which brings a test of the highs. This shows a reflex rally on the smaller monthly wheel of time after the bigger yearly wheel turned down. After 2 to 3 years of strong rally you would expect a tail month at a test of the high, which occurs in July 1957. The market then resumes its decline completing an ABC correction in October.

(C) Label (C) shows a down inside month and some time on the side after the three month decline. The compression led to a turn up in the yearly which bullishly kept going.

In 1960 the Dow gave a two-plot year down which, bullishly, did not lead to further weakness but was a warning flag as we have seen before. Despite the fact that the yearly turned up again there is no real momentum and the sharp break on the monthly chart in April suggests the possibility of a test or turndown of the yearly as the yearly low is not that far away.

(D) Label (D) shows that the yearly chart did in fact turn down. Note how the three big red bars down echo the pattern of five years earlier in 1957. Note, the down inside month at the low in 1962 followed by a turn-up that dies and then the second mouse signal when the monthly turns back up strongly as the Dow keeps going.

NOTES

(DJ-30) Dow Jones Indust-Monthly 12/29/1978 C=805.000 +6.000 +0.75% O=805.700 H=829.900 L=781.000 V=49244

1026.30
1007.80
792.80
888.90
848.60
619.10
570.00
904.00
1042.40
783.60
883.40
958.10
848.20
790.70
627.50
974.90
994.70
764.50
817.60
951.60
776.20
735.70
1001.10
976.60
832.70
897.00
760.30
773.10
643.60
741.30 734.40
524.60
606.10
588.20
564.20
683.90
571.70
587.40
434.00
523.10
416.20
524.40
458.20
490.80
385.70
20

3
2
1
X

1975
1970
1965
1960
1955

1000.00
900.000
800.000
700.000
600.000
500.000
400.000

Created with TradeStation 2000i by Omega Research © 1999

Unlocking the Profits of the New Swing Chart Method — | — PAGE 22

CHART 9

The important thing to understand in this chart is the X 1-2-3 Pattern or the 1-2-3 Swing-to-a-Test Pattern.

The red line at X represents the 1957 high which occurred 60 months prior which is an important time period. Note the three swings down towards this level which holds above the key low at X. After # three you have to look for a change in trend and a challenge of the prior highs.

The Bear market low in 1974 was also the bottom of a X pattern.

NOTES

(DJ-30) Dow Jones Indust-Monthly 05/31/2005 C=10315.400 +152.890 +1.50% O=10236.260 H=10454.400 L=10149.060 V=125056

Created with TradeStation 2000i by Omega Research © 1999

Unlocking the Profits of the New Swing Chart Method

CHART 10

This chart demonstrates how the market oscillated back and forth before giving a Rule of 4 Breakout in 1982 which signaled a low for a long time.

(A) Label (A) is the outside down year which led to a water fall decline and the low in 1974. 1980 is a 3 plot year. The chart turns up, down and then back up. This 3-plot year actually marks the low of a Bear market which gave birth to the mother of all Bull markets. 1982 is a successful test of the 1980 low which offers second chance graceful entry.

(B) Label (B) is point 3, of the three tops prior to the breakout on the fourth attempt. A rule of 4 Breakout is a breakout over triple tops.

(C) Label (C) is the outside up year in 1982 which triggers the Rule of 4 Breakout.

NOTES

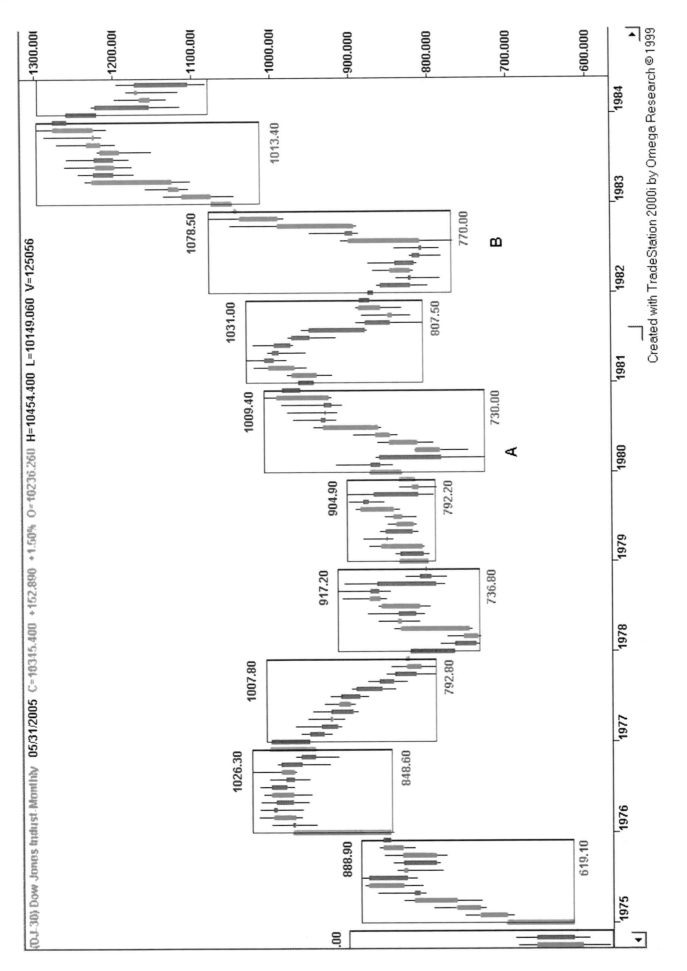

(DJ-30) Dow Jones Indust Monthly   05/31/2005   C=10345.400 +152.890 +1.50%   O=10236.260   H=10454.400   L=10149.060   V=125056

1300.00

1200.00

1100.00

1000.00

900.000

800.000

700.000

600.000

1975 1976 1977 1978 1979 1980 1981 1982 1983 1984

619.10

888.90

1026.30

848.60

1007.80

792.80

736.80

917.20

792.20

904.90

730.00

A

1009.40

807.50

1031.00

770.00

1078.50

B

1013.40

Created with TradeStation 2000i by Omega Research © 1999

Unlocking the Profits of the New Swing Chart Method   PAGE 26

CHART 11

1975 shows a down inside set up and the expectation is for the yearly chart to turn up. The yearly does in fact turn up in 1976 and finds high on the third month up in March. You will notice going thru these charts that many important turns have occurred in March. There is a fake-out move to the upside in Sept. which leaves a bearish tail as the subsequent break leaves a corresponding large range bar — leaving what is referred to as Train Tracks. Note, the graceful exit into the end of the year and another January turn.

Note, when the monthly turns back down and continues immediately lower taking out the low of the Train Tracks it confirms the case for lower prices. Note, the 2-plot March. 1978 shows a minus 2 year with a low early in the year---in the first two months of the year.

(A) Label (A) shows how the yearly chart turns up in Feb. 1980; back down in March and back up again in the 7th month, July, leaving a 3-plot year. The mother of all Bull markets comes off this 3-plot year.

(B) Label (B) is a good example of the Principle of Tests as the first pull back after the 3-plot year carves out a successful test of the 1980 low in August 1982. The notion of an important test is captured by the large range outside up month in August 1982. Note the symmetry in as much as the large range up in August was the largest range since the low in March 1980 (another March turn). Here again we see the Principal of Fractals play out as an outside up month led to an outside up year.

NOTES

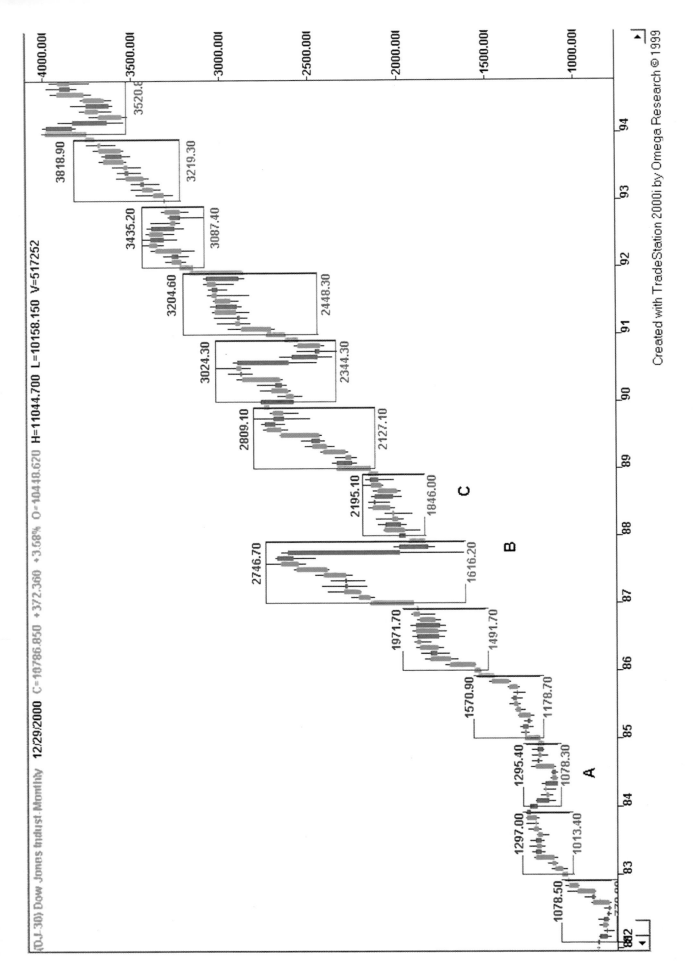

(DJ-30) Dow Jones Indust Monthly   12/29/2000   C=10786.850 +372.360 +3.58%   O=10448.620   H=11044.700   L=10158.150   V=517252

Created with TradeStation 2000i by Omega Research © 1999

Unlocking the Profits of the New Swing Chart Method |————| PAGE 28

CHART 12

(A) Label (A) shows the up inside pattern on the yearly chart. The expectation would have been for the yearly chart to turn down. Not only does the market not turn down but you get a momentum move in the opposite direction. When the price action doesn't do what history suggests it ought to do you usually get a strong move the other way. However, the important thing to remember is that usually markets walk before they run, which is the case in 1985. Note how the failure to turn down from the 1984 up inside year led to a 3 year rally.

(B) Label (B) represents the crash of 1987. Most technicians at the time were expecting the yearly chart to turn down after such a violent decline especially as the market ended up near the low of the year. Instead the Dow goes down inside.

(C) Label (C) represents the down inside yearly set up which indicates a turn up. The Dow does turn up in early 1989 and the behavior is bullish as the index continues higher immediately, a sign of the Bull. In another sign of bullish behavior, the monthly chart turns down in March defining an immediate low. Note the tail at the July high in 1990, three years from the 1987 top, and the subsequent sharp three month sell off.

NOTES ~~~~~~

(DJ-30) Dow Jones Indust-Monthly 05/31/2005 C=10281.110 +88.600 +0.87% O=10236.260 H=10454.400 L=10149.060 V=168538

Created with TradeStation 2000i by Omega Research © 1999

Unlocking the Profits of the New Swing Chart Method — PAGE 30

CHART 13

(A) Label (A) demonstrates the series of higher highs and higher lows on the yearly chart giving the analyst no choice but to be bullish. The higher highs and higher lows persisted for 18 years.

(B) Label (B) shows the high in 2000 and the two "green feet" in March and October 2000. These lows are broken when the yearly chart turns down in March 2001.

(C) Label (C) represents the yearly turn down in March 2001. Note the immediate reflex rally into May 2001 leaving a -1 + 2 sell setup and a 'graceful exit'. The important thing to remember is that since the yearly has turned down for the first time in 18 years (and after a blow off move) the first -1 + 2 set up is just a reflex rally. When the monthly chart turns down and continues lower it is confirmation of lower prices. Note, the seven bars down to low in Oct. 2002.

(D) Label (D) shows that after two lower lows on the yearly chart you need to think about getting bullish.

(E) Label (E) shows the down inside yearly set up in 2003.

(F) Label (F) shows the yearly turn up in early 2004. In typical fashion, the market pulls back for 7 to 8 months demonstrating once again the immediate reaction after a big wheel of time turns up or down. (The Principal of Reflexivity)

NOTES

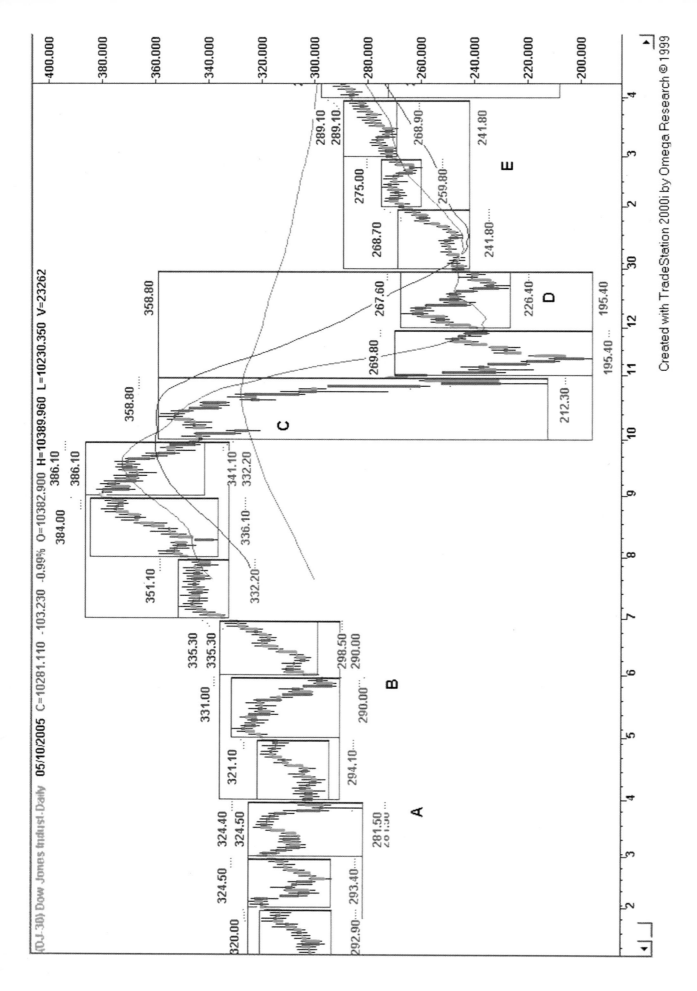

(DJ-30) Dow Jones Indust-Daily 05/10/2005 C=10281.110 -103.230 -0.99% O=10382.900 H=10389.960 L=10230.350 V=23262

Created with TradeStation 2000i by Omega Research © 1999

Unlocking the Profits of the New Swing Chart Method   PAGE 32

CHART 14

Chart #14 is a chart of quarterly/monthly boxes. The quarterly and monthly boxes are the meat and potatoes of swing charts and determine the trend that you can actively trade.

(A) Label (A) shows a 2-plot March to the downside that doesn't follow thru. Then the monthly gives a down inside April followed by another 2 plot down in May. June turns back up triggering a Double Slingshot buy signal which gives the final run to the top which lasts approximately, 3 months.

(B) Label (B) is the quarterly chart where these plots took place. The low of the quarterly chart at 290 represents the Dow's Maginot Line.

(C) Label(C) shows how the Quarterly chart turns down after the 1929 high and finds low immediately leading to a reflex bounce that tests the Dow's overhead 50 DMA as well as the prior breakdown level which tests the low of the high bar month. Note, that the bounce cannot even generate a 50% retracement of the decline off the top. When the low at point C is broken (bearishly on a gap down) it is time to batten down the hatches. You don't know that it's a crash. But, when the daily chart turns up and immediately turns down it is the kiss of death signal.

(D) Label (D) represents a down inside month. You expect a turn up and that is what occurs.

(E) Label (E) represents a down inside quarter. You expect a turn up and that is what occurs. Once again the action on the monthly leads to a similar set up on the quarterly. (The Principal of Fractals)

NOTES

(DJ-30) Dow Jones Indust-Daily 05/10/2005 C=10281.110 -103.230 -0.99% O=10382.900 H=10389.960 L=10230.350 V=23262

358.80

297.30
297.30
276.90

282.00

289.10
289.10

275.00

268.70

268.90

259.80

249.80

272.20

241.80

241.80

226.40

195.40

243.70

241.40

247.20
247.20

216.90

214.60

214.50

207.70

202.00

A

B

C

D

Created with TradeStation 2000i by Omega Research © 1999

— Unlocking the Profits of the New Swing Chart Method — PAGE 34

CHART 15

This chart shows monthly and quarterly boxes, on a daily chart.

(A) Label (A) represents the quarterly turn-up which sees the price action run up somewhat higher to tag the 200 DMA and then roll over. Note how the monthly turns down in short order to be followed by an a-b-c retracement rally to the overhead 50 DMA.

(B) Label (B) shows how the quarterly then turned back down which was foreshadowed by the gap down and the roll over from the 50 DMA. This turn down in the quarterly gives a 2-plot quarter or an outside down quarter which would indicate lower prices to follow. The outside down big quarterly wheel is not a good sign and it does continue to plot lower into June.

(C) Label (C) shows that July and August 1930 are both inside months, giving substantial time-on-the side. You expect a turn up and you get one. However, tellingly, no real momentum is created on the monthly turn-up and consequently a high is defined as the market rolls over. Note how the Dow could not even get to its 200DMA.

(D) The failure to gain traction on the turn-up is bearish and the result is a turndown in the monthly chart leaving an outside down month. Failed moves lead to fast moves in the opposite direction. The 2-plot quarter, in the second quarter of 1930 and the 2-plot month in Sept. 1930 said the Bear was going to get worse. The market was talking.

NOTES

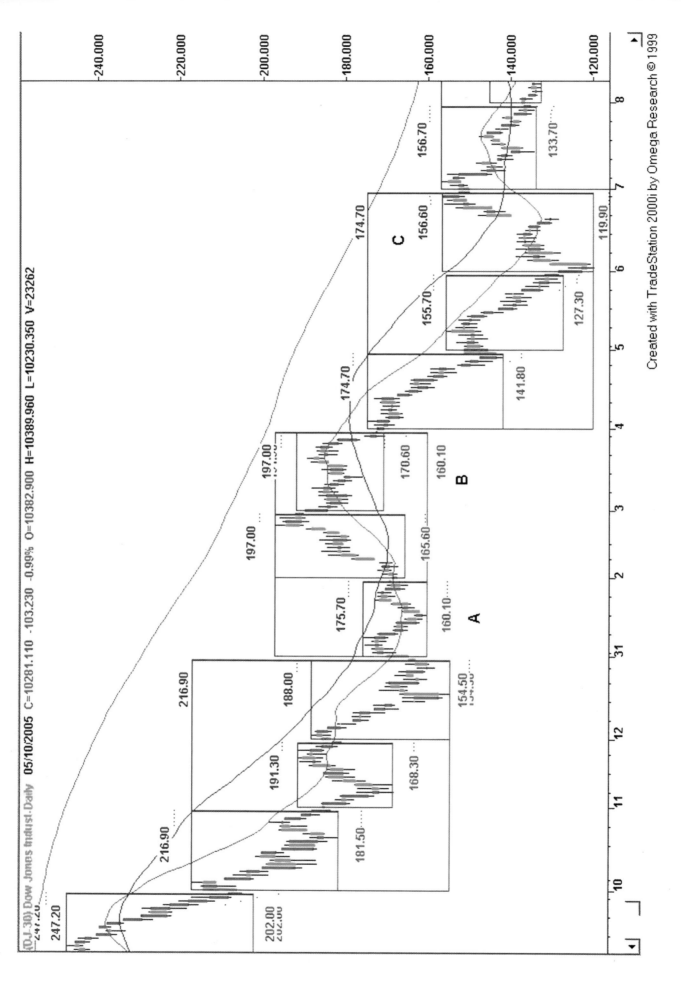

CHART 16

The outside down month in Sept. led to a persistent decline for another three months as the quarterly chart continues to plot lower.

(A) Label (A) shows a down inside month set up and the expectations for a turn up. The turn up occurs and a rally ensues, for a while. Also, note that the first quarter goes down inside, once again demonstrating the Principal of Fractals.

(B) Label (B) shows the subsequent up inside month. The expectation is for a turn down and it is important to remember this is within the context of an ongoing Bear market and that the up inside sell setup occurs below a declining 200 DMA which has well confined the Bear market. At this juncture the quarterly chart is down inside suggesting a possible advance while the monthly chart is up inside suggesting a decline. What do you do? You wait for the market to decide. You do nothing until you get a resolution. In April 1931 the market talks as it gives a get-out-of-Dodge signal when the monthly turns back down and downside momentum explodes.

C) Label (C) shows a 2-plot month back up which should have led to strength but did not as a bearish -1 +2 pattern is traced out.

NOTES

Unlocking the Profits of the New Swing Chart Method   PAGE 38

Created with TradeStation 2000i by Omega Research © 1999

CHART 17

(A) Label (A) is another picture of the bearish -1 +2 setup into July 1931. The very next month fulfills the bearish indication of the set up as the monthly chart turns down. The turn down finds an immediate low and a reflex rally is traced out. This is typical behavior. What is important to note is that the month of August is an N/R (narrow range) 7 month, the narrowest range of the last seven months which suggests a volatility move as expansion follows contraction or compression in markets.

(B) Label (B) shows that the monthly turns up and dies which is bearish behavior and in fact defines another high. The chart demonstrates a market trying to be bullish but failing to generate follow thru on turn ups.

(C) Label (C) shows the close near the low of the turn down month of November which suggests lower prices to come.

NOTES

(DJ-30) Dow Jones Indust-Daily 05/10/2005 C=10281.110 -103.230 -0.99% O=10382.900 H=10389.960 L=10230.350 V=23262

119.20

119.20

93.40

89.40

71.80

87.80

69.90

89.80

70.60

A

89.90
89.90

72.60
69.90

74.40

74.40

55.40

B

59.80

44.30

51.40

42.30

C

54.70

40.60

D 77.00

52.40

E

81.40
81.40

64.30

40.60

40.60

Created with TradeStation 2000i by Omega Research © 1999

Unlocking the Profits of the New Swing Chart Method   PAGE 40

CHART 18

The long Bear market continues to give bad buy set ups which is emblematic of the downtrend. The quarterly wheel of time continues to plot lower lows and lower highs determining that the downtrend is entrenched.

(A) Label (A) represents the -1 + 2 bearish pattern into March 1932; another important March turn. Note, the bearish behavior as the price action dies after the turn up, tests the high and then rolls over. It is important to remember that it takes TIME for the market to play out.

(B) Label (B) shows that when the monthly chart turned down and the quarterly chart plotted lower on the second day of the new quarter in April 1932 the market accelerated lower. Remember that many important turning points come at the end/beginning of new months and quarters. After the significant pause in the first quarter, volatility expands. This behavior from thrust to pause is the underlying nature of price action and exists on all time frames. Note, how the decline after the turn in April 1932 generates a 3 month (90 days or 90 degrees of the year) decline into the low of the Bear market in July 1932.

(C) Label (C) is the outside up month at the July 1932 low which is a fractal of the outside up 3rd quarter of that year. (the Principal of Fractals)

(D) Label (D) denotes the turn-up in the quarterly chart near the end of August 1932 that does not see much follow thru and defines a high. But, in a possible change in character, the market is trying to do something bullish as the Dow carved out a potentially bullish outside up quarter.

(E) Label (E) shows the important observation that for the first time in a long time the monthly chart traces out 3 higher highs. This portends a change in character of the market. The important thing to understand is that the change in character has occurred and that despite the 'failure' to move immediately higher after the 2-plot quarter, the reflex pullback is a natural expectation. This demonstrates the principle of turning the main trend and getting a test. The Dow pulls back to test towards the high of the signal month--the outside bar up in July 1932.

NOTES

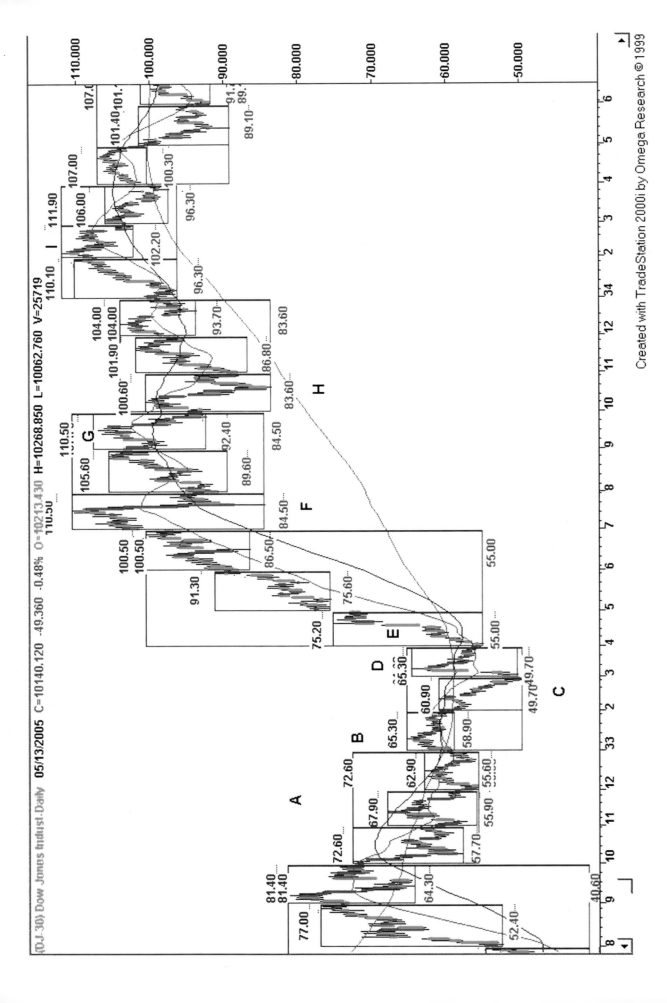

(DJ-30) Dow Jones Indust-Daily   05/13/2005   C=10140.120 -49.360 -0.48%   O=10213.430 H=10268.850 L=10062.760 V=25719

Created with TradeStation 2000i by Omega Research ©1999

Unlocking the Profits of the New Swing Chart Method   PAGE 42

CHART 19

(A) Label (A) shows an up inside quarter giving the expectation for a turn down in the quarterly chart to test the low and provide a higher low if the trend has turned.

(B) Label (B) shows that after the monthly turn up which sees the Dow die.

(C) Label (C) shows that the failure when the monthly chart turned up did in fact lead to a turn down in the quarterly chart as a low is made within a few weeks. If the trend has changed from 1932 based on the prior observations we want to careful watch for the possibility of a higher low on the quarterly chart.

(D) Label (D) represents the turn up in the monthly chart which gives a relatively short-lived reflex reaction back down. The important thing to understand is that trade back above the level where the high was made after the monthly turned up confirms the notion of a higher month and gives a Second Mouse buy signal on the monthly chart by plotting higher: the second mouse gets the cheese!

(E) Label (E) shows the 'cascade' action in as much as at the same time the as the Dow gives trade above the recent monthly turn-up, the quarterly chart also turns back up and price, bulllishly, continues higher. Note, how the large range on the monthly bar and the upside momentum is a recognition by the market/players that a higher low (on the quarterly chart) has been confirmed. Note, how the large range on the monthly is a fractal of the large range on the quarterly bar for the 2nd quarter in 1932. The large range of the quarterly bar tells you a low is in for a while. At (E) you knew the bottom was in because you have the first higher low on the quarterly. The market advanced into 1937.

(F) Label (F) reflects the 2-plot month down. The monthly turns down but does not go lower, going inside instead.

(G) Label (G) shows the monthly turns up and dies. Interestingly (G) is a 1-2-3 swing to a test sell pattern on the daily chart. The outside down month and the ensuing reflex rally suggest caution. The monthly does turn down.

(H) Label (H) shows where the quarterly turned back down. The important thing to understand is that if the trend is still up we would expect the market to find low soon after the quarterly turndown. The quarterly turn did represent a change in character as a low was put in immediately which saw stocks march higher.

(I) Label (I) shows a turn back up in the quarterly in January which runs into Feb. However, Feb. sees a close near the low indicating a possible downturn in March which occurs.

NOTES

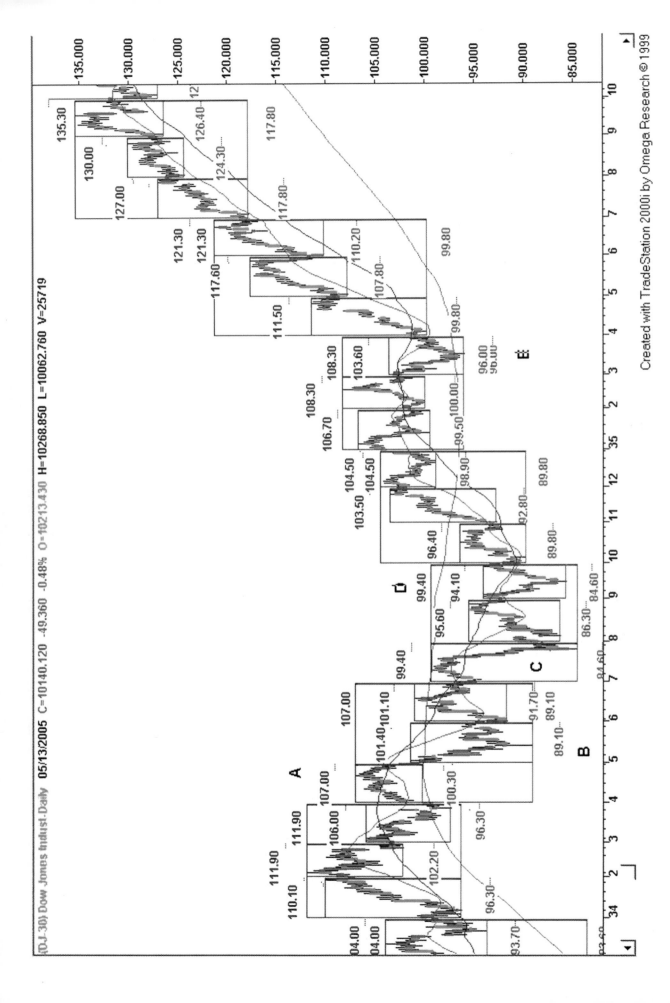

(DJ-30) Dow Jones Indust-Daily 05/13/2005 C=10140.120 -49.360 -0.48% O=10213.430 H=10268.850 L=10062.760 V=25719

Created with TradeStation 2000i by Omega Research © 1999

Unlocking the Profits of the New Swing Chart Method   PAGE 44

CHART 20

(A) Label (A) shows where the monthly chart turned up and died. Why would you expect a decline to follow? Well the monthly chart turned down in March closing near the low of the month and the low of the quarter therefore the expectation would be for the second quarter to see a turn down in the quarterly chart.

(B) Label (B) shows that the monthly chart turns back down quickly and accelerates implying a turndown in the quarterly chart which occurs in May shortly after the monthly turned back down. Note, the tail down at the low of the month in May, June is a down inside month setting up the expectation for a rally. However, instead the monthly does not turn up and plots lower.

(C) Label (C) Shows the flush out or mini 'whoop 'em down' following the 'failure' to turn up.

(D) Label (D) represents the +1 -2 on the quarterly chart that results from that flush out which is a bullish set up. After a double down inside month, the monthly turns up in Oct and bullishly price action accelerates. Note, how the Dow gains traction when the quarterly turns up as well--bullish behavior and the subsequent pullback in Dec. to the level where the quarterly turn up. These levels where the monthlies and quarterlies turn up represent important levels of future support and resistance and are True Trend Lines. After two quarters up the monthly chart turns down.

(E) Label (E) shows that turndown for another important March turn. Note, how the monthly turns back up immediately and generates acceleration approximately 3 years from the Bear market low.

NOTES

Created with TradeStation 2000i by Omega Research © 1999

Unlocking the Profits of the New Swing Chart Method — PAGE 46

CHART 21

The quarterly low in 1934 was at 84.60. Chart 21 shows what happens when a third higher low is carved out. Third higher lows many times generate what we call Power Surge moves. This is exactly what played out from the third higher low in 1935.

(A) Label (A) represents the first monthly turndown of the year and again reflects an important March pivot. Note, the solid accelerations as the monthly chart turns immediately back up in April. Note, the tag of the important 200 DMA in March helps to put the pieces together for a buy set up confirming the notion of a significant low.

(B) Label (B) shows how the monthly chart remained up for eight months before tuning back down and defining yet another low in December. Remember the end of December/early January often represents many good turns. The monthly chart turns back up in January and runs into the end of March which leads to a two-plot month down early in the second quarter in April. Note the acceleration to the downside when the monthly turns down running directly to, yep, the 200 DMA.

NOTES

6/1/36 High 154.00

(DJ-30) Dow Jones Indust-Daily 05/13/2005 C=10140.120 -49.360 -0.48% O=10213.430 H=10268.850 L=10062.760 V=25719

Created with TradeStation 2000i by Omega Research © 1999

Unlocking the Profits of the New Swing Chart Method   PAGE 48

CHART 22

(A) Label (A) is another look at how the monthly chart turned down after 3 months up. Note how the gap on the daily chart thru the 50 DMA indicates a turndown in the monthly and a tag of the 200 DMA. The important thing to understand is that the Quarterly chart turns down the same month and finds low on the very day of the turndown as the 200 DMA is tagged. It is also important that this is the first hit the 200 DMA in a substantial period of time, which is nearly always a good trading opportunity.

(B) Label (B) gives a down inside month and the anticipated resumption of the up trend. Note, the Theory of Reflexivity at work with the pullback in July to test near the level where the monthly chart turned up.

(C) Label (C) shows an outside down month at the top and a reflex bounce to test the level of the turndown. The outside down month after an extended period of higher highs and higher lows suggest a turndown in the larger quarterly wheel of time.

(D) Label (D) shows that in fact the quarterly chart does turn down makes a low immediately giving a reflex bounce but when the quarterly plots lower you can expect lower prices and/or at least more time consolidating at least into the end of that quarter which is exactly what occurs. Note the gap thru the 200 DMA as the monthly and quarterly plotted lower in April 1937. There is really no set up at the low in June. However, when the monthly chart turns back up and accelerates thru the 200 DMA you can expect a test of some sort of the high which occurs where?--near the level where the monthly chart two plotted down in March (another March turn).

The moral of the story is that the 2-plot down month was a warning, signal bar, a caution flag, and after 3 to 4 months down into the end of the second quarter a rally ensued. However, when the quarterly turned up in August, no momentum was generated which defined a high. Note, the angle of attack which confirmed the markets bearish action as well as the gap through the 200 DMA.

NOTES

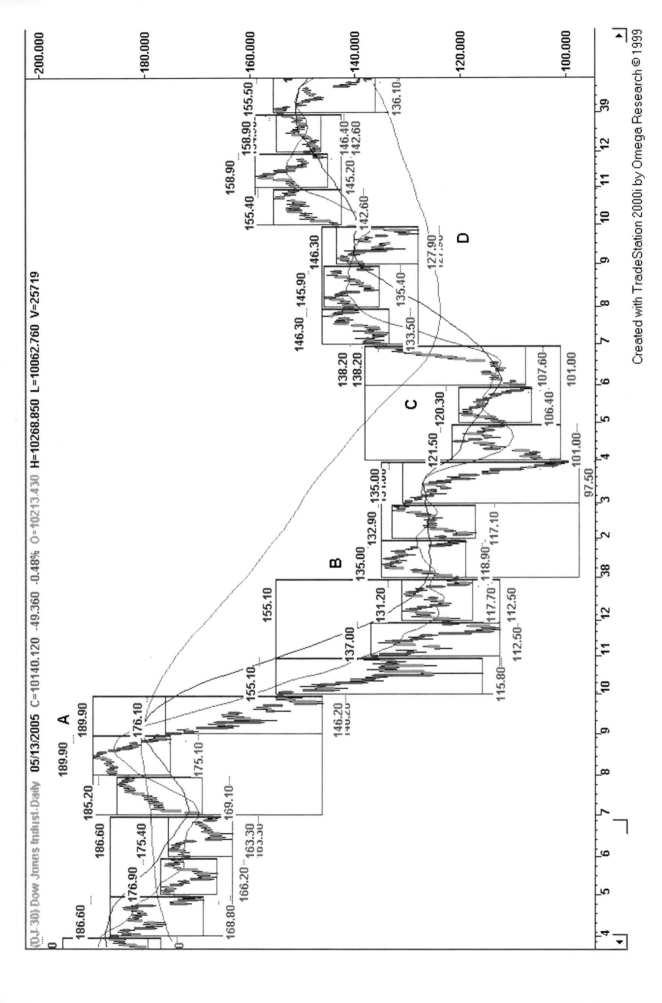

(DJ-30) Dow Jones Indust-Daily   05/13/2005   C=10140.120   -49.360   -0.48%   O=10213.430   H=10268.850   L=10062.760   V=25719

CHART 23

(A) Label (A) is another look at what does happen coming off the June low. The important thing to recognize is the -1 +2 sell pattern at the test of the outside down month which coincides with a turn up in the quarterly chart. Note the acceleration to the down side when the quarterly chart turns back down underscoring the failure to follow thru to the upside when it turned up. This is what we mean by observing behavior. The outside down quarter suggests a sharp decline and we get it.

(B) Label (B) represents the down inside month from which we expect a monthly turn up and it occurs but importantly defines a high as the price action dies. Subsequently the monthly turns down and finds low immediately generating a rally to test the last level where the monthly turned up. See how the market has a memory. The failure to turn the monthly back up and the roll over after the test suggests that the monthly chart will plot lower again and it does. Note the -1 +2 on the daily chart in March just prior to the downside acceleration into the end of March for another important March turning point. The final decline which breaks the multiple bottoms of November, December 1937 and February 1938 leads to a 'whoop 'em down' or flush out of approximately 8 days.

(C) Label(C) demonstrates the action after the double down inside months of April and May 1938. Double inside 'time on the side' especially after a flush out move that 'pulls back the rubber band' should create good compression that can generate solid momentum. That's exactly what we get when the monthly turns up in June. Note the acceleration on the turn up, the lack of reflexivity and the immediate drive over the important 200 DMA which are clues that a meaningful bottom has occurred. Note how the consolidation occurs just after and just above where the quarterly chart turns up as the advance is digested.

(D) Label (D) shows that after an up inside month you get the anticipated turn down. Bullishly the Dow makes low relatively quickly as the 200 DMA is approached. Note that the 200 DMA is rising on this second chance entry.

NOTES

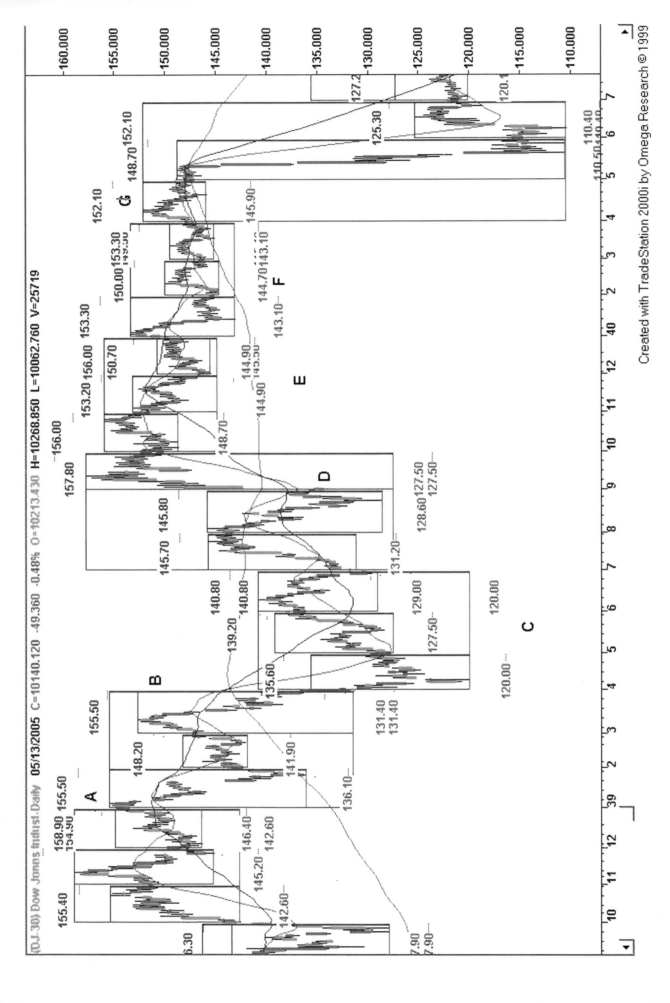

Created with TradeStation 2000i by Omega Research © 1999

CHART 24

(A) Label (A) shows an up inside month with trade slightly higher in Jan. 1939 for another important turn at the end/beginning of the year. When the monthly failed to actually plot higher the Dow rolled over as the gap down suggested a decline that would see the monthly chart turn back down which it does as price is magnetized to the 200 DMA once again as the quarterly chart turns down making a low relatively quickly in terms of time in January 1939.

(B) Label (B) shows how the monthly turns back up for another important March pivot. The important thing to note is how the replot or turn back down of the monthly chart in March leads to a sharp decline which one would expect. The expectation would be for the 2-plot month to lead to a test of the next larger wheel, the quarterly, while the sharp angle of attack to the down side suggests that the quarterly may actually plot lower which occurs for a few days. Note, the break of the 200 DMA and reflex move back to kiss it goodbye in March as the monthly chart turned back down.

(C) Label (C) gives no real buy set up as a low is made and the monthly chart turns up. Note, the reflexivity in May from where the quarterly chart initially plotted lower. Note, the 3 month rally from the low at C.

(D) Label (D) shows a 2-plot month back down which is bearish behavior but the market then does something you would not expect: downside momentum dies shortly after the turndown (which is constructive action in and of itself) and the market runs back up. Remember, false setups lead to fast moves: the tail day at the August low and the subsequent gap higher suggest a drive thru the 200 DMA which is exactly what occurs as the highs from November 1938 are tested.

(E) Label (E) shows the Principle of Fractals as the up inside month leads to an up inside quarter, the last quarter of 1939. The up inside quarter indicates a turndown in the quarterly chart hence; note how the turn up in the monthly chart in Jan. 1940 (another important Jan. turn) defines high leading to the expected turndown in the quarterly the same month.

(F) Label (F) shows the quarterly turndown and the reflex rally back. The double down inside month suggests a rally phase if the market is bullish but at the very least a turn up in the monthly chart. The behavior after such a turn up especially after an Narrow Range month will be important to observe.

(G) Label (G) shows how in fact the monthly chart did turn up immediately in the new quarter and died. You expect a rally but you don't get it. When the monthly turns back down with conviction (note the large range red day and the gap the following day) the market is talking. When the monthly turned back down undercutting the double down inside months as well, it was a Get Out of Dodge Set Up. Note, the angular rule of 4, break down as the monthly turns back down in May 1940 and the 200 DMA is decisively broken.

NOTES

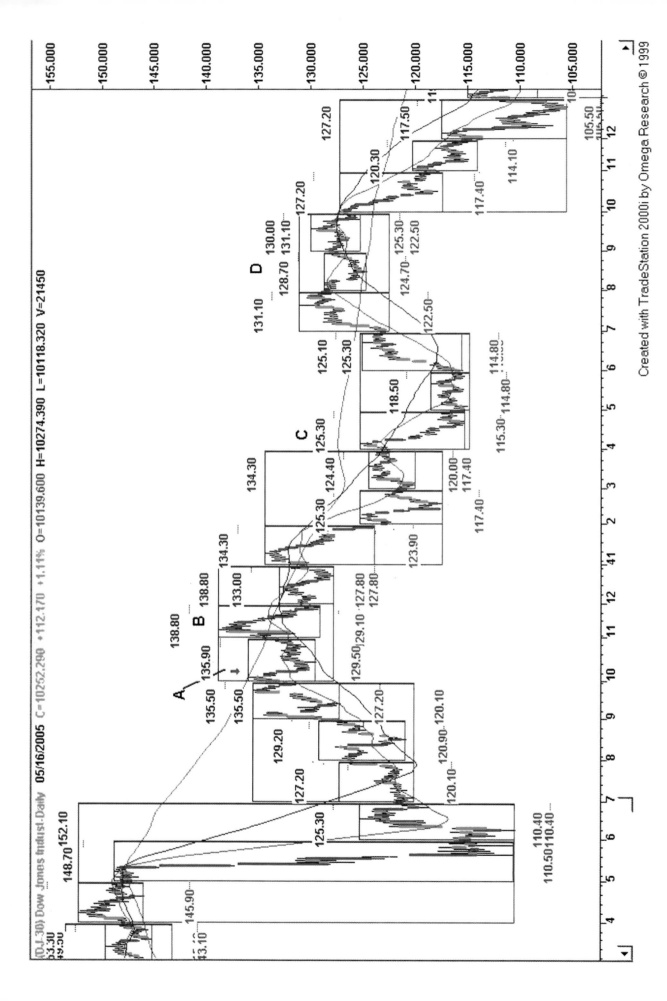

Created with TradeStation 2000i by Omega Research © 1999

Unlocking the Profits of the New Swing Chart Method   PAGE 54

CHART 25

(A) Label (A) shows the set up from a down inside quarter that leads to a turn up in the quarterly chart. The turn up defines an immediate high in the beginning of the new quarter which leads to a reflex pullback.

(B) Label (B) shows the ensuing rally which leads to a test of the high which is quickly 'souped' giving way to a 2-plot month to the downside. Not a good sign. Note, how the close near the low of December and the low of the final quarter in 1940 is also not a good sign and although the market gives a reflex rally which tests the level where the quarterly chart last turned up, it is important to see that the market died and rolled over as the monthly turned up defining another important January turning point. The failure of the market to gain traction as the monthly turned up combined with the low close of the 4th quarter of 1940 suggests that the quarterly chart is primed to turn back down and it does. The drive down through the 200 DMA virtually assures that will occur as well.

(C) Label (C) reflects the down inside month in March 1941 indicating a turn up which does occur early in the next quarter. Note, the bearish behavior as the turn up immediately defines a high leading to a low six months from point B which as you know is an important time span. C is a 2-plot month down and one would expect acceleration lower. However, the market finds lows quickly instead and the loss of downside momentum leads to a Narrow Range 7 month. The compression in volatility suggests a probable turn up after six months down and you get it. Note the acceleration on the turn up.

(D) Label (D) shows where the quarterly chart turned up and ran a little further making a high at the end of the month which leads to a reflex pullback to test the level where the quarterly chart turned up and the 200 DMA in the process. The monthly chart trades up inside giving the expectation for a turndown. This is important to understand: although the monthly chart trades higher, in September there is NO NEW PLOT ...it is already up inside and does not make a new high. The rally towards the end of September proves to be only a test of the July high which is confirmed by the behavior when the monthly chart turn back down and the market accelerates below the 200 DMA turning the quarterly back down in early October. The momentum suggests a probable 3 month decline into the end of the year as the break occurs from a lower high in the quarterly chart.

NOTES

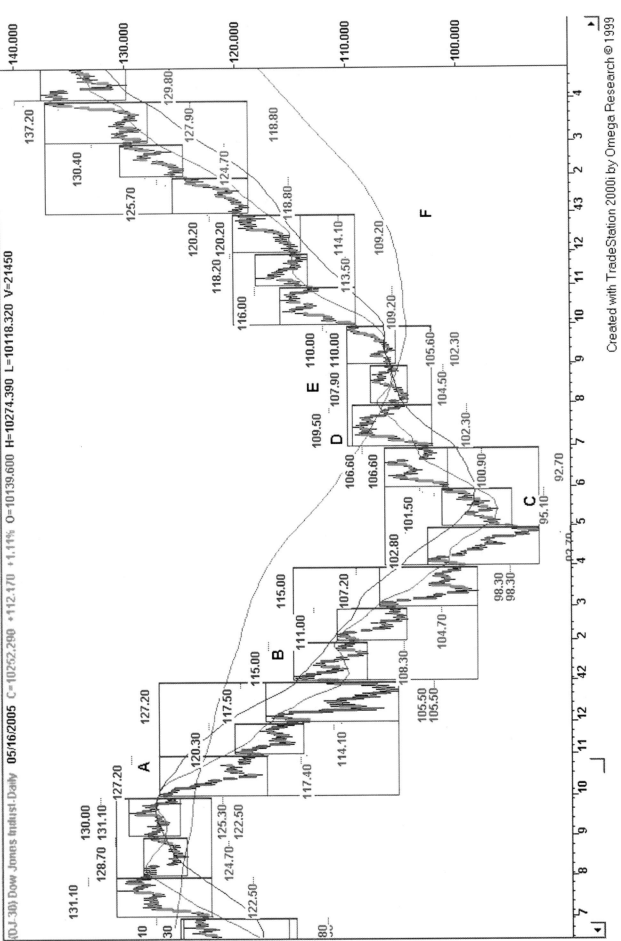

Created with TradeStation 2000i by Omega Research © 1999

CHART 26

(A) Label (A) shows the turn down on the monthly chart after the double up inside pattern on the monthly. Note, how the behavior of the acceleration on the turn down and the weak reflex rally indicate lower prices and you get them.

(B) Label (B) shows that after a 3 month decline you expect a pause and you get a sharp rally. The monthly should turn up but instead the early January pivot defines another high and bearishly the market closes near the low of the month: look out below.

(C) Label (C) shows that after plotting lower in February the market declines for another 3 months! However after six to seven months down you might expect at least a countertrend rally and the down inside month sets up the expectation for a turn up and the behavior following that turn up was constructive as momentum picked up and then after a reflex pullback the market gave a second mouse move (the second mouse gets the cheese) above the 200 DMA signaling higher.

(D) Label (D) shows that the 'second mouse' turned the next larger wheel, the quarterly wheel up, and that although the market did not really advance going largely sideways for the balance of the quarter, bullishly the quarter closed near the high.

(E) Label (E) is an up inside month and it is important to note that the expectation would be for the monthly chart to turn down. Instead, the market pauses after the up inside Narrow Range 7 month at E suggesting a volatility move. Fast moves occur when what the majority may expect does not play out. When the market does something it normally shouldn't do it is talking. Note the major up move that results from the N/R 7 month, the ability of the quarterly chart to hold after it turned up as the market built a platform from which to launch. The key was an explosion over the up inside month instead of the turndown.

(F) Label (F) shows the power of following the monthly chart and how it DETERMINES TREND as 12 monthly higher lows are traced out. It is interesting to note the acceleration up above the 107-111 area in November just as there was acceleration below the 107-111 level in February 1942. The market truly has a memory.

NOTES

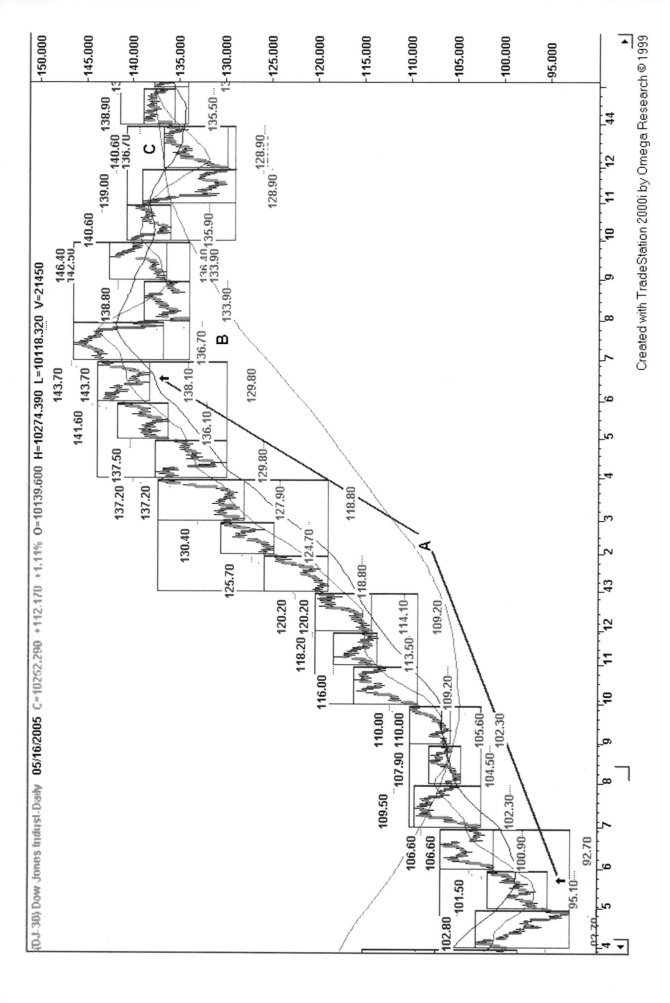

(DJ-30) Dow Jones Indust-Daily   05/16/2005   C=10252.290 +112.470 +1.11%   O=10139.600   H=10274.390   L=10118.320   V=21450

Created with TradeStation 2000i by Omega Research © 1999

Unlocking the Profits of the New Swing Chart Method   PAGE 58

CHART 27

(A) Label (A) shows the 14 month run of higher lows. This demonstrates how long the market can run without even giving a +1 -2 set up on the monthly chart. The market does not always accommodate with picture perfect buy set ups. We've mentioned before how the market many times plays out in threes and sevens. June 1943 represents the 14th (7X2) higher low and the last higher low in this run. Note how after the seventh higher low in November 1942 the 200 DMA is just beginning to turn up at this mid point of this advance in time.

(B) Label (B) is the first turndown in the monthly chart in a substantial period of time and is a 2-plot month down. Note the +1 -2 buy set up as the market pulls back. Note, the +1 -2 pattern is established, the reflex bounce and the rest of the low. Note, how the monthly turns up but turns right back down early the next month at the beginning of the new quarter suggesting the quarterly chart will turn down...when? Likely after an intervening reflex bounce which occurs into late October. It is interesting to note how again the turndown in the quarterly chart coincides with a convincing break of the 200 DMA.

(C) Label (C) shows a down inside month. You expect a turn up and you get it at the 200 DMA.

NOTES

(DJ-30) Dow Jones Indust-Daily 05/18/2005 C=10464.450 +132.570 +1.28% O=10329.400 H=10518.170 L=10329.370 V=29601

Created with TradeStation 2000i by Omega Research © 1999

CHART 28

(A) Label (A) shows a turndown on the monthly chart that finds low immediately and rallies strongly turning the monthly chart right back up the following month. Note that the quarterly low turns up in March. This is bullish BEHAVIOR and suggests a potential up trend will unfold. Note, the thrust above the 200 DMA in March, and the reflex pullback on the quarterly.

(B) Label (B) shows that when the monthly chart turns back down that once again a low is found quickly. The ensuing thrust above the 200 DMA is a 'second mouse move' above this important moving average which confirms that the higher True Swing low on the monthly chart underscores the up trend to follow. Importantly, see how the quarterly chart plots higher up on the second thrust through the 200 DMA and bullishly the market accelerates higher. Note, that the market rallies THREE months from pt. B.

(C) Label (C) represents +1 -2 monthly buy set up as the market pulls back towards the 200 DMA. As anticipated the monthly turns back up and after the three month consolidation ABOVE a rising 200 DMA.

(D) Label (D) shows the monthly turns back down by the smallest of margins (10 cents), tracing out a two step pullback prior too exploding again in a three month up trend. Note the reflexivity back to the turn up point after the market turns up in December and then again the same pattern in January and the reflex action gives a pullback to where the monthly plotted higher.

(E) Label (E) shows a 2-plot month high to low and you would expect this to signal that the market is prepared to go lower. But, instead, the market sticks it in your face and rallies another three months. Note the behavior of how the low is found quickly after the turndown AND near the rising 200 DMA.

(F) Label (F) simply shows an up inside month. You expect the monthly chart to turn down and it does. This first up inside month in this chart should put you on your toes: when the market does something for the first time in a long time you should pay attention.

NOTES

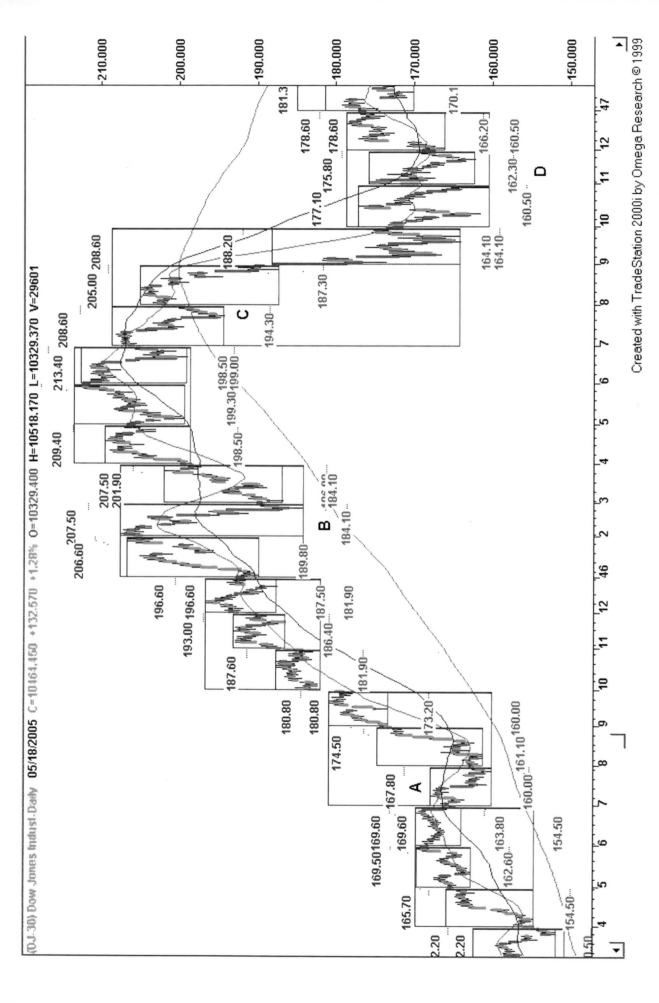

CHART 29

(A) Label (A) shows that you do get a turn down and a low is made relatively quickly in terms of both time and price. Then when the market turns back up it jams it in your face as a six month rally unfolds. Note the acceleration as the last swing high month is offset. This is how you identify a power move.

(B) Label (B) refers to the 2-plot month down. It is the first 2-plot month down. Note that a low is found quickly after the monthly 2-plots down from high and that the next top is three months later. The choppy nature of the two month rally after the sharp outside month down in February suggests distribution.

(C) Label (C) shows that after only two months up into the end of June 1946 the monthly chart turns back down which leads to a turn down in the quarterly chart followed by another reflex bounce that tests the 50 DMA. Once the quarterly chart plots lower again the monthly is in sync plotting lower at the same time suggesting a power move to the down side which corrects the whole move up through chart 29.

(D) Label (D) shows a down inside month after 'rapid flipping' on the daily chart. At the same time the market has traced out a +1 -2 buy set up on the quarterly chart. You expect a turn up and you get it.

NOTES ～～～～～～～～～～～～～～～～～～～～～～～～～～～～～

(D.J-30) Dow Jones Indust-Daily 05/24/2005 C=10503.680 -19.880 -0.19% O=10522.700 H=10550.240 L=10433.780 V=20325

Created with TradeStation 2000i by Omega Research © 1999

Unlocking the Profits of the New Swing Chart Method —— PAGE 64

CHART 30

(A) Label (A) shows the turn up in the quarterly chart which immediately defines a high and the reflex pullback to the 50 DMA which fills the gap. The pullback generates a one month rally towards the declining 200 DMA. You get a close near the low of the month in February and so you expect the monthly chart to turn down and it does followed by a reflex rally to the 50 DMA at the end of March which is now overhead resistance.

(B) Label (B) The quarterly chart turns down and you get a reflex bounce to the 50 DMA followed by a test of the last quarterly low in the 4th quarter of 1946 creating a higher low on quarterly chart. In June the monthly turns up driving through the 200 DMA with vigor suggesting higher prices.

(C) Label (C) The Principle of Fractals plays out as the up inside month in November leads to an up inside quarter for the 4th quarter of 1947. The up inside month and up inside quarter indicate a turndown and you get it at C. Again a convincing decline through the 50 DMA leads to a multi-month decline (two months to be exact). After a test of the low on the daily chart in March (another important March turn) the market gaps away as the monthly chart turns up and the 200 DMA is recaptured leading to a turn up of the quarterly chart which puts in a second higher low on the quarterly chart. When you turn a large wheel of time you expect a reflex the other way; consequently, when the monthly turns up in March 1948 and keeps plotting higher it suggest both higher prices and the notion that the quarterly wheel will turn up directly. Note, how the market marches up to turn the quarterly up with barely a pause. The important thing to understand in this chart is how the turn up in the monthly and quarterly give a 'cascade' higher.

(D) Label (D) reflects the reflexivity after the quarterly turns up. Note, how the pullback holds the vicinity where the quarterly turned up and the momentum as the monthly plotted higher.

NOTES

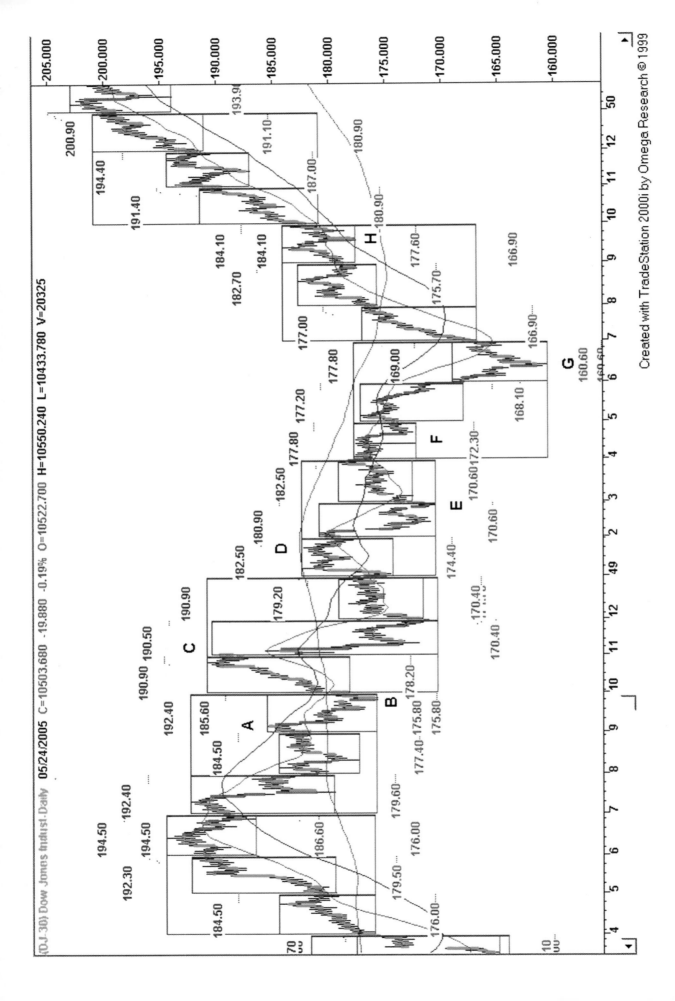

Unlocking the Profits of the New Swing Chart Method   PAGE 66

CHART 31

(A) Label (A) shows the behavior of the how the monthly chart turns up defining a high as the market rolls over immediately leaving a 2-plot month down.

(B) Label (B) is important as it shows how the quarterly chart turned down and found low immediately in a kind of mirror image fractal of the behavior at (A) where the monthly turned up. Note how the quarterly turndown was made with only a marginal new low. You expect a reflex bounce and when the monthly turns back up with conviction and the market powers back through the 200 DMA you can expect a test of the highs in June. The important thing to understand is the behavior that the quarterly failed to turn back up suggesting a 'test failure' at (C) as the market fails big-time accelerating back through its 200 DMA. It is important to understand that the marginal turndown of the quarterly chart at (B) was a bullish event as a rally unfolded immediately suggesting the expectation of a turn back up in the quarterly chart. When that does not occur, especially given the momentum of the advance an equally fast and furious move in the opposite direction takes place.

(C) Label (C) shows the failure of the quarterly chart to turn up despite the sharp rally in the monthly chart.

(D) Label (D) shows how a down inside month sets up a rally which takes the overhead 200 DMA. Note the mini test and two tails at the underbelly of the 200 DMA.

(E) Label (E) shows that the ensuing turn down of the monthly chart tests the low in early December 1948 and how the down inside month sets up a down inside quarter at the end of March 1949 and we expect a turn up. Once again the Principal of Fractals is at work.

(F) Label (F) shows a Narrow Range 7 inside month and that instead of the expected quarterly turn up both the monthly and quarterly plot lower: Failed moves or failed expectations lead to fast moves in the opposite directions.

(G) Label (G) shows the fast move or 'whoop'em down' of approximately 49 (7x7) days. These kind of flush outs or capitulations which undercut obvious bottoms often put in classic V Bottoms. There is no classic buy set up at the low. However, the clue to the low after (G) is the lack of reflexivity and the power move back through the bottoms of the price level at (E).

(H) Label (H) is a test of a test (of the September pullback) which occurs at the prior quarters high and the turn up level from August. Note how the market planted Two Feet, the second one at the 50 DMA prior to the market marching higher. Note how after the second foot the market accelerates as the quarterly plots higher. The bullish trend is underscored by the persistence of the monthly trend which produced nothing but higher highs and higher lows.

NOTES

(DJ-30) Dow Jones Indust.Daily 05/24/2005 C=10503.680 -19.880 -0.19% O=10522.700 H=10550.240 L=10433.780 V=20325

Created with TradeStation 2000i by Omega Research ©1999

CHART 32

(A) Label (A) shows that trends can persist without a turndown in the monthly wheel for a substantial period of time as there were 11 higher highs to the June 1950 high which gave a large range outside down 2-plot month. The low close near the end of June suggests lower prices and you get them into July.

(B) Label (B) shows the bullish +1 -2 month in July as the 200 DMA is violated. This is the first time the 200 DMA is tagged or undercut in a long time which typically presents a good buying opportunity. At approximately the same time the 200 DMA is broken the quarterly chart turns down and a low is made relatively quickly in terms of time. Many ingredients for a bullish posture present themselves at this juncture: the first tag of the 200 DMA in a long time, the +1 -2 monthly set up, the fact that the quarterly turned down and soon found low, and the ability of the market to climb back above the 200 DMA quickly and hold and gain traction demanded a bullish stance. The monthly chart turning back up in August and continuing higher confirmed the bullish bias. What is important to understand here is the interaction between the 200 DMA and the Quarterly chart which plays out over and over again. The outside down month and the break of the 200 DMA flushed enough buyers out and created enough bearish sentiment to define a significant low at the quarterly turndown. Happenstance? We don't think so. Once the market has shaken out many players, it says thank you and moves higher with their shares!

(C) Label (C) reflects the turn back up in the quarterly chart as a reflex pullback occurs. This time another '2-step' pullback which plants Two Feet as the monthly chart turns down and defines a low during this consolidation above a rising 200 DMA. December is an up inside month and you expect it to turn down but notice how the close of the month is near the high of the month and you get a breakout instead. The market is talking as it does something you don't expect. Notice how the fourth quarter of 1950 appears to have traced out a Head and Shoulders topping pattern. When the pattern is destroyed coincident with the unexpected move out of the monthly up inside position, you get a fast move up. This is how you put the pieces together. May 1951 gives another outside down 2-plot month after a strong advance. Notice how the 200 DMA is once again tagged at the end of the quarter in June 1951. Although the market gives a close near the low of the quarter and the low of the month, counter intuitively, the market runs up and when the monthly chart turns up and the rally continues you can expect higher prices and you get them.

NOTES

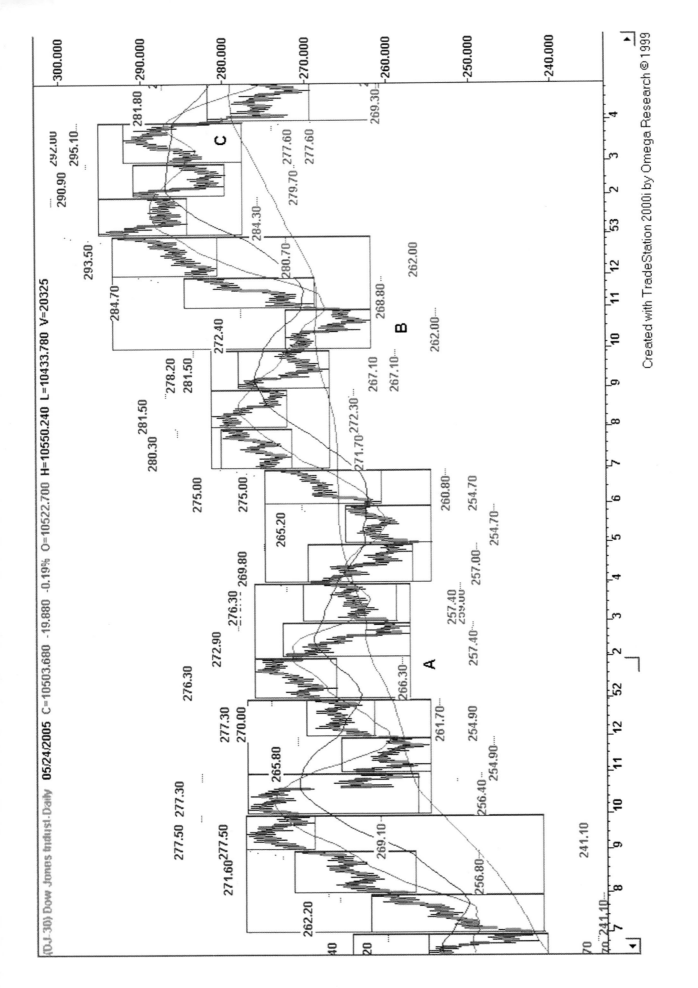

CHART 33

(A) Label (A) refers to the double up inside quarter and you expect a turndown and it occurs making a low immediately. Notice how the marginal turndown by a tick suggests the market is in a position to rally. Finding low immediately in time and price is bullish behavior. Note, how the down inside month suggests a rally but plots lower instead in a fake out move. When the monthly turns up and accelerates over the 200 DMA immediately you have to be bullish! Additionally, notice how the failure of any reflexivity in June 1952 after the monthly turned up also says the market wants to go higher which it does turning the quarterly up before making a high in August.

(B) Label (B) shows another +1 -2 pullback buy set up on the monthly chart. Notice how once again the quarterly chart turns down and the market finds low relatively quickly again before rocketing higher. The important thing to understand is that when the quarterly chart turns back up in November and the price action accelerates, closing at the high of the month, it is a better than average likelihood that the market will run into the end of the year.

(C) Label (C) shows how the monthly chart turned back up in March and immediately dies, 2-plotting down. The close near the low of the quarter suggests that the quarterly chart will turn down and it does. Once again we see an important March pivot.

NOTES

(DJ-30) Dow Jones Indust. Daily 05/25/2005 C=10457.800 -45.880 -0.44% O=10503.200 V=0 Mov Avg 3 lines(Close,21,50,200,0) H=10516.200 L=10396.500

This is a three plot month. A rare setup!.

Created with TradeStation 2000i by Omega Research © 1999

Unlocking the Profits of the New Swing Chart Method

CHART 34

(A) Label (A) is the same 2-plot month down which follows through but eventually gives a reflex bounce back to the 200 DMA.

(B) Label (B) the level where the quarterly chart turned down and the overhead 200 DMA. The failure to rally at this point suggests lower prices and you get them. Note how the 2-plot month at (A) led to a six month correction with a reversal in the seventh month. Many times the market plays out in threes and sevens. Notice how (B) is also a failure of a down inside month (the expectation is for a turn up) at a Necktie of the 200 and 50 DMA's.

(C) Label (C) shows the 2-plot month down which gives the 3rd drive to the low and the reversal in the 7th month. Notice how the turn up of the monthly chart at (C) defines another high and a high at the 200 DMA as well. See how valuable understanding the behavior of True Swing Charts at key moving averages is. In October the monthly chart turns up and accelerates suggesting the promise of a low. Notice how the market recaptures the 200 DMA and the reflex back to kiss the MA goodbye. Notice how after the reflex pullback the quarterly chart turns back up taking out two prior quarters high in one move. There is consolidation after this liftoff from low but no real pullback and when the monthly plots higher early in 1954 it suggests the market wants to move higher.

(D) Label (D) is important to understand because it is a rare setup. The monthly plots higher in June making a higher high then plots lower on trade below May's low. Note the 'tail' on the daily chart as the market tags the 50 DMA. Tails at a turn down are many times a bullish phenomena. As you can see in this case it was a bullish clue as to how the price action would unfold. When the monthly chart turns back up in the same month it is a Lace-Up-Your Shoes Buy Signal.

NOTES

(DJ-30) Dow Jones Indust.Daily   05/25/2005   C=10457.800   -45.880   -0.44%   O=10503.200   H=10516.200   L=10396.500   V=0   Mov Avg 3 lines(Close,21,50,200,0)

Created with TradeStation 2000i by Omega Research © 1999

Unlocking the Profits of the New Swing Chart Method   PAGE 74

CHART 35

(A) Label (A) is another look at how the market advanced solidly from the June 1954 3-plot month. At (A) One might have anticipated at least a test of the 200 DMA after it 2-plotted down but the immediate turn back up speaks to the strength of the market.

(B) Label (B) shows the strength of the market continues as the up inside set up which suggest a turn down in the monthly chart fails to pan out and instead the market accelerates as the monthly plots higher into the end of the quarter.

(C) Label (C) shows how the market finally tagged the 200 DMA for the first time making a low within days of turning the monthly chart down. This is very bullish action and suggests a test of the high. In addition, the quarterly chart turns down, marks low very quickly and two plots back up.

(D) Label (D) shows that after a line formation the monthly chart turns down as once again the 200 DMA is tagged defining support. After a reflex rally and a test which holds the 200 DMA we can expect a rally attempt which occurs and turns the monthly back up at the same time a 4 month consolidation is broken. Note the acceleration.

NOTES

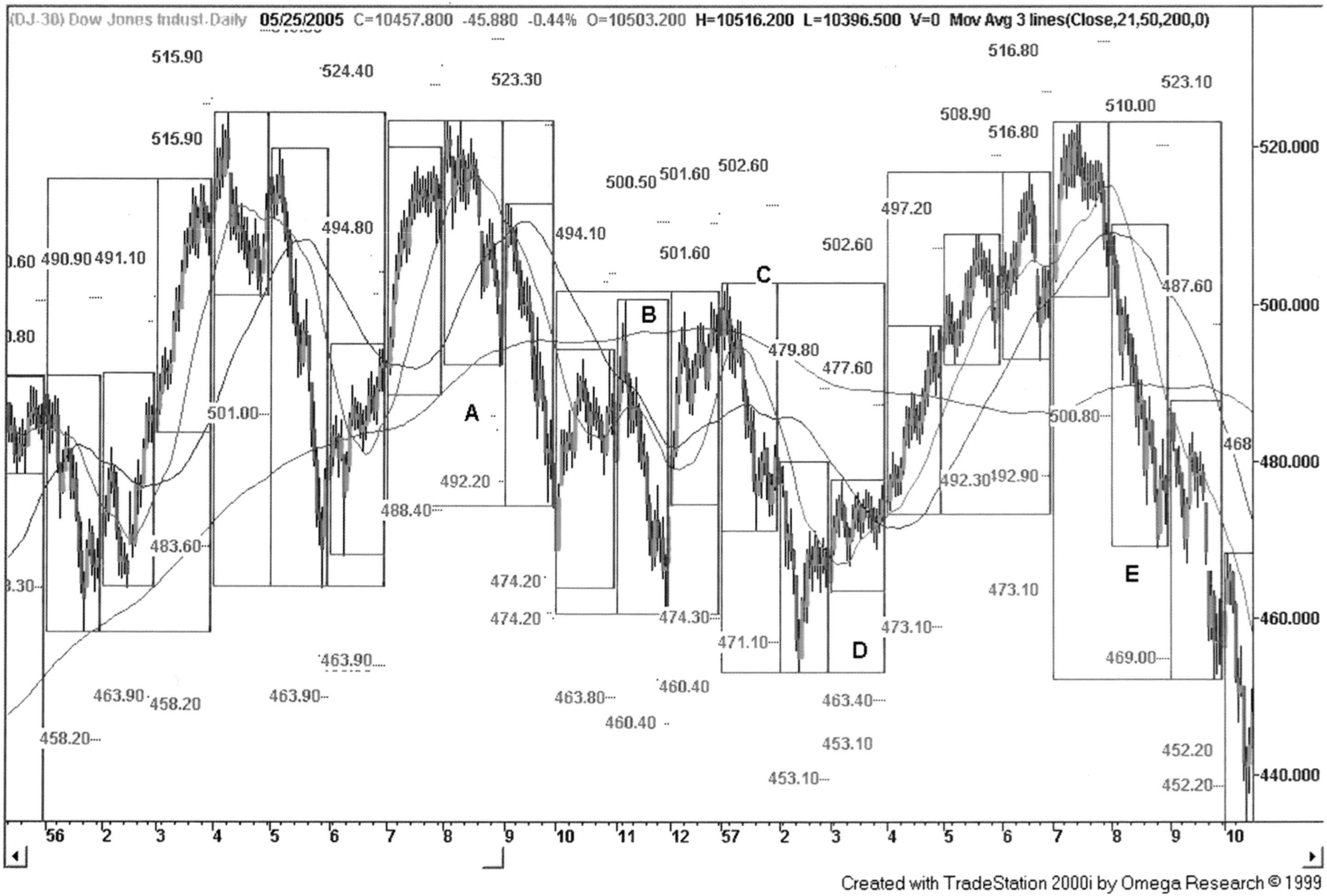
(DJ-30) Dow Jones Indust-Daily 05/25/2005 C=10457.800 -45.880 -0.44% O=10503.200 H=10516.200 L=10396.500 V=0 Mov Avg 3 lines(Close,21,50,200,0)
515.90
524.40
523.30
516.80
523.10
510.00
508.90
516.80
515.90
500.50
501.60
502.60
497.20
494.80
494.10
501.60
502.60
490.90
491.10
C
B
487.60
479.80
477.60
501.00
A
500.80
468
492.20
492.30
192.90
488.40
483.60
474.20
473.10
E
474.20
474.30
471.10
473.10
D
469.00
463.90
463.90
458.20
463.90
463.80
460.40
463.40
460.40
458.20
453.10
452.20
453.10
452.20
520.000
500.000
480.000
460.000
440.000
56
2
3
4
5
6
7
8
9
10
11
12
57
2
3
4
5
6
7
8
9
10
Created with TradeStation 2000i by Omega Research © 1999

CHART 36

The run up from March makes a high early in the second quarter in April. Note, how after that high is tested and the monthly turns down the market accelerates lower giving a mirror image test of the low in the first quarter. It is an interesting example of both the Principle of Tests and Principle of Fractals playing out as the test of the monthly high leads to a test of the quarterly low.

(A) shows a test of the quarterly high from April 1956. Notice how the market found high as soon as it plotted higher in August 1956. The important thing to understand here is the Rapid Flipping of the monthly chart since May 1956. Note the difference in behavior as the 200 DMA is tagged in late August which one would expect to carve out a low if the market were bullish. A rally develops but proves to be only a reflex rally as the 200 DMA is quickly broken. (Note how the overhead 50 DMA contained the reflex rally). The close near the low of the third quarter in September suggests a turn down of the quarterly chart which occurs. The turn down does define a low but the market stalls out as it finds resistance at its overhead 200 DMA early in November just as the monthly chart turns up. The failure to gain momentum as the monthly chart turns up indicates the bounce from the quarterly low is merely a reflex bounce. The market rolls over as the monthly 2-plots down. It's getting tough in here as the action is choppy. You would think the market would go much lower here but instead it jams it in your face turning the monthly chart back up.

(B) Label (B) shows the outside down two plot month which did not plot lower.

(C) Label (C) shows that the quarterly turn up defined a high tracing out a bearish monthly -1+2 sell signal. Once again the market 2-plots to the downside as the market fails to stabilize above the 200 DMA

(D) Label (D) refers to the 2-plot quarter which one might expect to be bearish and signal lower prices. However, the price action does not follow through and the market carves out a V bottom. Notice the THREE drives down into D and the fact that D was six months from the high at A. The down inside month sets up the run to test the high high. Notice the bullish behavior as the market accelerates when the monthly chart turns up and how the 200 DMA is easily converted. Note the 3 drives to a high are a fractal of the 3 drives to a low at D. Note, how the market waterfalls lower in July as the Two Feet in May and June respectively are broken.

(E) Label (E) shows the acceleration as the monthly chart turns down which is a mirror image of the upside acceleration as the monthly turned up in April. Notice the three tops in this chart through 1956 and 1957 which sets up a possible Rule of 4 Breakout.

NOTES

(DJ-30) Dow Jones Indust-Daily 05/25/2005 C=10457.800 -45.880 -0.44% O=10503.200 H=10516.200 L=10396.500 V=0 Mov Avg 3 lines(Close,21,50,200,0)

Created with TradeStation 2000i by Omega Research © 1999

Unlocking the Profits of the New Swing Chart Method   PAGE 78

CHART 37

(A) Label (A) shows a double down inside monthly buy set up (note how there are almost three months inside)

(B) Label (B) refers to the Principle of Fractals in as much as the down inside months led to a down inside quarter. At the end of March 1958 you've got to start getting bullish about the down inside quarter. With six to seven months on the side you know you've got a big turn coming. When the quarterly turns up the market accelerates through the 200 DMA. Note the reflex pullback in May that tests the 200 DMA. Remember from the prior chart that a Rule of 4 Breakout, a breakout over triple tops will occur at approximately 524. The persistence and power of the trend after the quarterly plots higher suggest the market will be magnetized to an attempt to break out over 524. The market never looks back. If you were waiting for the market to provide a second chance you had a long wait. Such is the lesson when the big wheels of time turn up and keep going after a substantial period of time on the side.

(C) Label(C) shows the power of the trend and that trends don't end easily: the monthly chart turns down for the first time in many months but bullishly finds low immediately and 2-plots back up.

NOTES

(DJ 30) Dow Jones Indust-Daily 05/25/2005 C=10457.800 -45.880 -0.44% O=10503.200 H=10516.200 L=10396.500 V=0 Mov Avg 3 lines(Close,21,50,200,0)

Created with TradeStation 2000i by Omega Research © 1999

Unlocking the Profits of the New Swing Chart Method   PAGE 80

CHART 38

(A) Label (A) shows how the trend from the prior chart continued from May 1958 to August 1959 (approximately 14 month months) where a 2-plot month down occurs. After a reflex rally the decline continues tracing out a +1 -2 buy pattern as the market tags its 200 DMA once again. You've got to start getting bullish here. When you've been above the 200 DMA for a substantial period of time and it is tagged for the first time, it is almost always a great buying opportunity.

(B) Label (B) That notion is confirmed by the down inside month buy set up. Note how B is an up inside quarter.

(C) Label (C) shows that the quarterly chart plots higher at the beginning of the New Year but bearishly does not follow through from the expectation of higher prices from the close near the high at the end of December and bearishly when the market stabs back below the consolidation: in December downside acceleration occurs as the monthly chart turns down. Note how the failure leads to a break of the 200 DMA. From the Rule of 4 break out near 524 the market ran to 683 carving out a top for a while with a fake out break out and a January turn at C.

(D) Label (D) refers to a down inside quarter from where you would expect a turn up but you do not get it. Instead the market bounces to test the level of the scene of the crime from the big top where the monthly 2-plotted down at C. The market has a memory. Keep track of these turn levels.

(E) Label (E) following the Principle of Fractals the down inside quarter leads to a down inside month. The inside/inside set up on these two big wheels suggests a possible cascade higher. But even though the market closes near the high of the month in August it does not follow through and you get a failure as the monthly and quarterly plot lower.

NOTES

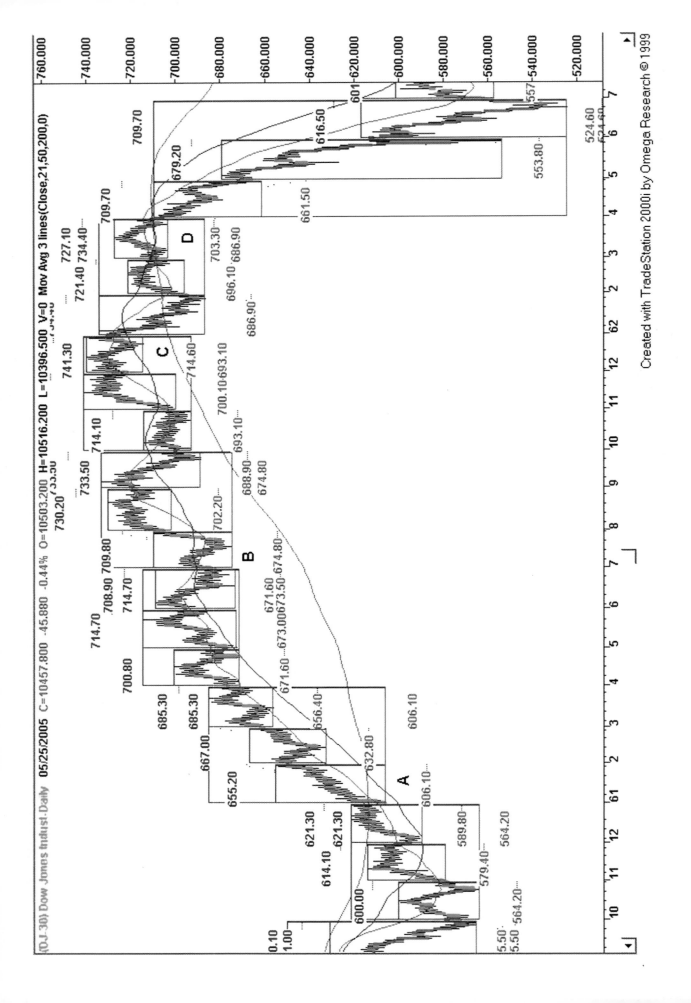

(DJ-30) Dow Jones Indust-Daily 05/25/2005 C=10457.800 -45.880 -0.44% O=10503.200 H=10516.200 L=10396.500 V=0 Mov Avg 3 lines(Close,21,50,200,0)

Created with TradeStation 2000i by Omega Research © 1999

— Unlocking the Profits of the New Swing Chart Method —   PAGE 82

CHART 39

There is no great set-up at the 1960 bottom. The monthly chart turned up and there was a reflex pullback that tested the 50 DMA. The market treaded water around the 200 DMA and then when the quarterly chart turned up; bullishly we get acceleration and no reflex pullback. You can see how the market recognizes and respects these two moving averages.

(A) Label (A) shows where the quarterly turned up and accelerated directly to the high of the 4th quarter of 1960 before pulling back. When the monthly plots higher the market is talking as momentum continues.

(B) Label (B) shows a double up inside month after the strong advance. You expect a turn down but the close near the high of the month in July suggests higher prices and the market powers higher into September. However, the last month of the quarter traces out a 2-plot month down. The 2-plot down does not deliver follow through and instead the down inside month suggests a turn up and a least a test of the high which occurs at (C).

(C) Label (C) shows an up inside month and you expect a turndown and you get it. Bearishly, the quarterly chart turns down in January 1962. This is important: Note the break of the 200 DMA and the close near the low the month of January suggesting a bullish resolution especially since this is the first time the 200 DMA has been tagged in a substantial period of time.

(D) Label (D) shows however that the behavior when the monthly chart turns back up is bearish as the market rolls over. The turn up of the monthly chart which defined a high as the monthly turned right back down knifing back below the 200 DMA was a Get Out of Dodge sell signal. When the quarterly starts plotting lower in April the nail is in the coffin and after a small reflex rally the market crashes lower. Note the cascade set up on the monthly quarterly wheels led to the waterfall.

NOTES

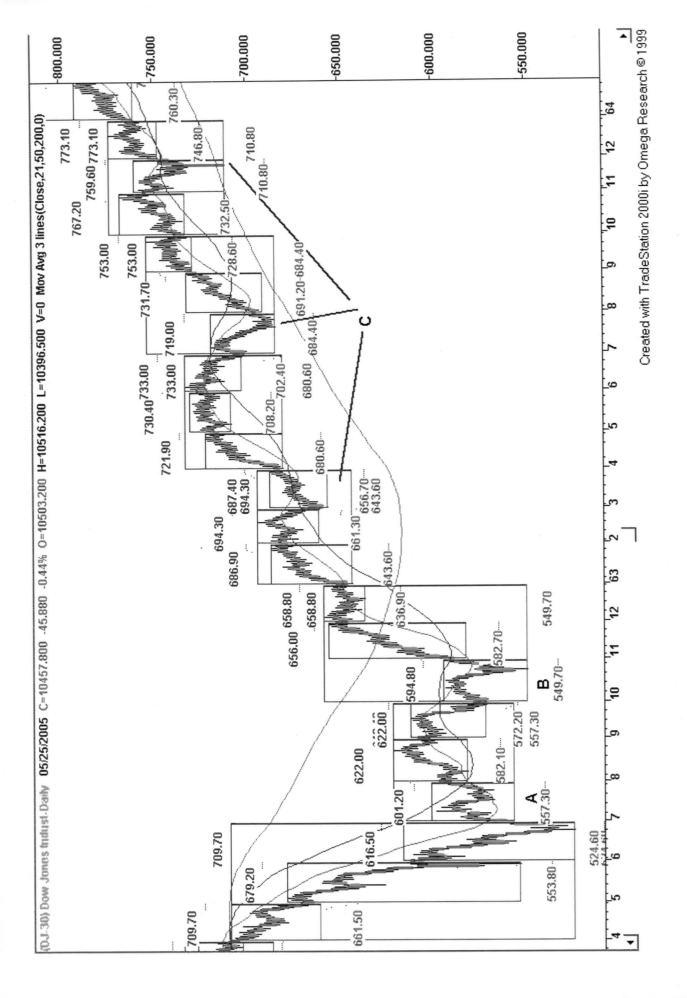

(DJ-30) Dow Jones Indust. Daily   05/25/2005   C=10457.800   -45.880   -0.44%   O=10503.200   H=10516.200   L=10396.500   V=0   Mov Avg 3 lines(Close,21,50,200,0)

Created with TradeStation 2000i by Omega Research © 1999

Unlocking the Profits of the New Swing Chart Method   PAGE 84

CHART 40

(A) Label (A) shows the down inside month after the three month smash down into the end of the second quarter in 1962. Notice how the down inside month led to a down inside quarter, once again demonstrating the Principal of Fractals.

(B) Label (B) is important. Why is (B) not a plot? Because, it's already down, it didn't go lower, and it's not a 2-plot quarter since it didn't plot lower. It is an outside quarter up but is not a 2-plot quarter. This is the distinction between True Swing Charts and traditional swing charts most technicians are familiar with. Bullishly, the market accelerates higher upon the quarterly turn up. The lack of reflexivity at the turn up is a sign of strength. Notice how the acceleration coincides with a break-out above the 200 DMA once again.

(C) Label (C) marks the only turndowns in the monthly chart in this advance. The first one is a March turn down that finds low immediately. The second one traces out a + 1- 2 buy pattern. The third one gives a turn down that delivers a pullback to the 200 DMA which is the first tag of this moving average all year. Notice how from the outside up quarter at the end of 1962 the quarterly carves out higher highs and higher lows throughout the following year, a Sign of the Bull.

NOTES

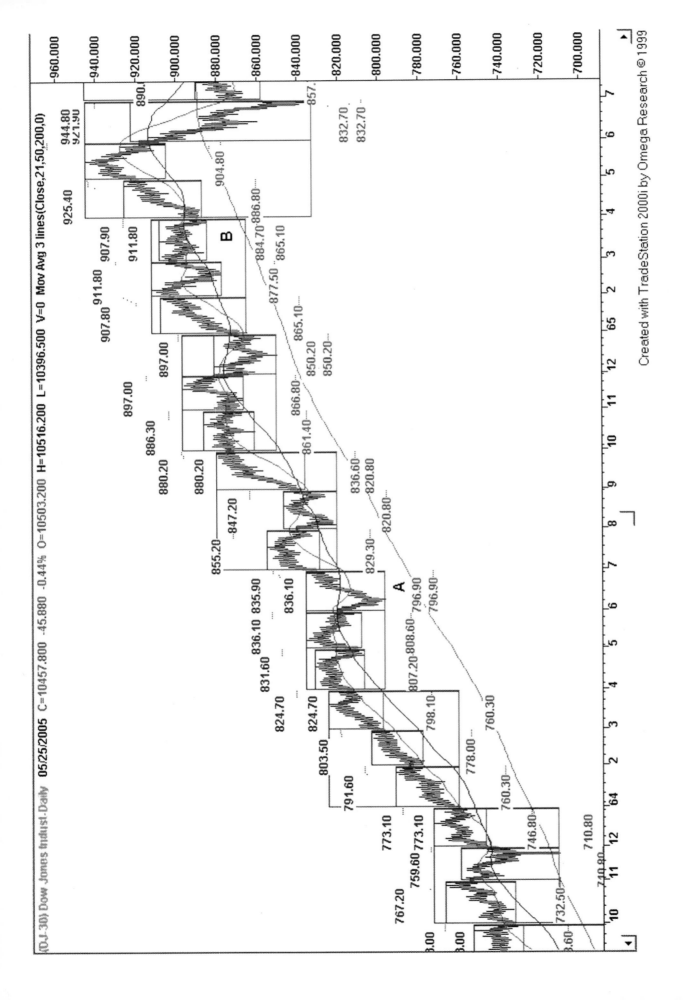

(DJ-30) Dow Jones Indust-Daily   05/25/2005   C=10457.800   -45.880   -0.44%   O=10503.200   L=10396.500   V=0   Mov Avg 3 lines(Close,21,50,200,0)

Created with TradeStation 2000i by Omega Research © 1999

Unlocking the Profits of the New Swing Chart Method   PAGE 86

CHART 41

(A) Label (A) refers to the first monthly turndown after a long period--in this case six months. This is the first monthly turndown after six higher lows. A turn down after substantial time without turning down is almost always a buy. In a persistent strongly trending market these turndowns typically define a low: they are like the inhale a long distance runner takes.

(B) Label (B) shows the first up inside month in a while. This is a warning flag. The expectation is for a turn down but it doesn't occur. However, (B) was the 11th quarter up from the low in 1962. When the market doesn't do what you expect you can usually get a significant move in the opposite direction. Notice how that although the market closes at the low of the month in March 1965 there is not the expected downside follow through. Contrary to expectation you get another March turn up which runs up to a 3 year anniversary (less one month) of the last major low. Remember, the market tends to play out in threes. A move below the breakout point in April and particularly a move below the up inside month defined by (B) confirms the notion of the warning flag and raises a red flag----literally. The run up into the three year anniversary of the low was a 'whoop 'em up' --the opposite of the flush out that we have seen that occurs at many lows. Notice how the market picks up steam to the downside as the monthly chart turns down in June indicating the likelihood of a failure of the support from the first quarter to hold. It doesn't. Notice, also, how the close near the low of the month in May from the rally high suggested a monthly turn down and how the acceleration indicated a nosedive to the 200 DMA. Bearishly, although the 200 DMA has not been tagged in a long period, the market knifes through the 200 DMA convincingly and gives a reflex bounce to kiss it goodbye. Notice how the quarterly turns down just after the 200 DMA breaks and how this important relationship between the two echoes throughout market history. The important thing to remember is that it took 12 quarters for the quarterly chart to turn down: there were no bearish setups for 12 quarters!

NOTES

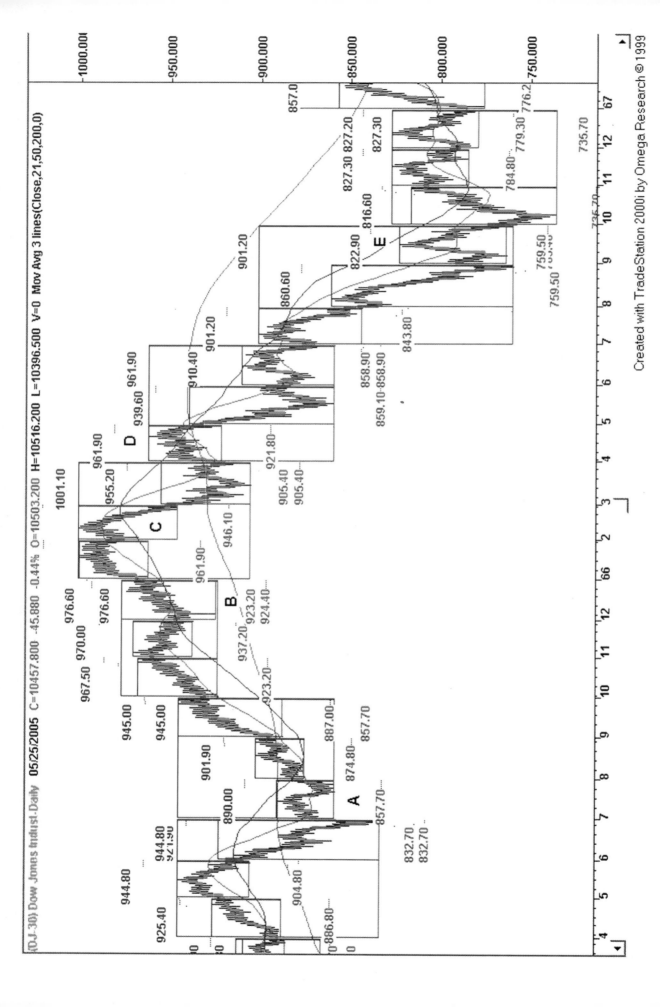

Unlocking the Profits of the New Swing Chart Method   PAGE 88

CHART 42

(A) Label (A) shows the turndown in the quarterly chart, which was a 2-plot outside down quarter, and the ensuing bounce back to the 200 DMA. The market oscillates creating an inside month indicating a rally. The monthly does turn up. After a 2-plot reversal quarter you would expect a turn up in the monthly to define a high. Instead, after the monthly turns up you get a small reflex pullback and then bullishly the monthly plots higher. Notice how the plot higher on the monthly coincides with acceleration back over the 200 DMA which leads to a close the high of the month in September and a turn back up in the quarterly chart at the end of the 3rd quarter. Importantly, this turn up leads a higher quarterly low sparking two more quarters of rally.

(B) Label (B) shows how the monthly turned down and the market found low right away leading to a run to 1000 for the first time ever.

(C) Label (C) shows the low close in the month of February does not follow through but instead leads to a test of the high. The move 'soups' the old high leading to an outside month down which following the Principle of Fractals leads to an outside down quarter.

(D) Label (D) shows that shortly after the quarterly turns down it relatively quickly defines another critical March turn as the 200 DMA is undercut. The important thing to understand is that after the bearish outside down quarter the first time the monthly turns up, as one might anticipate, it defines a high. When the quarterly plots lower in May you know there is trouble ahead. After four years of advance, you have to be thinking about a correction based on the behavior and it happens. All the other times throughout the advance when the monthly turned up the market did not roll over.

(E) Label (E) shows a down inside month after a waterfall decline which suggests stabilization and a possible set up for a low. This is a mirror image of the top. Notice, however, the close near the low of the month and the market flushes out to make the low followed by rapid flipping of the monthly chart putting in some time on the side.

NOTES

Unlocking the Profits of the New Swing Chart Method — PAGE 90

Created with TradeStation 2000i by Omega Research © 1999

CHART 43

(A) Label (A) shows a 2-plot up January which is bullish and which turns the quarterly up as well. The market gains traction over the 200 DMA and gives a reflex pull-back towards the 200 DMA.

(B) Label (B) shows a monthly turndown that, bullishly, finds low immediately, and you get 1-2-3 bars higher on monthly. Following the Principle of Fractals, notice how after the quarterly chart turns up in the first quarter of 1967 you get 1-2-3 quarters up to a high as well as a test of historic highs plays out. The monthly turns down and keeps going and the quarterly turns down giving another break of the 200 DMA. This confirms the idea of a test failure and the notion that the market has work to do.

(C) Label (C) shows an outside down month which leads to two lower lows on the monthly as the quarterly plots lower but no real downside momentum is established.

(D) Label (D) shows a double bottom on daily chart in March for another critical March turn followed by a turn up in the monthly and bullish behavior as the market accelerates back above the 200 DMA. Once again, this action occurs six months from high. Notice the sharp gap up after the double bottom suggesting a bottom is in. Notice also how the quarterly turns up and the market goes nowhere suggesting consolidation.

(E) Label (E) shows a rare 3-plot month as the market tests the 200 DMA and the level of the acceleration in April. Notice how the undercut and recapture of the 200 DMA in August implies an advance defined by a turn up in the monthly that accelerates.

NOTES

DJ-30-Daily 05/27/2005 C=10542.500 +4.900 +0.05% O=10535.800 H=10579.900 L=10489.300 V=16736 Mov Avg 3 lines(Close,17,50,200,0)

-1 Volume Average(50,50,Green,Red) 16736.00 25797.96

Created with TradeStation 2000i by Omega Research © 1999

Unlocking the Profits of the New Swing Chart Method   PAGE 92

CHART 44

If you take out December lows in January or February you have to be careful.

(A) Label (A) shows such a set up as the monthly and quarterly turn down. But, the important thing to remember is that it takes time for the market to do its thing. (A) Also shows how a down inside month sets up a turn up.

(B) Label (B) shows a bearish -1 +2 set up after a two month rally. Note, how the quarterly turns up and the market dies. The pieces are coming together for a decline phase.

(C) Label (C) shows once again that acceleration through the 200 DMA is not a good thing as the quarterly chart turns down leaving an outside down quarter and confirming a bear market. Note the acceleration after the March low is broken. The quarterly is now plotting lower for the 3rd quarter in a row something it has not done since 1966.

(D) Label (D) shows 7 plots in 5 bars on the monthly as the market is not going anywhere as it skates BELOW its 200 DMA which suggest distribution before lower prices. Notice the behavior where all the monthly turn ups just before (D) define a high.

NOTES

DJ-30-Daily 05/27/2005 C=10542.500 +4.900 +0.05% O=10535.800 H=10579.900 L=10489.300 V=16736 Mov Avg 3 lines(Close,17,50,200,0)

Created with TradeStation 2000i by Omega Research © 1999

Unlocking the Profits of the New Swing Chart Method   PAGE 94

CHART 45

(A) Label (A) refers to the down inside month at the low after five lower quarters as the Dow went from 1000 to 620.

(B) Label (B) shows a down inside quarter as the Principle of Fractals plays out. Notice, how after the monthly plots higher in August the 200 DMA is recaptured and how the market skates ABOVE this important moving average in a mirror image of the prior pattern where the market skated below the 200 DMA. A Fractal of Pattern. The inside month and the inside quarter led to a big rally back towards the 1000 level.

(C) Label (C) shows there were 10 higher lows on monthly before a turn down. Note, the up inside month prior to the turn down.

(D) Label (D) shows the bullish +1 -2 buy set up on the quarterly chart. Notice, how the low is near the high of the inside quarter at (B) one year later. The market does have a memory.

NOTES

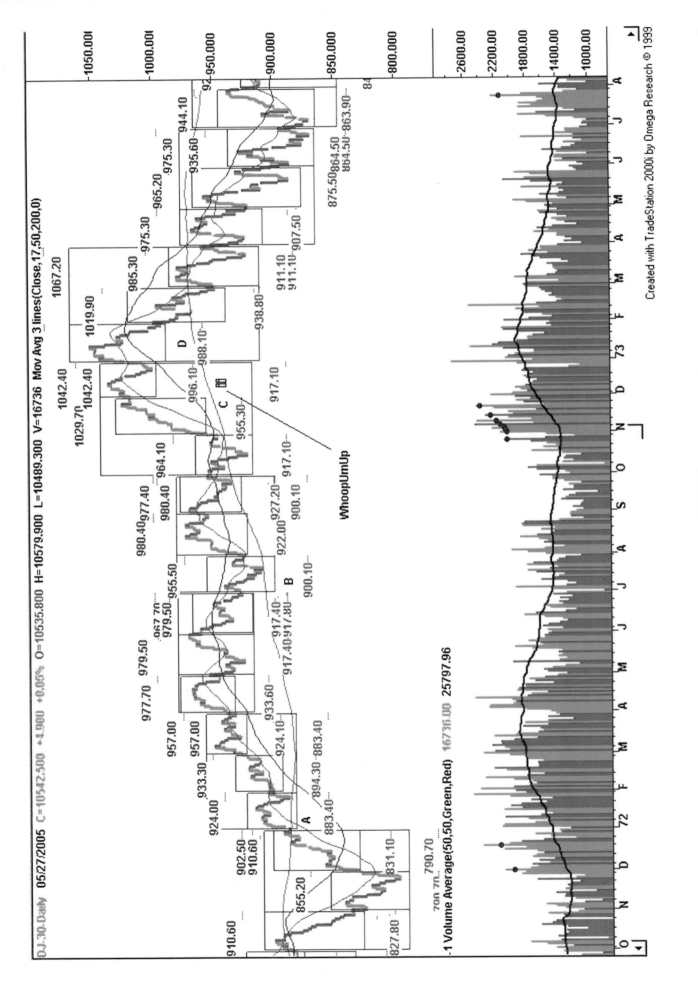

Unlocking the Profits of the New Swing Chart Method

PAGE 96

CHART 46

(A) Label (A) shows where the monthly accelerates on the turn up and its a good bet that you'll get a quarterly turn up as well and you do....at the beginning of the year.

(B) At Label (B) you get an up inside month which turns down and bullishly makes low immediately as the market kisses the 200 DMA. The quarterly also turns back down here and makes a low. Notice the Rapid Flipping of the monthly chart and that when you break out of that range you get a fast move.

(C) Label (C) shows a change in behavior from the 'flipping' as the monthly turns up followed by acceleration and you get a run for the roses or a "whoop 'em up". Notice the three higher highs into a high and the reversal on the third month which 2-plots down.

(D) Label (D) shows how the outside down month leads to an outside down quarter. Does this pattern remind you of the pattern into the 1929 top? Tops are many times made with these "whoop 'em ups". Back below the consolidation at 900 was bearish as the market went down for 1 1/2 years into October 1974 to 570.

NOTES

DJ-30-Daily 05/27/2005 C=10542.500 +4.900 +0.05% O=10535.800 H=10579.900 L=10489.300 V=16736 Mov Avg 3 lines(Close,17,50,200,0)

Similar to 911 Setup.

-1 Volume Average(50,50,Green,Red) 16736.00 25797.96

Created with TradeStation 2000i by Omega Research © 1999

Unlocking the Profits of the New Swing Chart Method   PAGE 98

CHART 47

This chart shows the continuation of the bear market of 1973/1974. The remarkable thing is that based on True Swing charts the market did nothing bullish giving only bearish symptoms all the way down. It never got anything bullish going.

(A) Label (A) shows a 2-plot month to the upside and a close at the high of the month but the market sticks it in your ear. However, when the monthly turns back down the market finds a low quickly suggesting a rally phase to come. The 50 DMA is regained with vigor indicating a turn back up in the monthly which occurs, leading to a turn up of the quarterly.

(B) Label (B) reflects that as the quarterly turned up momentum died and that the turn up coincided with the market carving out a bearish -1 +2 monthly sell set up. This is bearish behavior: the big quarterly wheel turned up and the rally died. Contrary to expectation, October closes near the high of the month and dies. Notice how the monthly turns back down and the decline accelerates as the market crashes through the quarterly and the 200 DMA. The high defined by the turn up in the quarterly coupled with the monthly -1 +2 led to a cascade to the downside.

(C) Label (C) refers to the fact that every turn up on the monthly chart defined a high---bearish behavior which foretold the lower prices to follow. The important thing to remember is that it typically takes time for the market to play out its agenda. (C) Traces out a lower high on the monthly chart. We have been mentioning the importance of March in many of these charts. Look what happens when the March pivot is broken to the downside. Notice also how the turn up at (C) finds resistance at the 200 DMA.

(D) Label (D) shows that once again the line formation lasts six months or one-half the wheel of the year. Notice the down inside month at (D) fails to deliver a rally which foreshadows the plunge to come. The quarterly was already down but when it plots lower the decline is in full force. In a fractal of the consolidation, the drop lasts six months. When the quarterly plots after a long period on the side without plotting the market is talking. This is similar to the set up prior to 9/11/01. Notice the quarterly rally to kiss the 50 DMA good-bye: the market often offers a graceful exit but; you have to take it. Notice the second minor bounce to the 50 DMA which is a heartburn rally for the bears at that time: the market doesn't like to accommodate. Be that as it may, the market has spoken and the whoop 'em down decline occurs followed by a low. Notice how the Principle of Tests plays out.

NOTES

DJ-30-Daily 05/27/2005 C=10542.500 +4.900 +0.05% O=10535.800 H=10579.900 L=10489.300 V=16736 Mov Avg 3 lines(Close,17,50,200,0)

-1 Volume Average(50,50,Green,Red) 16736.00 25797.96

Unlocking the Profits of the New Swing Chart Method — PAGE 100

CHART 48

(A) Label (A) shows the formation at the bottom in 1974 (it is analogous to the bottom in December 1987). The monthly turns up and dies and makes a slightly lower low on turning down at a test of the October low. This is often the signature of bottoms (reversed for tops). Note the N/R 7 month in December and the acceleration as the October low is 'souped' in a convincing manner. The next time the monthly turns up we get acceleration over the 200 DMA confirming the notion of the successful test in December. Moreover, the lack of reflexivity (lack of pullback) also confirms the significance of the double bottom.

(B) Label (B) shows where the market ran up for three quarters after the low. The quarterly turns down and makes low quickly which is bullish behavior. Once again note the relationship between the quarterly turndown and the 200 DMA. The sign of the bull is delivered as the monthly chart 2-plots back up. Note the low of the quarter occurs at the beginning of the quarter.

(C) Label (C) shows how The Principle of Fractals plays out and how the monthly chart turns down making the low at the 200 DMA. Bullishly, when the quarterly turns up the market accelerates. Note the six months of basically sideways consolidation from July 1975.

(D) Label (D) shows that the kind of momentous momentum that occurred at the beginning of January 1976 does not roll over easily. The big rally gives very little further gain as the market walks off the advance as the monthly flips around at the 1000 level.

NOTES

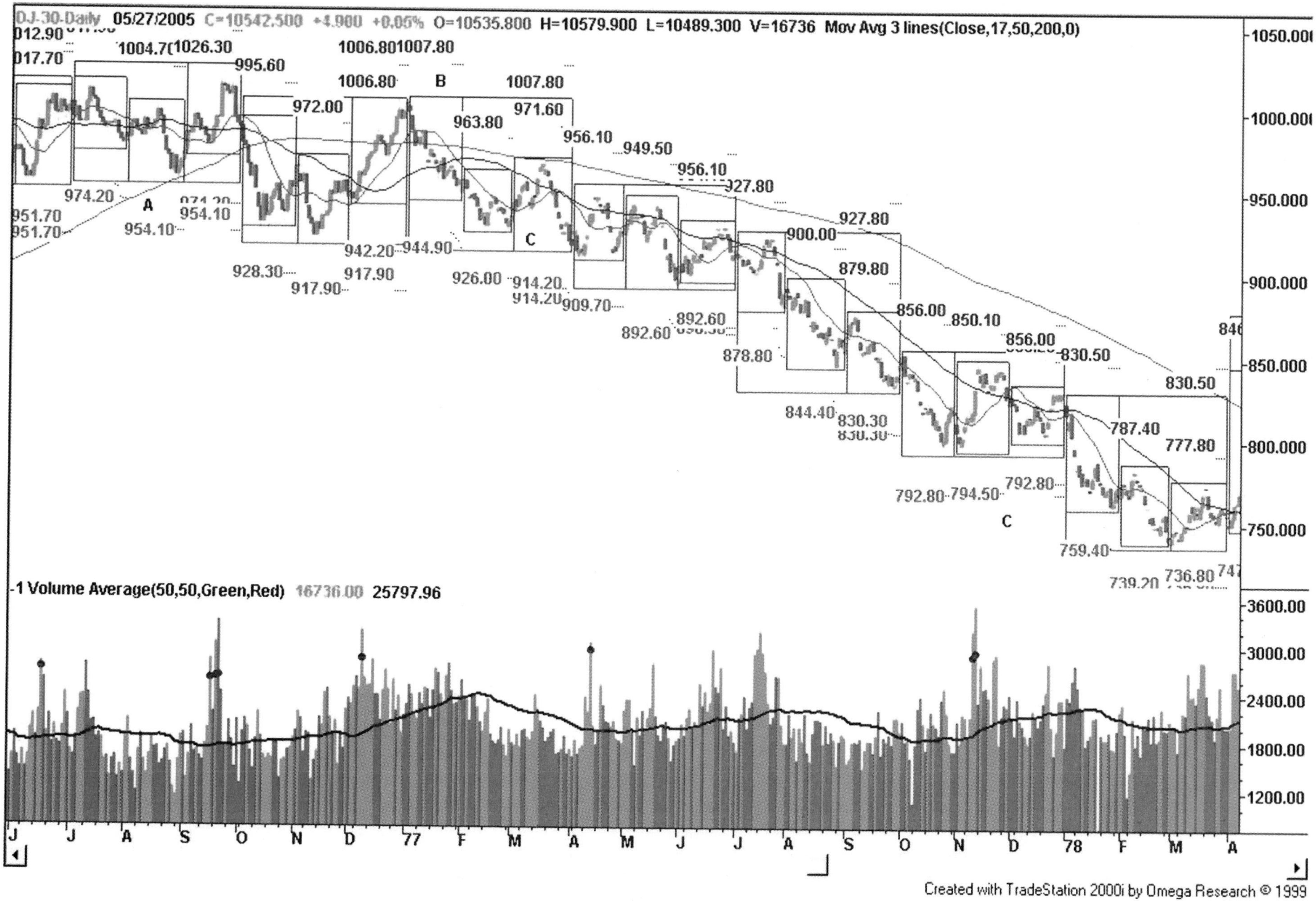
DJ-30-Daily 05/27/2005 C=10542.500 +4.900 +0.05% O=10535.800 H=10579.900 L=10489.300 V=16736 Mov Avg 3 lines(Close,17,50,200,0)
1004.7(1026.30
995.60
1006.801007.80
1006.80
B
1007.80
972.00
971.60
963.80
956.10
949.50
956.10
927.80
974.20
A
954.10
951.70
942.20
944.90
C
928.30
917.90
926.00
914.20
909.70
892.60
927.80
900.00
879.80
878.80
856.00
850.10
856.00
830.50
844.40
830.30
830.50
787.40
777.80
792.80
794.50
759.40
739.20
736.80
1050.000
1000.000
950.000
900.000
850.000
800.000
750.000
-1 Volume Average(50,50,Green,Red) 16736.00 25797.96
3600.00
3000.00
2400.00
1800.00
1200.00
J J A S O N D 77 F M A M J J A S O N D 78 F M A
Created with TradeStation 2000i by Omega Research © 1999

CHART 49

(A) Label (A) shows a higher low on quarterly which then plots higher as the market makes a higher high which is twice tested as the market goes nowhere that third quarter. Notice the second tag of the 200 DMA in a long time which leads to a turn up of the monthly chart in September.

(B) Label (B) shows where the quarterly turns up as the market attempts to recapture its 200 DMA. The turn up however defines a high immediately and that's bearish. Notice how the market proceeds to close at the low of the month and you kiss the 200 DMA good-bye.

(C) Label (C) shows the quarterly chart turns back down. Notice the Principle of Fractals at work as the outside down quarter synchronizes with an outside down month. Once again March proves pivotal as it is that month which produces an outside down month. Label (C) shows the failure of the potentially bullish double down inside month to generate a rally and the failure leads to lower prices.

NOTES

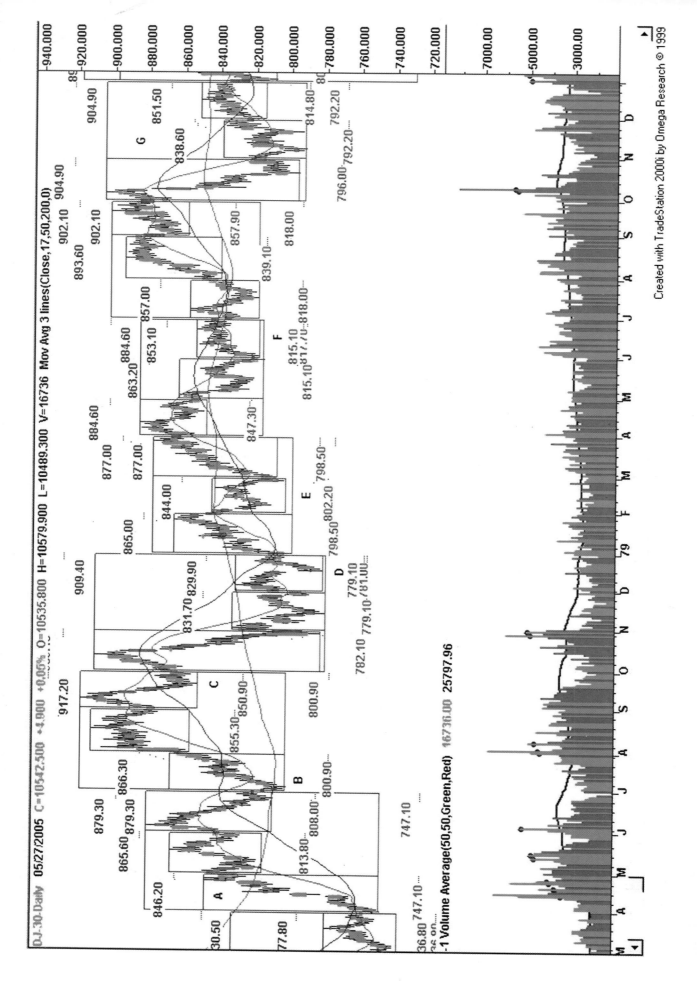

DJ-30-Daily 05/27/2005 C=10542.500 +4.900 +0.05% O=10535.800 L=10489.300 V=16736 Mov Avg 3 lines(Close,17,50,200,0)

-1 Volume Average(50,50,Green,Red)   16736.00   25797.96

Created with TradeStation 2000i by Omega Research © 1999

Unlocking the Profits of the New Swing Chart Method   PAGE 104

CHART 50

(A) Label (A) shows where the monthly and quarterly turn up in April after a March low and you get three higher highs on the monthly wheel immediately. The market plays out in threes.

(B) Label (B) shows a monthly +1 -2 pullback right at the 200 DMA. The set up leads to a new high as the monthly chart, as would be expected, turns right back up.

(C) Label (C) shows a mini fractal of the pattern we have seen at highs in the past and an outside down month. The outside down month doesn't kill you but it is a warning flag. The market finds low on the turn down and rallies back to test the high offering a graceful exit. Notice the fractal outside months down at the end of the second and third quarters in 1978. The bottom line is the market by its price action is talking in October and should put you on your toes.

(D) Label (D) shows how a down inside month leads to a down inside quarter.

(E) Label (E) an up inside month fails to generate a decline despite the close near the low of the month. When the market does not do as anticipated you get a strong move in the opposite direction which recaptures the 200 DMA.

(F) Label (F) a down inside month oscillates around the 200D DMA suggests a rally and you get one---a three month run.

(G) Label (G) many important turns come at the beginning and end of new quarters. Here you have a third quarter up and the third month up and the market falls out of bed as the monthly turns down immediately and the market knifes below the 200 DMA. The outside down month and the outside down quarter in the same month suggest downside follow through. Note the reflex rally back to the 200 DMA after the triple bottom on the daily chart.

NOTES

DJ-30-Daily   05/27/2005 C=10542.500 +4.900 +0.05% O=10535.800 H=10579.900 L=10489.300 V=16736   Mov Avg 3 lines(Close,17,50,200,0)

-1 Volume Average(50,50,Green,Red)   16736.00 25797.96

Created with TradeStation 2000i by Omega Research © 1999

CHART 51

(A) Label (A) shows that the quarterly turned up and died. The monthly and quarterly both turned down again in March, producing a second outside down quarter in a row. Again, March produces a key low.

(B) Label (B) is an inside month and another March turn which leads to a down inside quarter. The Principal of Fractals is evident once again.

(C) Label (C) shows the acceleration over the 200 DMA which suggests a turn up in the quarterly chart and you get it in July.

(D) Label (D) is a crazy month. It looks like a 3-plot month. The rapid flipping makes it very tricky to read the market here. Constructively, the 200 DMA and the quarterly chart hold up all through this period until (F).

(E) Label (E) shows the rapid flipping action in the monthly chart. It has 7 plots in 6 months.

(F) Label (F) shows an angular Rule of 4 Breakdown. The market breaks its 200 DMA, as the quarterly and monthly both turn down giving us our "Get-Out-of-Dodge" sell signal. After beating you up for months the market gave a great set up to the down side when these pieces came together. From (D) to (F) there were 13 plots on the monthly chart!

NOTES

DJ-30-Daily 05/27/2005 +4.900 +0.05% O=10535.800 H=10579.900 L=10489.300 V=16736 Mov Avg 3 lines(Close,17,50,200,0)

Unlocking the Profits of the New Swing Chart Method   PAGE 108

Created with TradeStation 2000i by Omega Research © 1999

CHART 52

(A) Label (A) is a down inside quarter which fails to generate an advance.

(B) Label (B) is a -1 +2 sell set up on the monthly which gives lower prices. The market spent 12 months making the prior high and the 13th month down gives low at (C).

(C) Label (C) everyone is loaded for bear here as the market makes a new low undercutting the March and June low (Two Feet). However, the momentum dries up at the new low and the market 'soups' the June low. Note how the quarterly barely plotted lower. (Mirror image of the 1929 high). Note how the turn up of the monthly in July dies at the 200 DMA leading to the final low. The monthly turns up in August as the acceleration back above the 200 DMA suggests the move to new lows was a fake out. Notice the fractal of how the 2-plot month led to a 2-plot quarter. Very bullish. The monthly turns down and dies by a tick at 50 DMA. That's bullish and a change in character. The bull market is on! In the fourth quarter of 1982 the market breaks out over 1000 for the first time. Note how the Dow held over the breakout point.

NOTES

〰〰〰

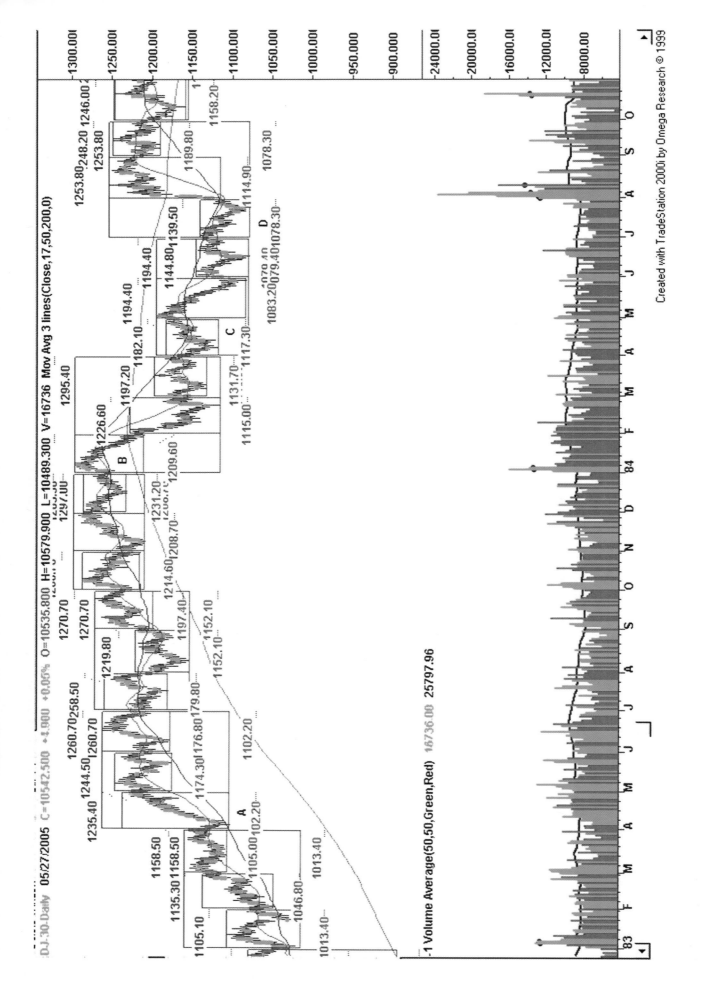

DJ-30-Daily 05/27/2005 C=10542.500 +4.000 +0.05% O=10535.800 H=10579.900 L=10489.300 V=16736 Mov Avg 3 lines(Close,17,50,200,0)

-1 Volume Average(50,50,Green,Red) 16736.00 25797.96

Created with TradeStation 2000i by Omega Research © 1999

CHART 53

This chart shows the powerful rally persisting from the low in 1982. The change in character from bear to bull market is demonstrated by six higher highs on the quarterly chart. It is interesting to note the fractal in as much as we have seen many six month advances, declines and consolidations.

(A) Label (A) refers to the fact that the whole rally never gave a +1 - 2 buy opportunity on the monthly chart. There was only one bar turndown as the market only took a single breath in the run up. Note, the marginal monthly turn down in April that found low immediately.

(B) Label (B) shows a monthly turndown that gives acceleration--a change in character. How was this top formed? It took TIME for the January 1984 top to be put in place. Firstly, November 1983 was a 2-plot month, down to up. The expectation would be for an advance, but contrary to expectation, you get an up inside month. The market goes higher but you do not plot higher because (B) is not higher than the November high. Many important turns, as we have seen occur at the end/beginning of the year. Consequently, with the rally in January 1984 I would be thinking it's a breakout, especially as the market is doing something again contrary to expectation: moving higher after an up inside month. However, look what happens. Early January defines a fake out breakout high as the monthly turns immediately back down with the market smashing concurrently through the 200 DMA and turning down the quarterly chart as well. All go within a few days triggering a "Get-Out-of-Dodge" sell signal.

(C) Label (C) is a double down inside set up. You expect a rally but instead you turn up and die, 2-plotting back down indicating the notion of much lower prices. You don't get them. Interestingly, the 2-plot month down does not follow through suggesting a possible mirror image of the November 2-plot month up that did not follow through putting in a top six months prior! As above so below.

(D) Label (D) notice the six month line formation as July traces out an N/R 7 month suggesting a pick up in volatility. You get it as the monthly chart turns up and accelerates gapping through the 200 DMA. The quarterly also turns up coincident with the 200 DMA once again. Note, the reflex pullback that tags the key 200 DMA.

NOTES

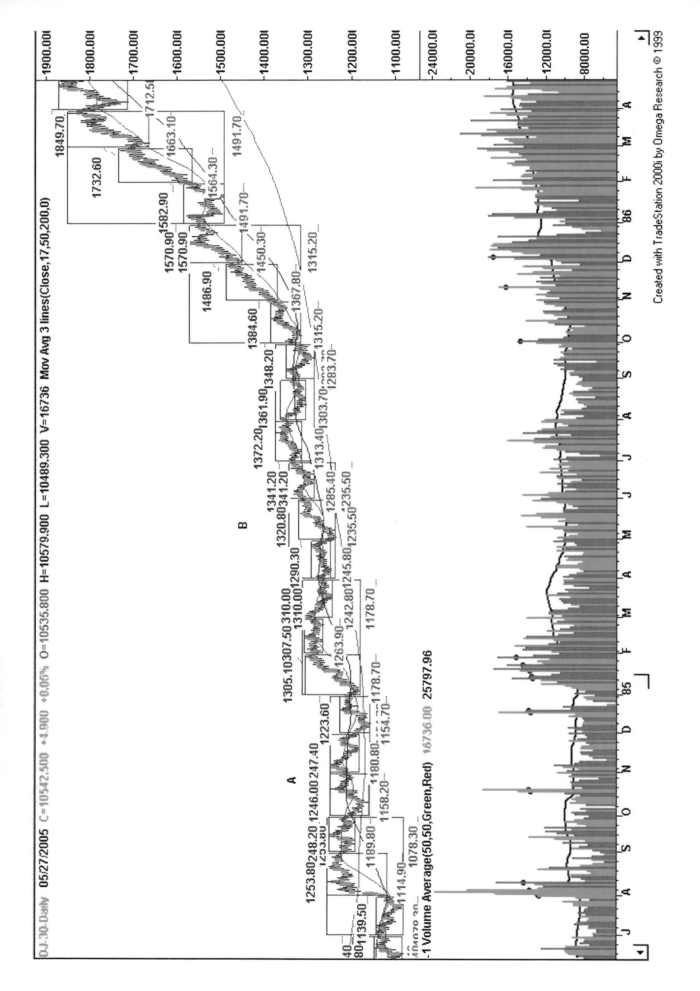

Unlocking the Profits of the New Swing Chart Method   PAGE 112

CHART 54

The bull is in charge. Despite the sleepiness of the advance and the labored nature of the advance the bull market is intact: the market has done nothing wrong so the bias and benefit of the doubt must go to the bull camp.

(A) Label(A) The up inside quarter suggests lower but the monthly turns down defining a low which leads to a beginning of the year turn as the monthly turns up and rallies convincingly off its 200 DMA. Note how the quarterly plots higher as the monthly chart makes higher highs and higher lows.

(B) Label (B) April is a down inside month and instead of generating a rally you plot lower below March but only by a tick or two. Remember, these MARGINAL plots and turns often indicate the market is ready to talk. And it does. The monthly 2-plots up leaving the sign of the bull. The low of the quarter is in May near the 200 DMA. Importantly, a +1 -2 bullish pattern in September 1985 leads to a Kick-Off Move after a final kiss of the 200 DMA. Does the market have order? Does this all look like happenstance?

NOTES

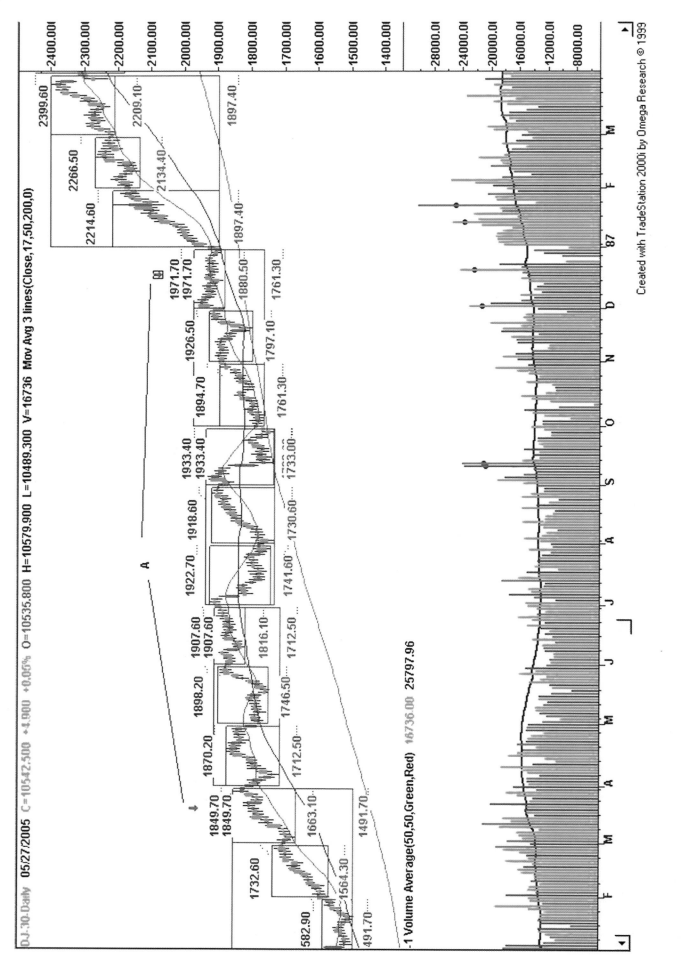

DJ-30-Daily 05/27/2005 C=10542.500 +4.900 +0.05% O=10535.800 H=10579.900 L=10489.300 V=16736 Mov Avg 3 lines(Close,17,50,200,0)

-1 Volume Average(50,50,Green,Red) 16736.00 25797.96

Created with TradeStation 2000i by Omega Research © 1999

Unlocking the Profits of the New Swing Chart Method   PAGE 114

CHART 55

(A) Label (A) refers to a long period of sideways action. Again, the market does nothing bearish. There are no quarterly turndowns despite lots of opportunities. The market crawls along the 200 DMA for 3 quarters. Note the last kiss of the 200 DMA in December 1986, as the second mouse gets the cheese. At the end of December/beginning of January you get a classic turn. Note the apparent breakout of the line formation in early December and the pullback to a low close for the month that does NOT give downside follow though.

NOTES

DJ-30-Daily   05/27/2005   C=10542.500   +4.900   +0.05%   O=10535.800   H=10579.900   L=10489.300   V=16736   Mov Avg 3 lines(Close,17,50,200,0)

2800.00t
2700.00t
2600.00t
2500.00t
2400.00t
2300.00t
2200.00t
2100.00t
2000.00t
1900.00t
1800.00t
1700.00t
1600.00t

2695.50
2662.40
2469.00
2391.30
2526.00
88.30
91.30

A
B
C

2027.50
2019.60
2075.30
2078.10
2110.90
2110.90
2121.40
2072.00
2169.10
2169.10
2169.50
2151.90
2140.30

1795.30
1846.00
1878.20
1951.30
1846.00
1968.00
1921.60
1921.60
2021.30
2047.30
1978.70
1988.40

1733.90
1616.20

-1 Volume Average(50,50,Green,Red)   16736.00   25797.96

55000.0t
45000.0t
35000.0t
25000.0t
15000.0t

A   S   O   N   D   88   F   M   A   M   J   J   A   S

Created with TradeStation 2000i by Omega Research © 1999

Unlocking the Profits of the New Swing Chart Method   PAGE 116

CHART 56

Here is the 1987 crash. In September the monthly chart turns down from an all time high planting Two Feet.

(A) Label (A) shows that a break of those Two Feet coincides with a break of the monthly, quarterly, 200 DMA all with in a few days triggering a "Get-Out-of-Dodge" sell signal.

(B) Label (B) refers to the double down inside monthly set up. You expect a turn up and you get it. Following the Principle of Fractals the double down inside monthly set up leads to a down inside quarter.

(C) Label (C) shows the expected quarterly turn up. The market is beginning to telegraph bullish confirming signals as the reflex pullback after the quarterly turn up holds at the 200 DMA. August is a turndown in the monthly which carves out higher lows. August 1988 is the 2nd higher monthly low since the crash and you would expect a little more bullish action here.

NOTES

DJ-30-Daily 05/27/2005 C=10542.500 +4.900 +0.05% O=10535.800 H=10579.900 L=10489.300 V=16736 Mov Avg 3 lines(Close,17,50,200,0)

-1 Volume Average(50,50,Green,Red) 16736.00 25797.96

Created with TradeStation 2000i by Omega Research © 1999

Unlocking the Profits of the New Swing Chart Method   PAGE 118

CHART 57

From the last chart we pointed out that one would expect to get some upside action from the 2nd higher low on the monthly chart. It didn't happen.

(A) Label (A) shows that from a THIRD higher low on the monthly chart in November 1988 the market is ready and explodes. Third higher lows are Power Surge Signals. In addition, the market shows strength by trading higher after an up inside month in March.

(B) Label (B) shows an outside down month in October which one would have thought would turn the quarterly chart down. Instead, the market goes nowhere stabilizing just above the 200 DMA. The monthly goes inside and then plots higher for two more months testing the high at C. Then guess what?

(C) Label (C) shows that in January 1990, you get yet another outside down month and you'd be thinking bearishly that this 'second mouse' would get the cheese----- that the quarterly chart would definitely turn down on this event especially as the 200 DMA is undercut. However, nothing develops on the downside and the down inside month puts the bull in gear again. Notice the Fractal of Two Feet on the monthly and the quarterly.

NOTES

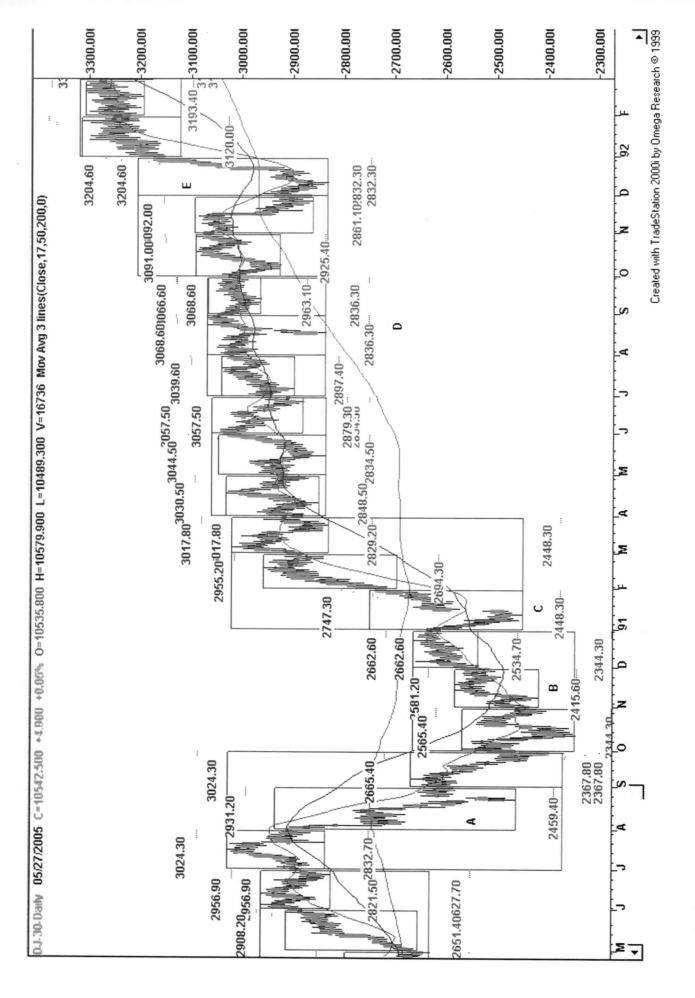

DJ-30-Daily 05/27/2005 C=10542.500 +4.900 +0.05% O=10535.800 H=10579.900 L=10489.300 V=16736 Mov Avg 3 lines(Close,17,50,200,0)

Unlocking the Profits of the New Swing Chart Method ——— PAGE 120

CHART 58

Remember the quarterly chart has been up since 1988.

(A) Label (A) is where the quarterly 2-plots down. Notice the three monthly higher highs going into the top before the break. Note the Two Feet that were planted in June and July and the waterfall after they were broken. The top before (A) was a mini-fractal of the 1929 top. When the market trades back below the breakout point and then back below the Two Feet it spells trouble. The monthly turns down on a big gap which is very bearish. Note how the close near the low of the month in June suggested a turn down but it did not come and instead we get a three week squeeze play up. It is typically not a good idea to chase strength in July.

(B) Label (B) shows the low after the waterfall decline which consisted of three drives to a low. At the low there is a +1 -2 buy set up on the quarterly chart. Note the ensuing 3 drives to the 200 DMA after the low which results in a test of the low. Note the two turns at the end of the year and at the beginning of the year. Notice how the market made a slightly lower low in the new quarter in October but bullishly reversed immediately.

(C) Label (C) shows the test and low after the -1 +2 on the monthly chart prior to the invasion of Iraq. Late January issues a "Get-Into-Dodge" buy signal as the quarterly, monthly turn up and the 200 DMA is recaptured concurrently. After a March high the market walks off the thrust into the end of the year.

(D) Label (D) shows where the market planted Two Feet again at the 200 DMA.

(E) Label (E) shows a monthly turndown that undercuts the 200 DMA. When the monthly turns back up 2-plotting with an expansion of range it signals another "Get-Into-Dodge" buy signal. Note the important low immediately upon the quarterly chart turning down and another end of the year turn.

NOTES

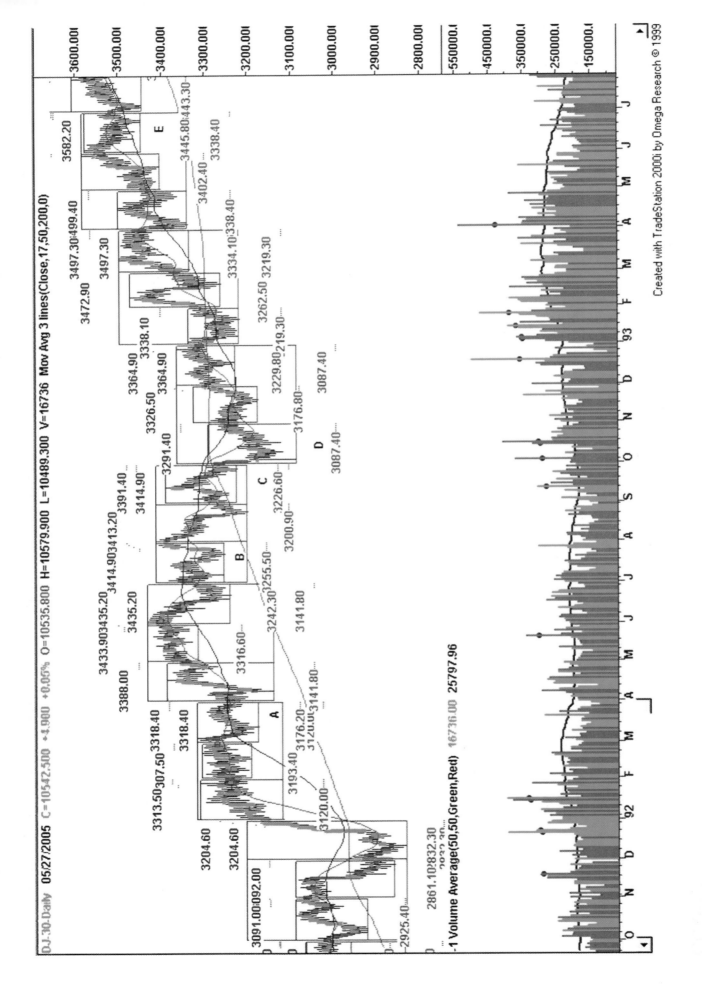

DJ-30-Daily 05/27/2005 C=10542.500 +4.900 +0.05% O=10535.800 H=10579.900 L=10489.300 V=16736 Mov Avg 3 lines(Close,17,50,200,0)

Unlocking the Profits of the New Swing Chart Method   PAGE 122

CHART 59

This chart shows a continuation of the advance from the prior chart.

(A) Label (A) is a 2-plot down month which gives a +1 -2 buy set up in April. Notice the slingshot right back up as the market stages an outside month up in April. If you didn't buy in the hole at the tail on the set up, it jammed it in your face. Note, how the rally led to three higher highs on the monthly with an outside down month in June.

(B) Label (B) is a down inside month that only leads to a test of the high. The close near the high of the month in July without the expected follow through suggests that this was a test failure. The down inside suggests a turn up and instead you roll over.

(C) Label (C) shows a down inside month after the market tags its 200 DMA finishing off an up inside quarter. The Principal of Fractals shows up once again.

(D) Label (D) you expect a turndown of the quarterly after the up inside pattern and you get one which flushes out the 200 DMA. Although you might expect much lower prices, the quarterly turndown defines an immediate low which should put you on your toes generating a bullish bias. After an attempt to recapture the 200 DMA there is a reflex pullback in January; which finds a low as soon as the monthly turns down. Note the acceleration as the monthly turns back up executing an Angular Rule of 4 buy set up causing a new high and the subsequent reflex back to the 200 DMA as the market marches higher without even an inside month.

(E) Label (E) is an up inside month and you expect a turn down, which occurs, carving out an immediate low.

NOTES

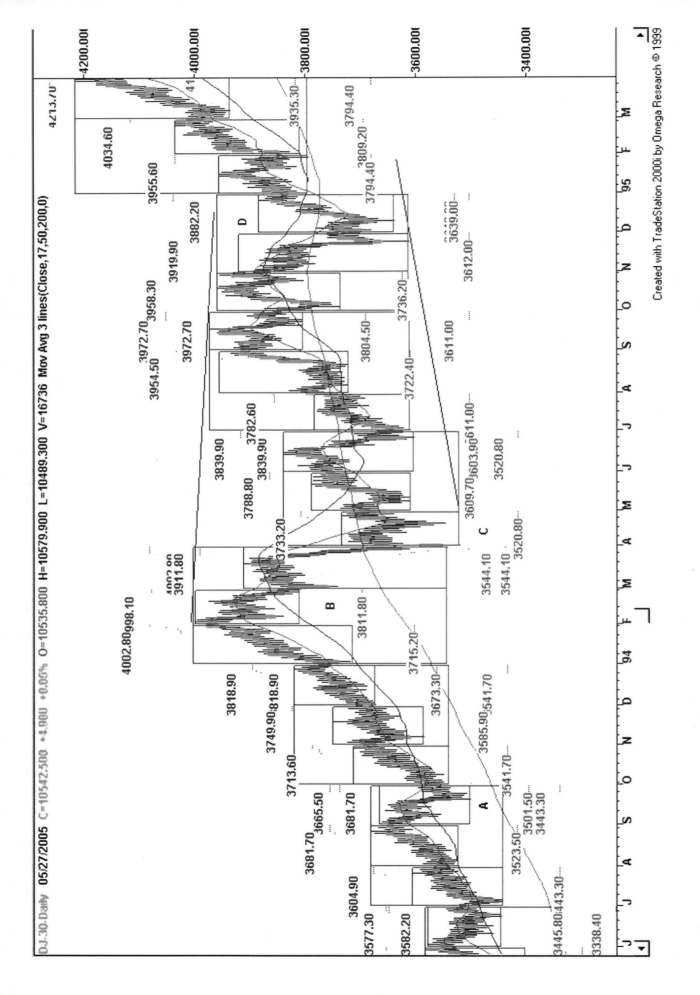

DJ-30-Daily 05/27/2005 C=10542.500 +4.900 +0.05% O=10535.800 H=10579.900 L=10489.300 V=16736 Mov Avg 3 lines(Close,17,50,200,0)

Unlocking the Profits of the New Swing Chart Method   PAGE 124

Created with TradeStation 2000i by Omega Research © 1999

CHART 60

This chart begins with another look at the turndown of the monthly in July from the prior chart which 2-plotted up.

(A) Label (A) is an important low as a monthly turndown occurs as it is a higher low, the third higher low on a True Monthly Swing chart from October 1992. Bullishly, these were all one month turndowns that found low quickly. Once again we see a power surge after the third higher low is confirmed in October 1993.

(B) Label (B) an up inside month after a significant run indicates a turndown and you get it right away as the close near the low of the month of February suggests. You get a quick reflex rally back to the 50 DMA. The subsequent gap down suggests a tag of the 200 DMA as the market makes a low near the end of March testing the low at (A)

(C) Label(C) shows the low made within a few days of the quarterly turn down.

(D) Label (D) here you get a down inside month but an up inside quarter and the close near the high of the month suggests a turn up. Notice the Rule of 4 Breakout after a reflex to the 200 DMA. A second mouse on the Rule of 4 really occurs in February 1995. Note the Two Feet on the daily chart in January and February.

NOTES

Unlocking the Profits of the New Swing Chart Method   PAGE 126

CHART 61

This chart shows the strong and relentless grinding advance after the Rule of 4 Breakout in November from the last chart.

(A) Label (A) the run up continues into the end of 1995. January 1996 (A) is interesting because it is the first monthly turn down in a substantial period of time specifically since the November 1994 low. The market had carved out 13 higher lows. We already know that many significant turns occur at the end/beginning of the year. Additionally, when the market does something for the first time in a long time it is typically an opportunity. In this case, the 'inhale' or breath in the trend as the monthly chart turned down defined an immediate low. Consequently, the expectation would be for higher prices and you get them. The monthly chart turns right back up in January leaving an outside up month.

(B) Label (B) notice the narrow range 7 month pattern just before (B). That whole six month pattern is analogous to the 1929 topping pattern. Here we also have a fractal to what happened at (A) when the monthly chart turned down and found support immediately at the 50 DMA. Here, in July, the first month of the third quarter, the quarterly chart turns down for the first time in a long time and a low is found at the 200 DMA relatively quickly. August is a down inside month which leads to the expected turn up.

NOTES

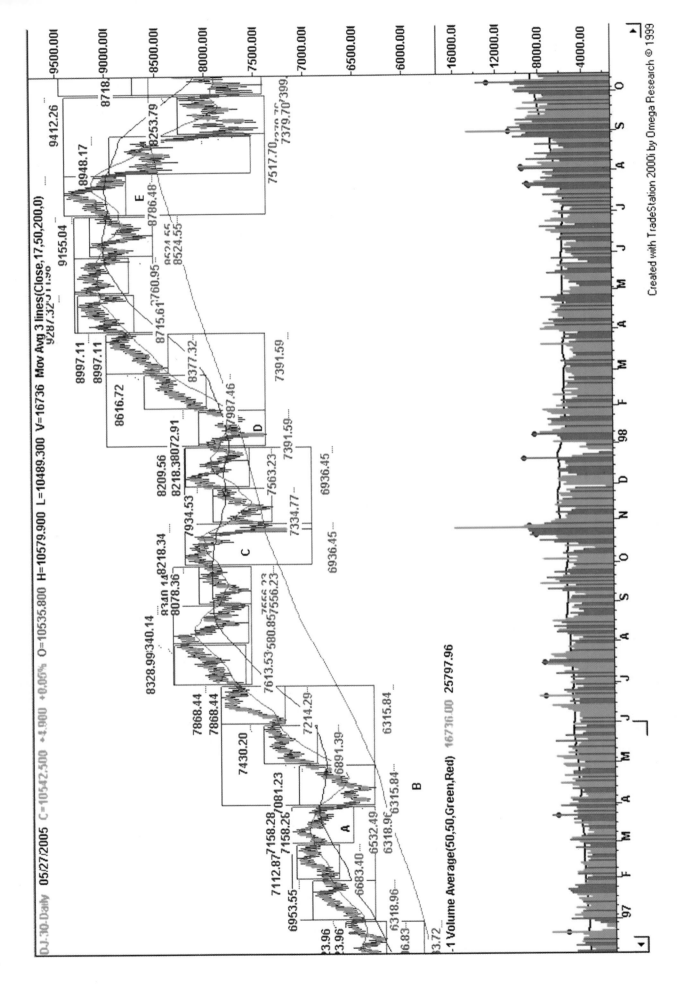

DJ-30-Daily 05/27/2005 C=10542.500 +4.000 +0.05% O=10535.800 H=10579.900 L=10489.300 V=16736 Mov Avg 3 lines(Close,17,50,200,0)

-1 Volume Average(50,50,Green,Red) 16736.00 25797.96

Created with TradeStation 2000i by Omega Research © 1999

Unlocking the Profits of the New Swing Chart Method   PAGE 128

CHART 62

(A) Label (A) is an outside month down in March; another potential important March turn. Legendary market technician W.D. Gann was one of the first to recognize the importance of the behavior in March because it is the Spring equinox.

(B) Label (B) the outside down March which saw a close near the end of the month led to follow through which generated the first +1 -2 buy set up on the monthly chart in some time. Here we show that at the same time the quarterly chart turns down early in the first month of the second quarter and the market finds low on the same day as the 200 DMA is approached. This is a bullish set up with bullish behavior. The market comes out of the pattern like a rocket ship. Happenstance? How does the market know? Could it be that the market has its own internal clock? Notice how the 2-plot quarter up signaled in May leads to a fast run as the market traces out three higher highs in May, June and July.

(C) Label (C) September is a + 1 -2 month. You expect a turn up and you get one. However, look at the ensuing behavior. Bearishly, the price action dies on the turn up defining a high and the monthly 2-plots down turning the quarterly down concurrently leading to an undercut of the 200 DMA. The outside down October and turndown of quarterly suggest at the minimum a tag of the 200 DMA and potentially substantially lower prices. But, it turns out to be only a flush out as there is no follow through from the outside down October. You have to adopt a bearish posture here, but, November goes inside putting some time on the side as the market stabilizes suggesting a turn up. The turn up plays out testing the level of the last monthly turn up. The market has a memory.

(D) Label (D) Note the fractals of how one test leads to another test: the test of the highs leads to a test of the lows as the market plants Two Feet as the 200 DMA is once again tested. The notion of a successful test is demonstrated by the fact that a low was found immediately when the monthly turned back down in January 1998. (Another beginning of the year turn).Remember how the big advance began with a large Rule of 4 Breakout? Now we get a fractal of that, as smaller Rule of 4 Breakout occurs to mirror the initial one to end the advance. As above so below; as below so above. The quarterly turns back up and the market picks up momentum marching higher.

(E) Label (E) Another fractal of the 1929 pattern. The monthly turns down in June, back up in July, but, bearishly closes near the low of the month after making a new high. The low close generates follow through as you get a concurrent turn down of quarterly and a break of the 200 DMA. The decline leaves a 2-plot quarter down, a sign of the bear and lower prices follow. At the low in September there is a +1 - 2 buy pattern.

NOTES

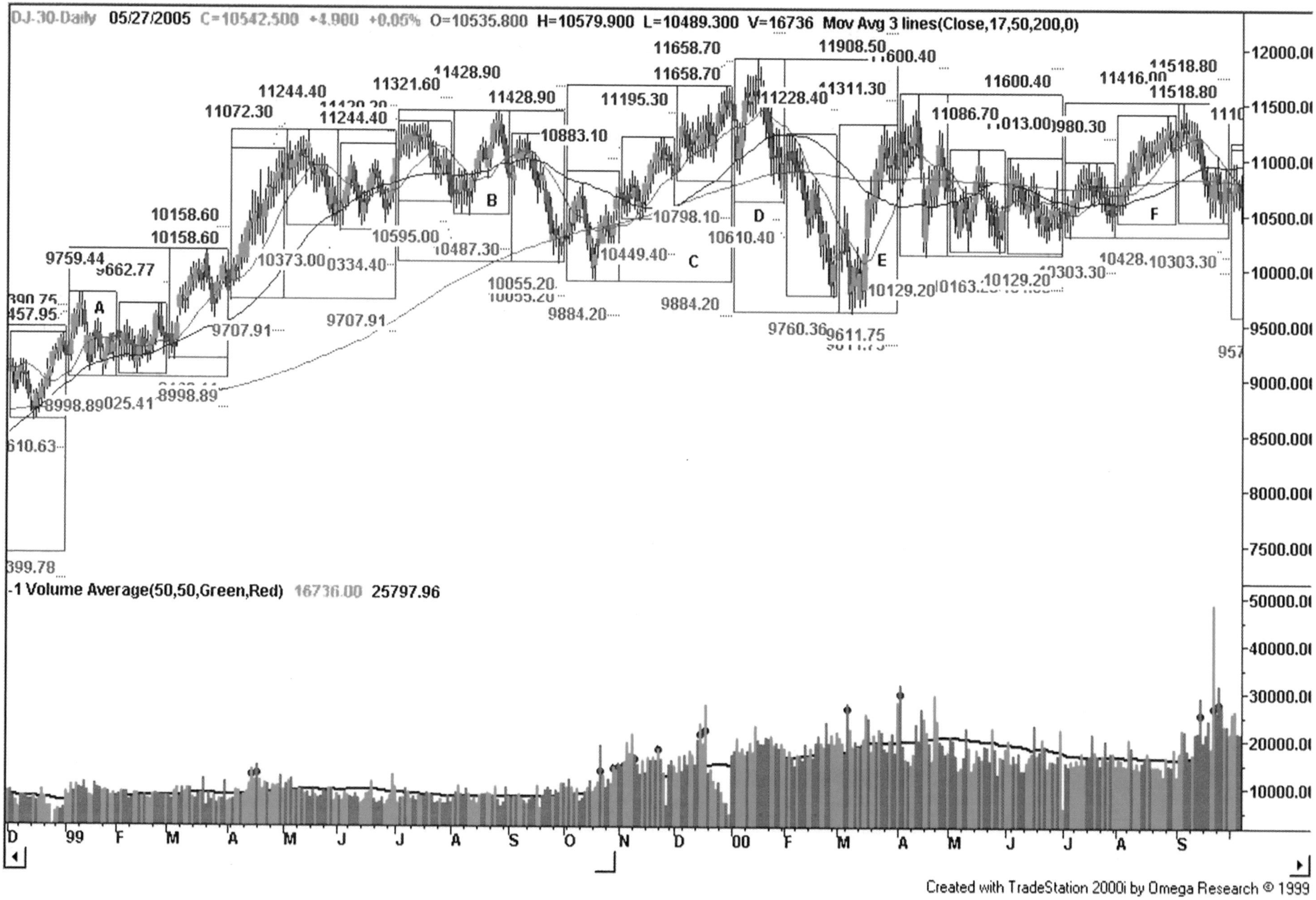
DJ-30-Daily 05/27/2005 C=10542.500 +4.900 +0.05% O=10535.800 H=10579.900 L=10489.300 V=16736 Mov Avg 3 lines(Close,17,50,200,0)
A
B
C
D
E
F
-1 Volume Average(50,50,Green,Red) 16736.00 25797.96
D 99 F M A M J J A S O N D 00 F M A M J J A S
Created with TradeStation 2000i by Omega Research © 1999

CHART 63

(A) Label (A) an up inside month does not give a turn down as would be expected. Instead, the market blasts higher in a sign of the bull.

(B) Label (B) is a 2-plot month up but no follow through indicates lower prices may follow. This failure leads to a test of the 200 DMA. It is important to note the three lower consecutive monthly lows turns the 3 month chart down.

(C) Label (C) shows that the market made low quickly after the quarterly chart turned down. Although one would anticipate lower prices, a rally materializes right in your face. The monthly chart turns back up and continues to rally for three months as the 3 month chart turns back up.

(D) Label (D) shows a 2-plot month down from a high, typically a sign of the bear. Importantly, you would expect a 2-plot up quarter to be bullish; instead you get a January high for a 2-plot month down which nails the quarterly leaving a 2-plot down quarter.

(E) This is a very tricky period as the monthly turns back up leaving an outside up month. However, the failure to generate momentum suggests that a test is playing out and that the rapid flipping of the monthly and quarterly wheels is signaling distribution.

(F) Label (F) is a big sell signal. You have two consecutive down inside quarters at a top area. This picture should have led to a rally. Instead, you break down after a long period on the side which is a nasty sell signal as the quarterly plots lower. When the March low is broken the market cascades lower. Notice how the test in September is a mirror image of the Two Feet or a Hand Stand, and the six month line formation. Additionally, there is a Slingshot on the 3 month chart from down to up to back down.

NOTES

〰〰〰〰〰〰〰〰〰〰〰〰〰〰〰〰〰〰〰〰〰〰〰〰

DJ.30-Daily 05/27/2005 C=10542.500 +4.900 +0.05% O=10535.800 H=10579.900 L=10489.300 V=16736 Mov Avg 3 lines(Close,17,50,200,0)

The Quarterly turned down on 9/17/01,
but the picture on the S&P was different
as we will see on the next chart.

-1 Volume Average(50,50,Green,Red)   16736.00 25797.96

Created with TradeStation 2000i by Omega Research © 1999

Unlocking the Profits of the New Swing Chart Method   PAGE 132

CHART 64

(A) Label (A) represents the mother of all sell signals. A double down inside quarter indicates substantial time on the side setting up a rally. However, plotting lower was a warning that distribution rather than accumulation was occurring. Of course the market is perverse and doesn't always like to accommodate immediately: when the market plotted lower it found low relatively quickly making it difficult to trade. The important thing to remember is that when the market does something you don't expect it is talking. Here it did something unexpected in a big way on a major wheel of time, the quarterly chart.

(B) Label (B) in a January turn, the quarterly and monthly turn up together defining an immediate high.

(C) Label (C) shows a 2-plot back down on quarterly for a low in March 2001.

(D) Label (D) the quarterly chart turns back up once again making a higher high than at (B). This is a real fake out move as it certainly looks like the market wants to go higher. However, the behavior is bearish as the quarterly turn up defines a high. It is the behavior of True Swing Charts as opposed to absolute price levels or breakouts that determines the trend. When the monthly turns down and keeps going it confirms the false 'breakout' in May.

(E) Label (E) the tag of the 200 DMA after the monthly turns down is the last graceful exit. (E) Shows another quarterly turndown. Notice how the quarterly was flipping back and forth like mad after an extended bull run in time. A sign of lower prices to come. It is important to realize that the market was unable to exploit bullish set ups during the entire period shown on this chart.

NOTES

The S&P penetrated the March Low of 1081.20 on 09/10/01. Plotting lower after five months was not bullish so we sold all positions that day. We were able to buy back after 9/21.

Created with TradeStation 2000i by Omega Research © 1999

Unlocking the Profits of the New Swing Chart Method   PAGE 134

CHART 64A

This chart compares the difference in the picture between the S&P and the Dow at the same time.

(A) Label (A) a down January (but not a turndown) is a clue as to the coming pressure.

(B) Label (B) the monthly turns down and tests the 200 DMA.

(C) Label (C) shows a 5 to 7 day run for the roses as the monthly chart turns back up. This was a 10 to 12% move which in such a short period indicates a potential blow off after an extended bull run. We call this a "Whoop-em-Up" sell signal.

(D) Label (D) shows a double up inside quarter and a 3 Drives to Test pattern, in this case a test of the all time high. The double up inside quarter suggests a turndown. The turndown occurs early in the beginning of the third quarter coinciding with a break of the 200 DMA, a turndown in the monthly chart and an Angular Rule of 4 sell signal. A "Get-Out-of-Dodge" sell signal is issued.

(E) Label (E) shows the drive into a March low followed by a -1 + 2 monthly sell set up. Note what happens after the down inside quarter (which one would expect to lead to some kind of rally) plots lower! The break of the March low led to a 12.6% decline in only 6 trading days, a classic "Whoop-em-Down".

NOTES

DJ-30-Daily 05/27/2005 C=10542.500 +1.900 +0.05% O=10535.800 H=10579.900 L=10489.300 V=16736 Mov Avg 3 lines(Close,17,50,200,0)

Created with TradeStation 2000i by Omega Research © 1999

Unlocking the Profits of the New Swing Chart Method   PAGE 136

CHART 65

(A) Label (A) shows a down inside quarter after a flush out. We expect a rally and a turn up and we get it.

(B) Label (B) shows three higher highs on monthly and a January turn at a test of the 200 DMA. This leads to an outside month down.

(C) Label (C) this is a good example of why it is not a good idea to chase strength in March after a down January. Note the downward acceleration after a 2nd mouse break of the 200 DMA.

(D) Label (D) the quarterly chart turns down at the same time as the three month chart turns down. The market accelerates lower after a small reflex rally.

(E) Label (E) a down inside month. You expect a rally but you do not get it. However, you do get a marginal plot lower on both the monthly and quarterly charts. These marginal undercuts often define lows just as marginal overthrows often define highs. Note the three drives down in September and October which are a fractal of the three drives down from the March 2002 high. Note the quick recapture of the July low on a gap up in October.

(F) Label (F) shows a -1 + 2 monthly sell signal at a test of the 200 DMA and another test rally (a heart burn rally for the bears at that time). Note how the market failed to give a "Get-Into-Dodge" buy signal as it failed to push over the 200 DMA and failed to turn up the quarterly chart here.

(G) Label (G) shows a down inside quarter as a Head and Shoulders Bottom is traced out. A 2-plot March indicates a possible kick off move. The Principal of Fractals says we should consider the possibility that a +1 -2 year could easily provide us with a down inside year in 2003. The fact that the first quarter of 2003 was a down inside quarter enhances that possibility.

NOTES

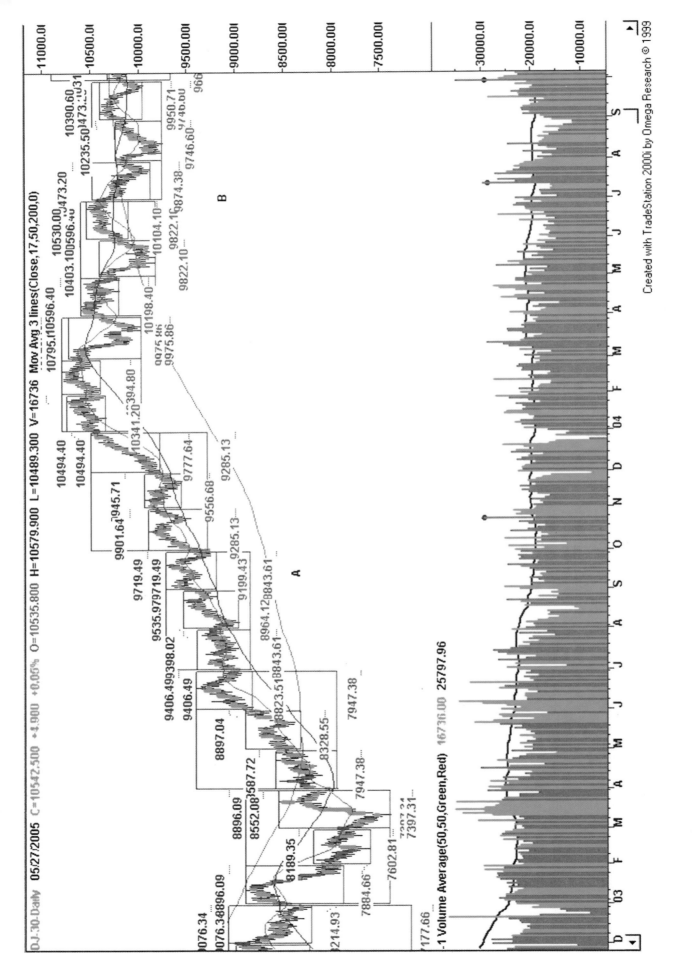

DJ 30-Daily 05/27/2005 C=10542.500 +4.900 +0.05% O=10535.800 H=10579.900 L=10489.300 V=16736 Mov Avg 3 lines(Close,17,50,200,0)

11000.0

10500.0

10500.00
10390.60 473.31
10235.50
10235.50
10403.10 10596.40
10530.00 473.20
10403.10 10596.40
10104.10
9822.10 9874.38
9950.71
946.60
9746.60
966

B

10795.10 10596.40

10000.0

9500.0

9000.0

1198.40
9975.86
9975.86

10341.20 10394.80
10394.80

9901.64 945.71

9777.64

9285.13

9556.68

9285.13

A

9719.49
9535.97 9719.49
9199.43 8843.61

8964.12 8843.61

8897.04

8896.09
8552.08 3587.72
8189.35

9406.49 9398.02
9406.49

8328.55

7947.38

8896.09

7947.38

7397.31
7397.31

076.34
076.38 8896.09

7884.66

7602.81

214.93

177.66

- 1 Volume Average(50,50,Green,Red) 16736.00 25797.96

30000.0

20000.0

10000.0

D   03   F   M   A   M   J   J   A   S   O   N   D   04   F   M   A   M   J   J   A   S

Created with TradeStation 2000i by Omega Research © 1999

Unlocking the Profits of the New Swing Chart Method   PAGE 138

CHART 66

(A) Label (A) simply shows the progression of the advance off the March 2003 low. The quarterly chart turns up in June and pulls back to the high of the down inside quarter and takes off again. The down inside quarterly at the low is a fractal of the down inside yearly being traced out.

(B) Label (B) the yearly turns up in January and a high is made in February for a -1 +2 quarter. Note how the low in August is three drives to a low and six months from the February high. Note that the Principal of Reflexivity is at work here again, as the turn up in the yearly chart in January 2004 leads to a top in February followed by a two quarter pullback.

NOTES

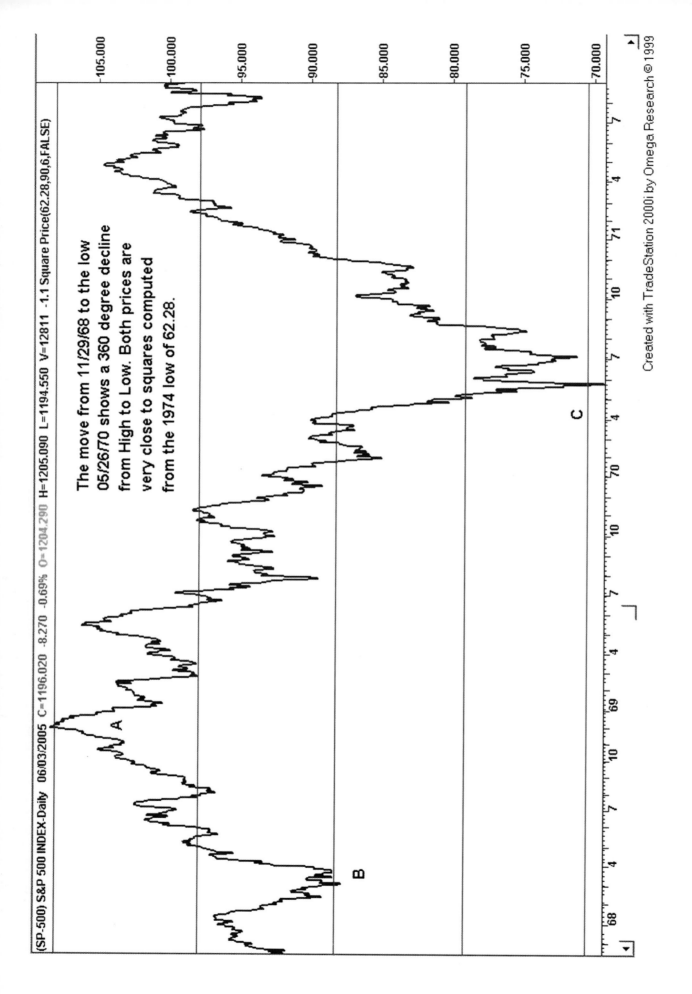

(SP -500) S&P 500 INDEX-Daily 06/03/2005 C=1196.020 -8.270 -0.69% O=1204.290 H=1205.090 L=1194.550 V=12811 -1.1 Square Price(62.28,90,6,FALSE)

The move from 11/29/68 to the low 05/26/70 shows a 360 degree decline from High to Low. Both prices are very close to squares computed from the 1974 low of 62.28.

Created with TradeStation 2000i by Omega Research © 1999

CHART 67

This is the first chart in the section on The Principle of Squares. These squares are 90 degrees apart in price. One of the concepts it is important to understand is that if it worked in the past, if it was important in the past, it will probably work in the future.

(A) Label (A) shows that looking back 180 degrees.

(B) Label (B) shows a significant low 'proving' the notion of a turn at (A). Further proving the significance of these levels is the drop of 180 degrees and the subsequent 90 degree bounce into November 1969.

(C) Label (C) shows that after oscillating around the market plunges a symmetrical 180 degrees into June of 1970. Hence, you have a 360 degree move or a complete circle or cycle from (A). Notice that the whole move from the October 1968 top at (A) to the low in June of 1970 was 18 months in time and 360 degrees in price for a TIME & PRICE SQUARE OUT.

NOTES

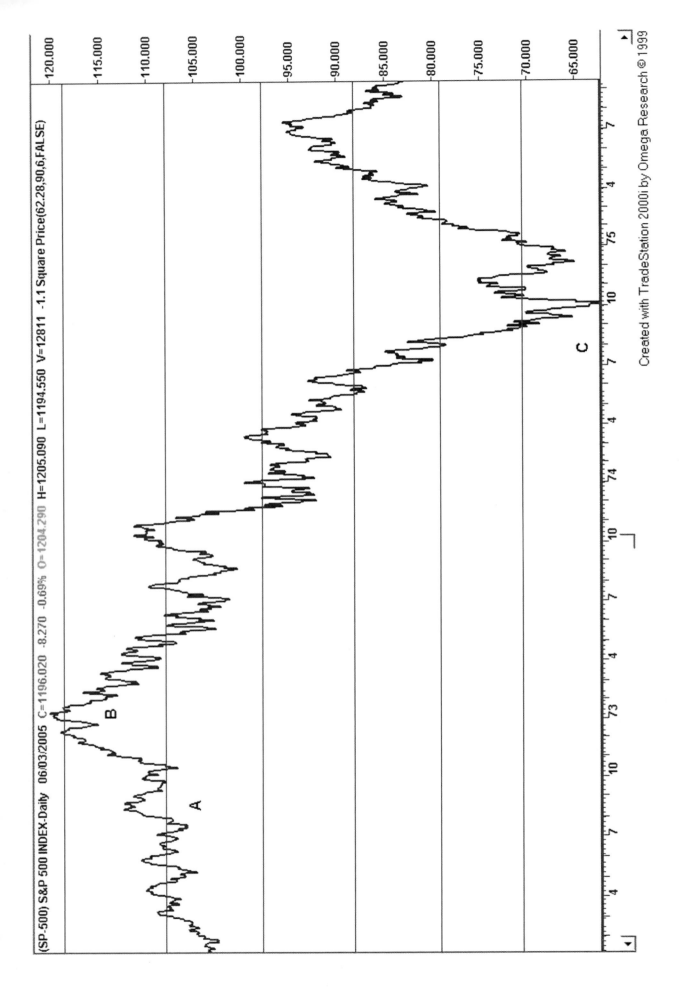

(SP-500) S&P 500 INDEX-Daily 06/03/2005 C=1196.020 -8.270 -0.69% O=1204.290 H=1205.090 L=1194.550 V=12811 -1.1 Square Price(62.28,90,6,FALSE)

Created with TradeStation 2000i by Omega Research © 1999

Unlocking the Profits of the New Swing Chart Method   PAGE 142

CHART 68

(A) Label (A) shows price oscillating around a square.

(B) Label (B) shows a top which was a 90 degree "whoop'em up".

(C) Label (C) was a decline of 540 degrees. This 540 degree move to the key 1974 low is important as it represents six squares of 90 degrees. Although 360 degrees is a full two dimensional cycle, a true three dimensional square is a cube which consists of six sides. Thus six 90 degree squares is a cube for a complete square out.

NOTES

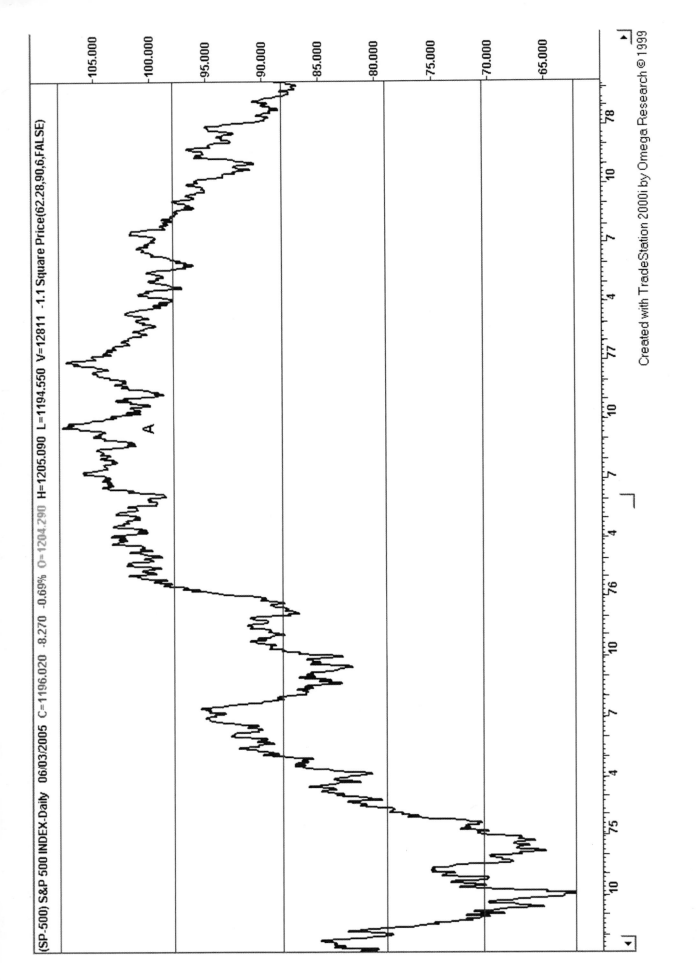

(SP-500) S&P 500 INDEX-Daily 06/03/2005 C=1196.020 -8.270 -0.69% O=1204.290 H=1205.090 L=1194.550 V=12811 -1.1 Square Price(62.28,90,6,FALSE)

Created with TradeStation 2000i by Omega Research © 1999

CHART 69

(A) Label (A) shows the rally off the 1974 low. The advance was 450 degrees or a 90 degree overthrow of the important 360 degree revolution. Note the Head and Shoulders topping pattern and choppy action during that 90 degree overthrow.

NOTES

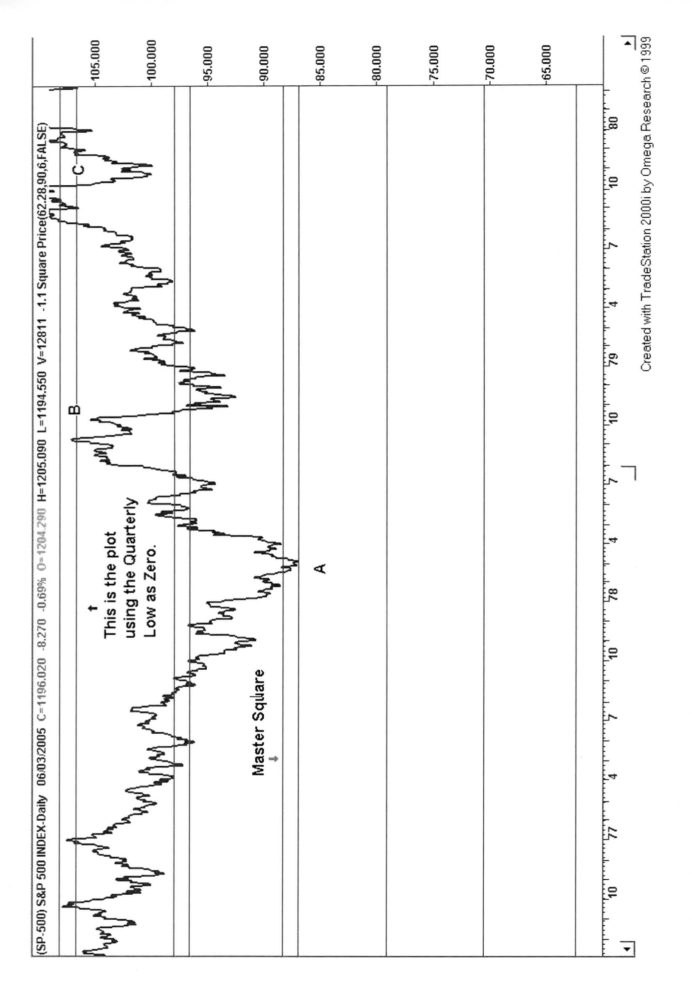

(SP-500) S&P 500 INDEX-Daily 06/03/2005 C=1196.020 -8.270 -0.69% O=1204.290 H=1205.090 L=1194.550 V=12811 -1.1 Square Price(62.28,90,6,FALSE)

C

B

This is the plot
using the Quarterly
Low as Zero.

A

Master Square

105.000
100.000
95.000
90.000
85.000
80.000
75.000
70.000
65.000

Created with TradeStation 2000i by Omega Research © 1999

CHART 70

In the same way that we have shown the interrelationship between the various wheels of time specifically the monthly and quarterly, it is important in using The Principle of Squares to measure from the master square as well as from the last major quarterly or yearly low or high.

(A) Label (A) shows a 180 degree move down to the Master Square from the last big high in 1976.

(B) Label (B) shows a 180 degree rally using the quarterly plot as the zero point. Note the 90 degree pullback followed by oscillation.

(C) Label (C) at this point you have to suspect that something new will play out.

NOTES

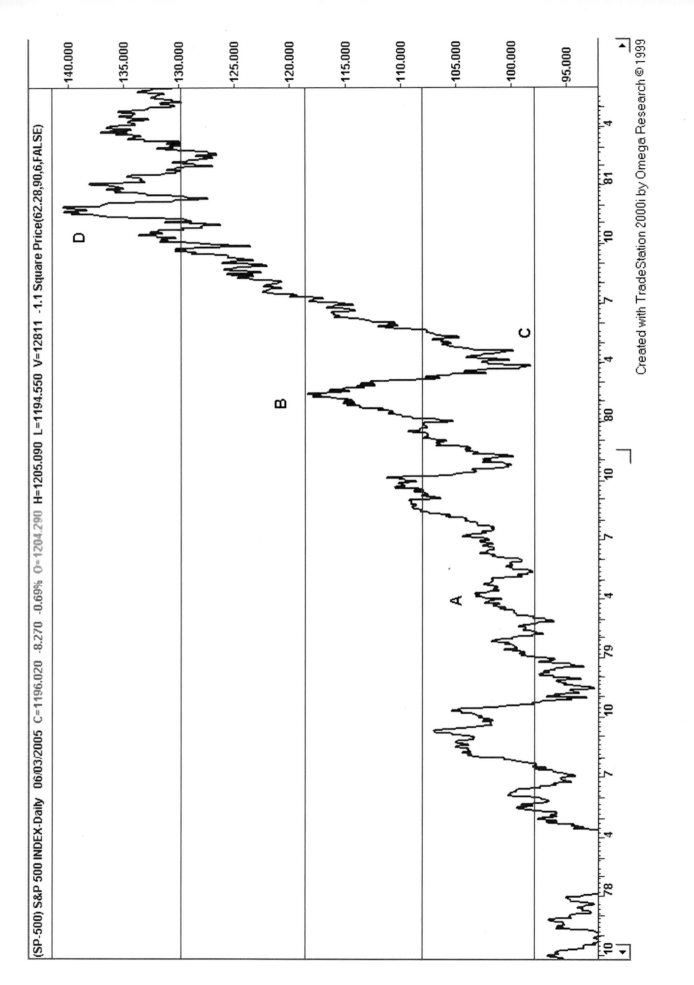

(SP-500) S&P 500 INDEX-Daily 06/03/2005 C=1196.020 -8.270 -0.69% O=1204.290 H=1205.090 L=1194.550 V=12811 -1.1 Square Price(62.28,90,6,FALSE)

Created with TradeStation 2000i by Omega Research © 1999

CHART 71

(A) Label (A) is the low after (B) from the prior chart. It shows the push up in the first quarter of 1979.

(B) Label (B) shows the 90 degree move up from the prior high. It looked like something different would play out and it did.

(C) Label (C) is a 180 degree move down.

(D) Label (D) is almost a precise 360 degree move. It is important to remember that although these wheels of time and price operate in the market, there will be some slippage in the majority of the cases. The market is not a fine Swiss watch.

NOTES

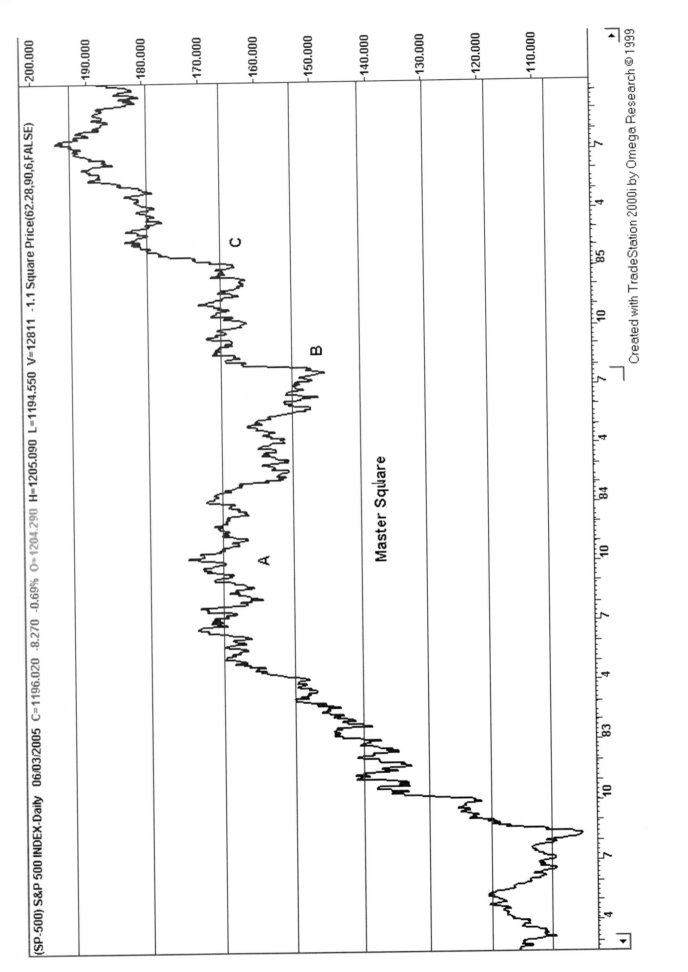

(SP-500) S&P 500 INDEX-Daily 06/03/2005 C=1196.020 -8.270 -0.69% O=1204.290 H=1205.090 L=1194.550 V=12811 -1.1 Square Price(62.28,90,6,FALSE)

Master Square

Created with TradeStation 2000i by Omega Research © 1999

Unlocking the Profits of the New Swing Chart Method   PAGE 150

CHART 72

In May 1982 we see the rally high at 120, the high before the major 1982 low in August.

(A) Label (A) demonstrates the approximately 360 degree move up from the 2nd quarter 1982 high.

(B) Label (B) shows an approximate 180 degree pullback. Notice how there will be an alternation between a precise hit on a square and how at other times price will oscillate above and below a square. In this case, plotting the squares down from the high at (A) shows a 180 degree move down from the last quarterly swing high.

(C) Label (C) shows more oscillation at the prior high which traces out a handle and then a 180 degree straight up move in July 1995.

NOTES

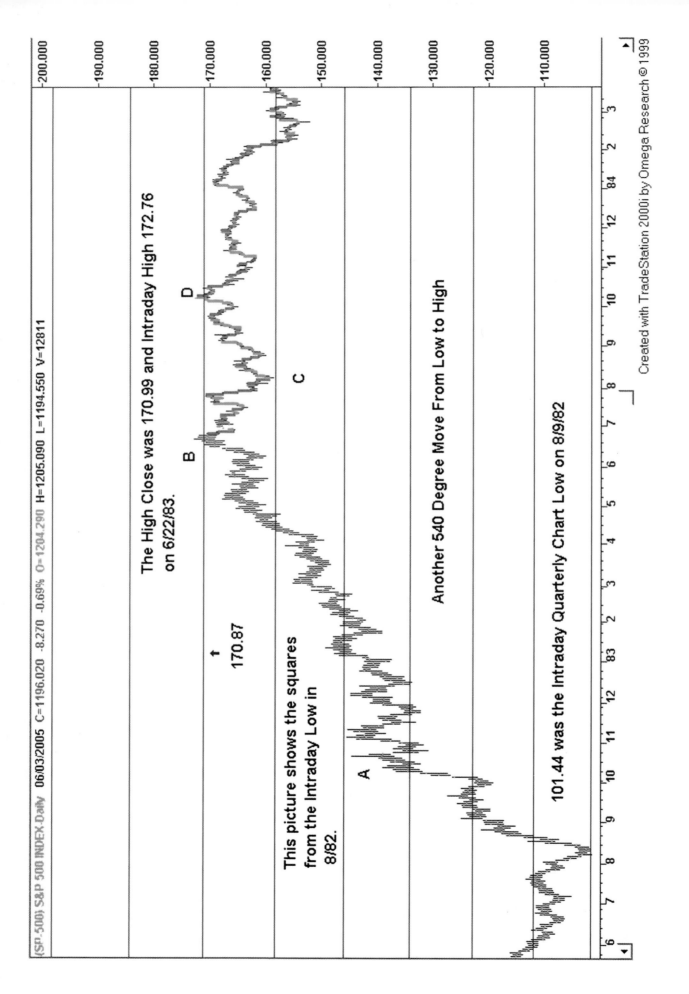

(SP-500) S&P 500 INDEX-Daily 06/03/2005 C=1196.020 -8.270 -0.69% O=1204.290 H=1205.090 L=1194.550 V=12811

The High Close was 170.99 and Intraday High 172.76
on 6/22/83.

↑
170.87

This picture shows the squares
from the Intraday Low in
8/82.

Another 540 Degree Move From Low to High

101.44 was the Intraday Quarterly Chart Low on 8/9/82

Created with TradeStation 2000i by Omega Research © 1999

Unlocking the Profits of the New Swing Chart Method   PAGE 152

CHART 72A

This chart shows the squares up measured from the major quarterly low in 1982.

(A) Label (A) shows a 360 degree move and the subsequent oscillation.

(B) Label (B) shows six squares of 90 degrees up from the August 1982 low. This is a move of 540 degrees which has characterized a point of significant completion many times in the past.

(C) Label (c) is a simple 90 degree pullback.

(D) Label (D) shows a 90 degree move to test the high. Note the 6 to 7 month line formation. The 540 degree move up was a high for more than a year!

NOTES ∼∼

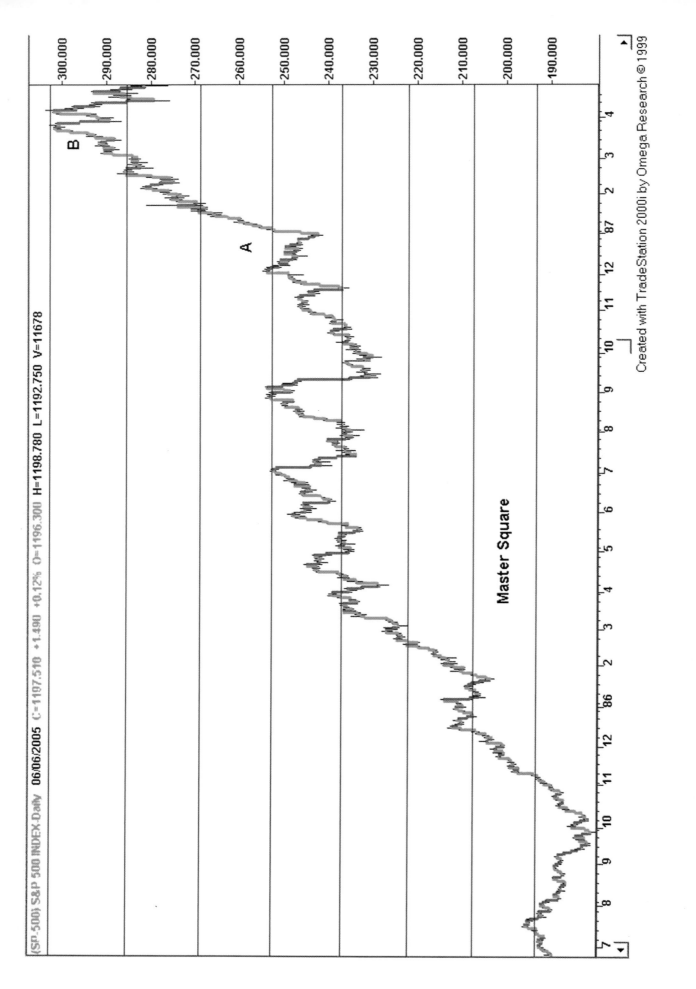

Master Square

(SP-500) S&P 500 INDEX-Daily 06/06/2005 C=1197.510 +1.490 +0.12% O=1196.300 H=1198.780 L=1192.750 V=11678

Created with TradeStation 2000i by Omega Research © 1999

Unlocking the Profits of the New Swing Chart Method | PAGE 154

CHART 73

This chart goes back to the Master Square.

(A) Label (A) is the Rule of 4 Breakout in 1987. What is incredible is that the market acknowledged that square, which was started from the low of 62.28 in October 1974. The price was 4 x 360 up from that low.

(B) Label (B) shows a 270 degree move up from the square at (A).

NOTES ∼∼

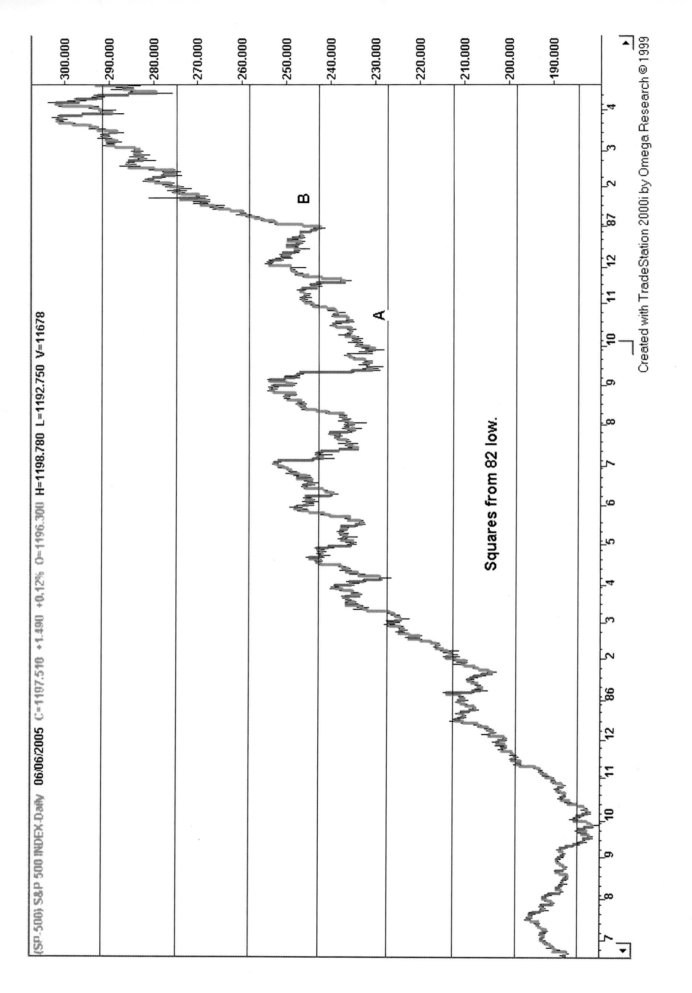

(SP 500) S&P 500 INDEX-Daily 06/06/2005 C=1197.510 +1.490 +0.12% O=1196.300 H=1198.780 L=1192.750 V=11678

B

A

Squares from 82 low.

Created with TradeStation 2000i by Omega Research © 1999

Unlocking the Profits of the New Swing Chart Method ———— PAGE 156

CHART 73A

(A) Label (A) shows three lows on a square from the 1982 low.

(B) Label (B) shows how the pullback before the blastoff tags a square from the 1982 low.

It is important to run squares concurrently from the Master Square and from quarterly and yearly highs and lows. These are the two strands of double helix at work in the Principle of Squares.

NOTES

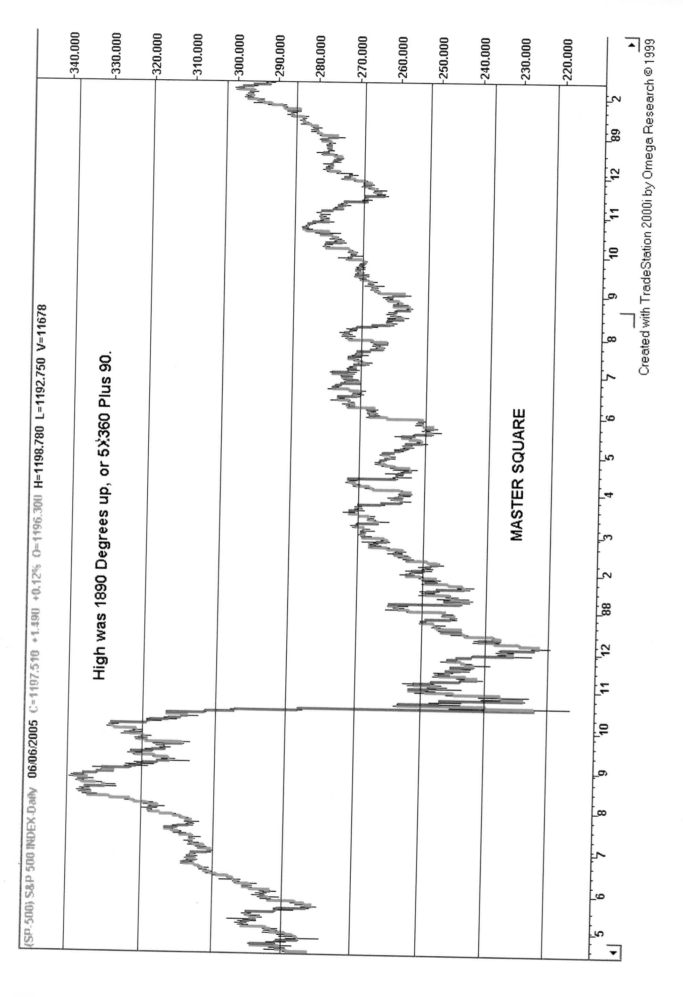

(SP 500) S&P 500 INDEX Daily 06/06/2005 C=1197.510 +1.490 +0.12% O=1196.300 H=1198.780 L=1192.750 V=11678

High was 1890 Degrees up, or 5x360 Plus 90.

MASTER SQUARE

Created with TradeStation 2000i by Omega Research © 1999

CHART 74

This is a chart with the master squares. The top prior to the 1987 crash was a dead hit on a master square which was 5 revolutions of 360 degrees up, plus a 90 degree overthrow. Many times blow off rallies and waterfall declines will overshoot by 90 degrees, and will appear to be a perfect harmonic. This is often a clue that you are in the final phase.

Note how the crash in 1987 found low 7 squares of 90 degrees from high. Seven is the number of panic.

The move up after the crash was 270 degrees followed by a 90 degree pullback.

NOTES

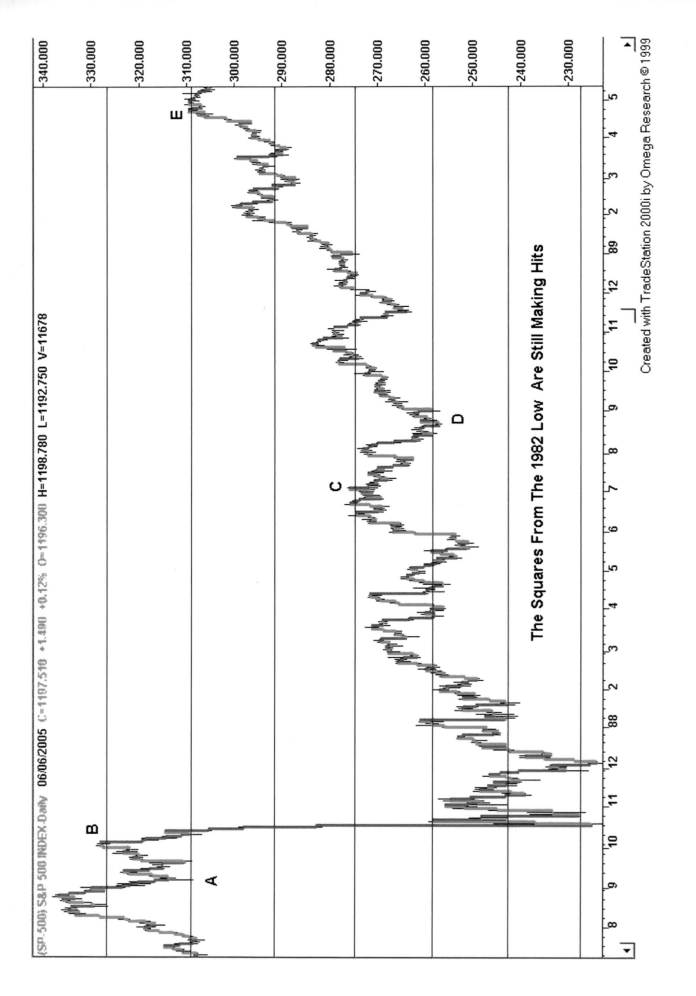

The Squares From The 1982 Low Are Still Making Hits

(SP-500) S&P 500 INDEX-Daily 06/06/2005 C=1197.510 +1.490 +0.12% O=1196.300 H=1198.780 L=1192.750 V=11678

Created with TradeStation 2000i by Omega Research © 1999

CHART 74A

This chart shows the squares from the 1982 low are still operative.

(A) The pullback after the August top tags a square precisely where Two Feet are planted. This is followed by a 90 degree bounce.

(B) From (B) to the low equals 540 degrees which is a true natural square and represents completion.

(C) The 1982 square nails the same level where the master square was oscillating.

(D) The 1982 square nails a 90 degree pullback.

(E) Label (E) shows a 270 degree move up from (D) which tags the underbelly where (A) was a critical pivot. This move was symmetrical from the crash low to point (C). The market knows geometry.

Many times 90 degree pullbacks define a pause in an ongoing trend.

NOTES

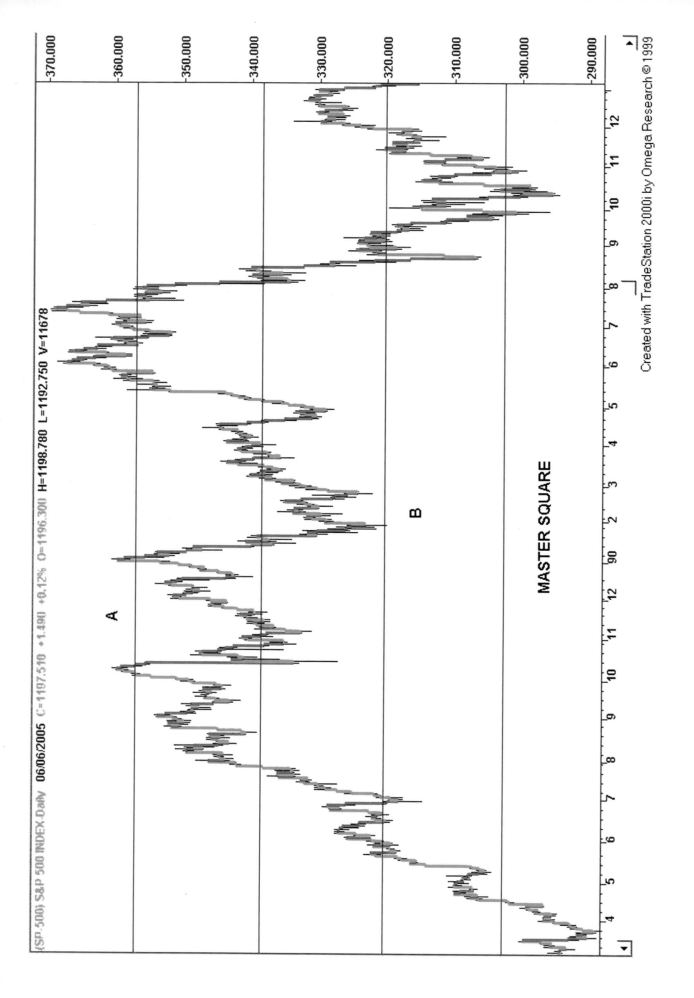

(SP 500) S&P 500 INDEX-Daily 06/06/2005 C=1197.510 +1.490 +0.12% O=1196.300 H=1198.780 L=1192.750 V=11678

MASTER SQUARE

Created with TradeStation 2000i by Omega Research © 1999

A

B

Unlocking the Profits of the New Swing Chart Method — PAGE 162

CHART 75

(A) Label (A) shows a double top at a master square.

(B) Label (B) shows a 180 degree pullback after the test of the high which is a perfect hit. The message is after all these years the master square is still in play. Note the fractal between the top in July and the top in January and the move down into October, of 360 degrees.

NOTES

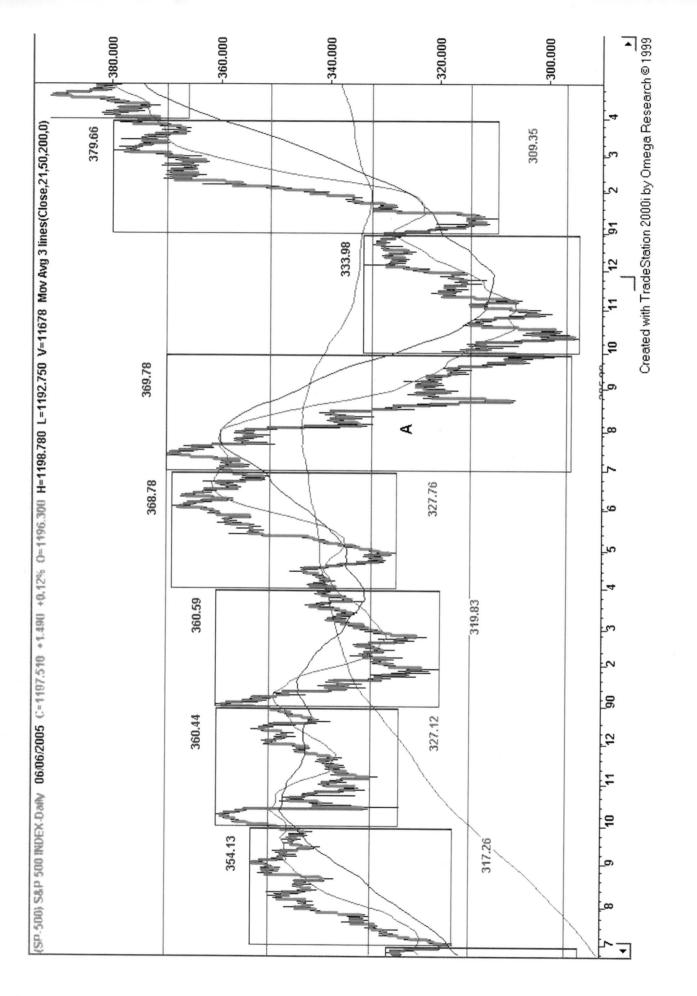

CHART 75A

Here is a chart showing the True Quarterly Swings and the Squares from the 1982 low.

(A) Notice how the high at (A) in 1990 nailed the top to the tick. This was a Test Failure of the high in June. Many times precise hits signify a completion and a square out when time and price are up. This circumstance can be particularly powerful at a test failure. Note how the Marginal plot higher on the quarterly does not generate follow through and instead Jack-knifes back through the original high leading to a 2-plot quarter. The 2-plot quarter sets up a potentially bullish +1 - 2 quarter at the October low. Note the marginal plot just below the September low without follow through and the dead hit on the square at the low 360 degrees or a cycle or circle, one full revolution down from high in 3 months or 1/4 of the year.

NOTES

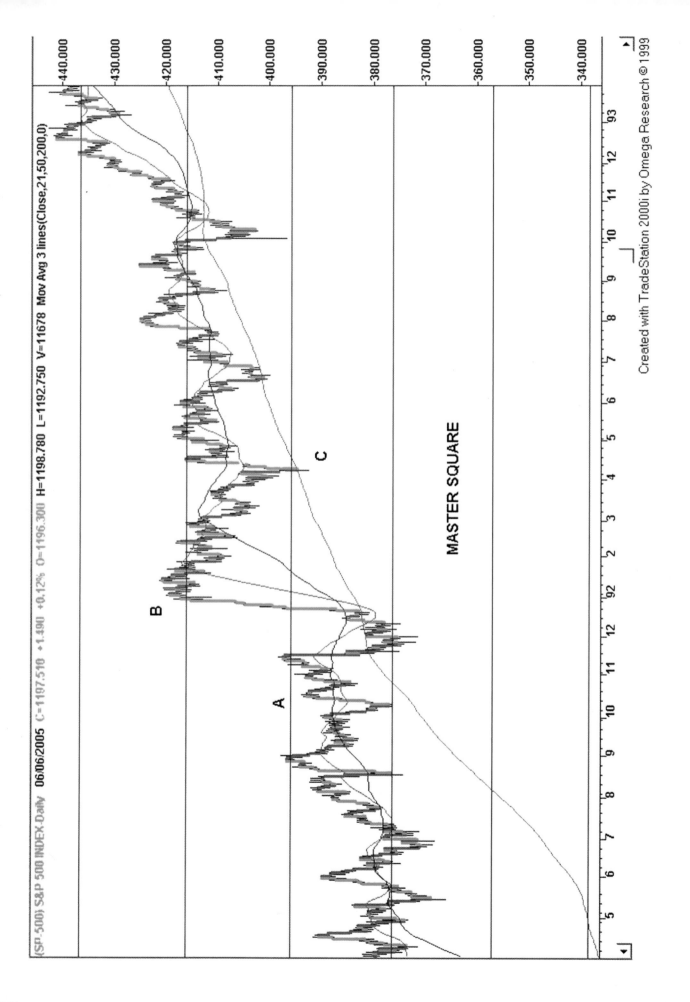

MASTER SQUARE

(SP-500) S&P 500 INDEX-Daily 06/06/2005 C=1197.510 +1.490 +0.12% O=1196.300 H=1198.780 L=1192.750 Mov Avg 3 lines(Close,21,50,200,0)

Created with TradeStation 2000i by Omega Research ©1999

CHART 76

(A) Label (A) shows 5 swings at the master square. Note how after an undercut of the 200 DMA flushes some market participants out, the market runs up 180 degrees.

(B) Label (B) or 90 degrees after breaking out over the tops at (A).

(C) Label (C) shows a 90 degree pullback which tags the 200 DMA for a solid buy set up. The important thing to understand is that the squares from 1974 are still working. The second foot was planted in September after a shake out below the 200 DMA.

NOTES 〜〜〜

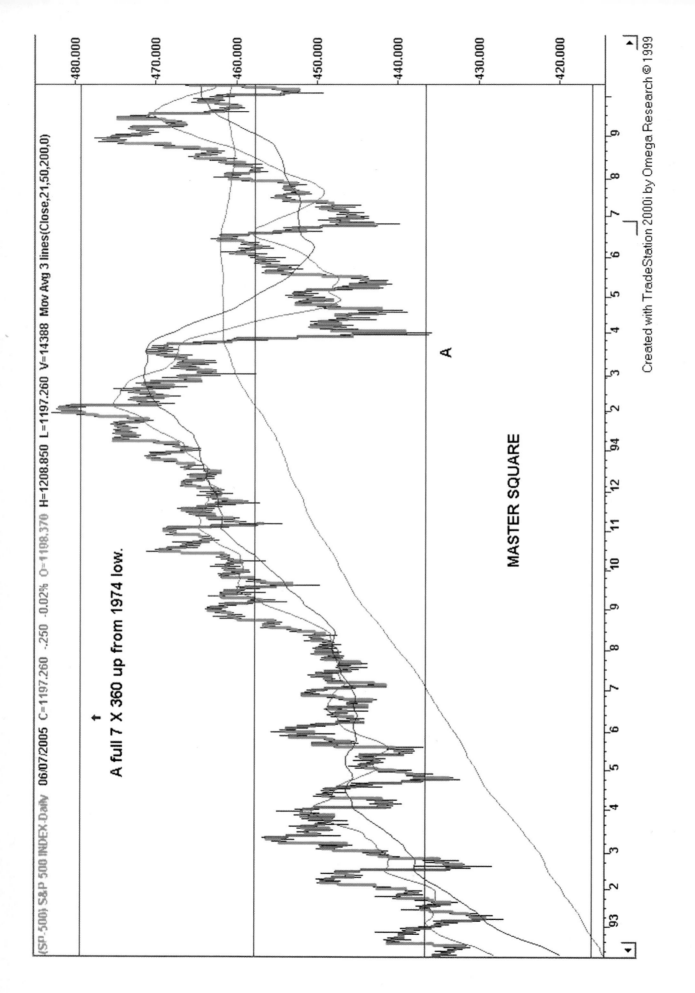

(SP-500) S&P 500 INDEX-Daily 06/07/2005 C=1197.260 -.250 -0.02% O=1198.370 H=1208.850 L=1197.260 V=14388 Mov Avg 3 lines(Close,21,50,200,0)

A full 7 X 360 up from 1974 low.

A

MASTER SQUARE

Created with TradeStation 2000i by Omega Research © 1999

Unlocking the Profits of the New Swing Chart Method   PAGE 168

CHART 77

Here's another picture of the master square still working from 1974. The market DOES have a memory. We know that 360 degrees is an important cycle. We know that 7 is an important cycle and that it represents the number of panic according to W.D. Gann. In February 1994, the market is 7 cycles of 360 degrees up from the 1974 low and 'genuflects' with a waterfall decline acknowledging that price cycle. Notice the first reaction 90 degrees down, the pullback to the 50 DMA and the subsequent dead hit 180 degrees down from the top.

NOTES

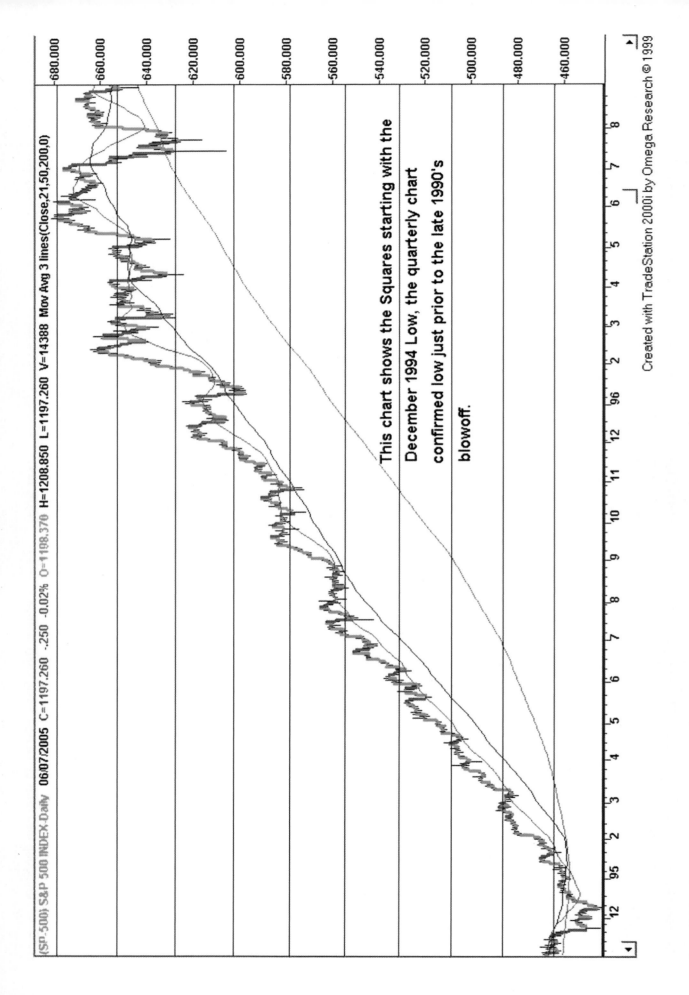

(SP 500) S&P 500 INDEX-Daily 06/07/2005 C=1197.260 -.250 -0.02% O=1198.370 H=1208.850 L=1197.260 V=14388 Mov Avg 3 lines(Close,21,50,200,0)

This chart shows the Squares starting with the

December 1994 Low, the quarterly chart

confirmed low just prior to the late 1990's

blowoff.

Created with TradeStation 2000i by Omega Research © 1999

CHART 78

We have stated that it is necessary to measure price from the Master Square as well as important quarterly and yearly highs and lows.

This chart shows the squares from the critical fourth quarter low in 1994 prior to the mother of all blow offs—the five year run that was a fractal of the five year run in time from the major 1982 low and the five year run into the important top in 1987 preceding the crash.

Notice how the consolidation in August 1995 is four squares or 360 degrees up from the breakout point and the kickoff of the advance in January 1995. Notice how when the market knifes back through the mini Angular Rule of 4 Buy Signal (generated in May 1996) in July the market drops a symmetrical 270 degrees.

NOTES

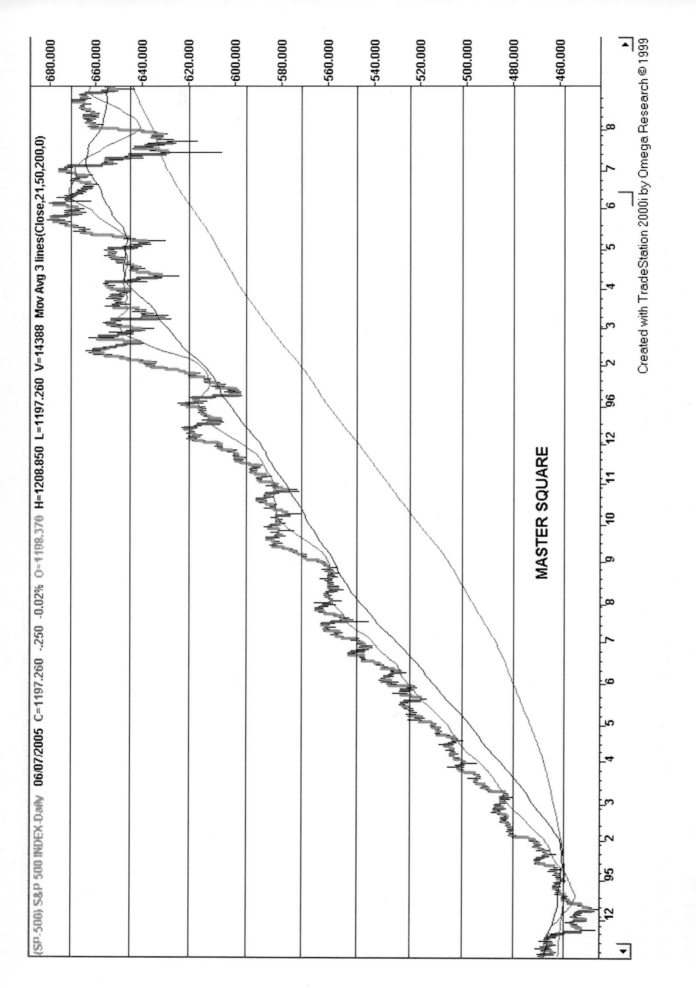

(SP-500) S&P 500 INDEX-Daily 06/07/2005 C=1197.260 -.250 -0.02% O=1198.370 H=1208.850 L=1197.260 V=14388 Mov Avg 3 lines(Close,21,50,200,0)

MASTER SQUARE

Created with TradeStation 2000i by Omega Research © 1999

Unlocking the Profits of the New Swing Chart Method —|— PAGE 172

CHART 78A

This chart is the same time frame as the previous chart but with the master squares.

There are not a lot of direct hits here, mostly oscillation around these squares. This time the master square is no real help.

NOTES

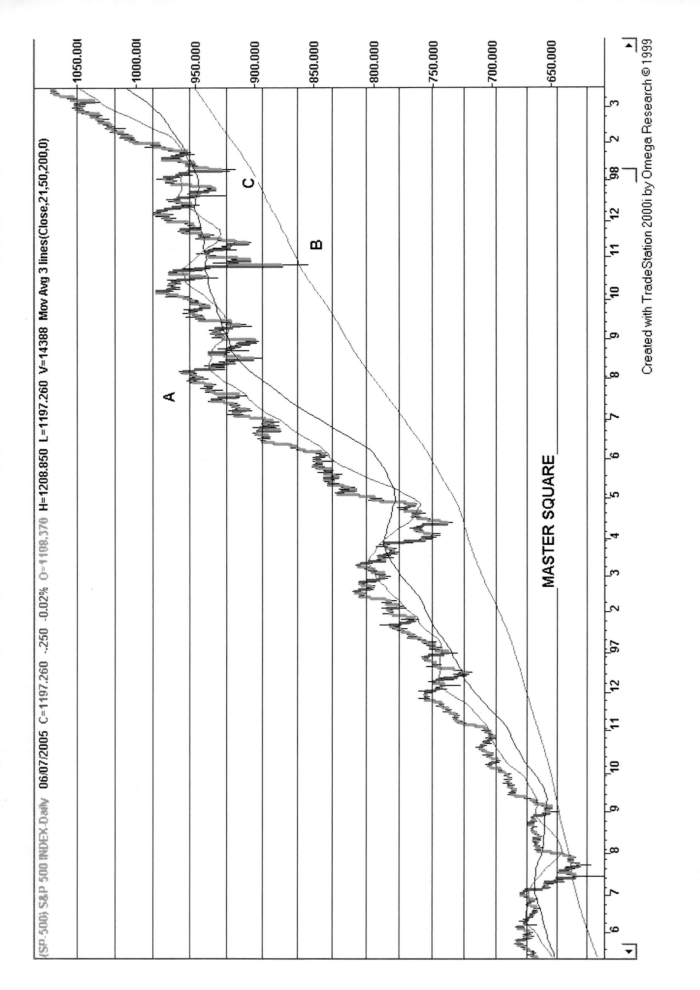

(SP 500) S&P 500 INDEX Daily 06/07/2005 C=1197.260 -.250 -0.02% O=1198.370 H=1208.850 L=1197.260 V=14388 Mov Avg 3 lines(Close,21,50,200,0)

A

C

B

MASTER SQUARE

Created with TradeStation 2000i by Omega Research © 1999

Unlocking the Profits of the New Swing Chart Method   PAGE 174

CHART 79

Again on this chart using the master squares there are few direct hits. However, note the precise hit in September of 1996 prior to the breakout and another kickoff move. Precise hits many times indicate important square outs and should put you on your toes for a potential big move to follow.

(A) The move ending at A, up from the low in April 1997, is a near perfect 720 Degrees.

(B) Label (B) shows a 360 degree pullback which tags the 200 DMA as the quarterly chart turns down. It's hard not to be interested in that kind of a buy setup for a test of the high at a minimum. Note the 90 degree overthrow prior to the decline into (B).

(C) After a test of the high you get a 180 degree pullback to launch a new bull run. It is important to note the bearish 3 swings to a test of the high after point (B). This is a potentially very bearish pattern. However, the pullback held the square 180 degrees down and importantly held above the supportive rising 200 DMA. When the market broke out triggering a mini Rule of 4 Breakout buy signal, it was talking. As you know, many times the market plays out in threes.

NOTES

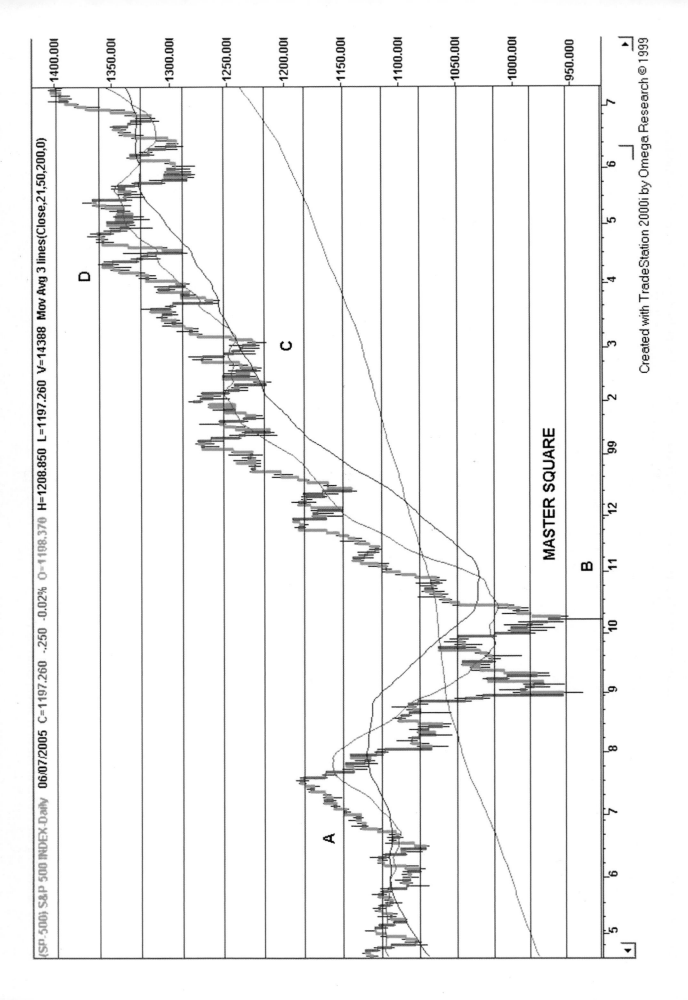

(SP-500) S&P 500 INDEX-Daily 06/07/2005 C=1197.260 -.250 -0.02% O=1198.370 H=1208.850 L=1197.260 V=14388 Mov Avg 3 lines(Close,21,50,200,0)

D

C

A

MASTER SQUARE

B

Created with TradeStation 2000i by Omega Research © 1999

— Unlocking the Profits of the New Swing Chart Method ———— **PAGE 176**

CHART 80

(A) Label (A) shows the 270 degree "Whoop-'em-Up" into the July 1998 high. Notice how the top was a fractal of the pattern into the 1929 high.

(B) Label (B) shows a decline that goes 7 squares down followed by a bounce of 360 degrees and the marginal new low that is a dead hit. The whole decline is 8 squares for 2 cycles of 360 degrees.

We have noticed how there have been lots of turns in March, July, and October; the 3rd, 7th and 10th month. 3 plus 7 gives a composite 10th month turn. Notice how the move down into the end of 1998 carves out a 90 degree 'handle'.

(C) Label (C) shows triple bottoms on the master square.

(D) Label (D) shows a 360 degree move up followed by a 180 degree move down. After a long period of not providing much help, the master square is working again.

NOTES

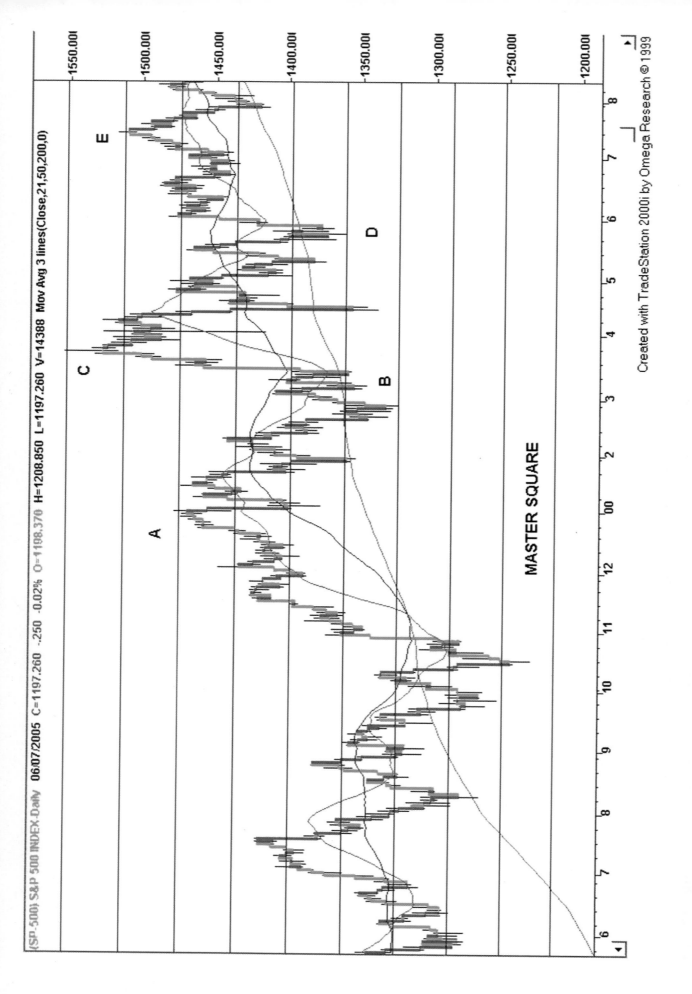

(SP-500) S&P 500 INDEX-Daily 06/07/2005 C=1197.260 -.250 -0.02% O=1198.370 H=1208.850 L=1197.260 V=14388 Mov Avg 3 lines(Close,21,50,200,0)

MASTER SQUARE

Created with TradeStation 2000i by Omega Research © 1999

Unlocking the Profits of the New Swing Chart Method —— PAGE 178

CHART 81

Not labeled is the 360 degree move down from the July 1999 high and the 270 degree bounce back.

The move down into the October low is a symmetrical 360 degree move down. The complete sequence down is 5 squares of 90 degrees.

(A) Label (A) shows a direct hit at a master square at the beginning of the year. The move up from the October low is a 'complete' 540 degrees which we have stated is a move of completion as a true 3-dimensional square is a 6-sided cube (6 sides of 90 degrees). This is important to understand as the move above the January high proves to be a failed 180 degree move, an overthrow that did not hold. Note the lack of longevity above (A) suggesting the notion of a false move.

(B) Label (B) shows a 360 degree correction which traced out 3 drives to a low.

(C) Label (C) shows a completion move six squares or 540 degrees up to the historic March 2000 top. The Principal of Fractals plays out against the prior 540 degree move.

(D) Label (D) is a correction of 5 squares down to a test of the April low. Note the Principle of Fractals again as three swings to a test pattern plays out.

(E) Label (E) is a 360 degree rally from (D). Note how the master square is providing some near perfect hits from the major low 26 years prior in 1974. It is interesting to note that the 50 day average volatility (Reif AVX) in 2000 was 2.4%. The 200 DMA Reif AVX hit an amazing 1.84% during the summer of 2000. The more volatile NASDAQ 100 hit 6.3% on the 50 day Reif AVX.

NOTES

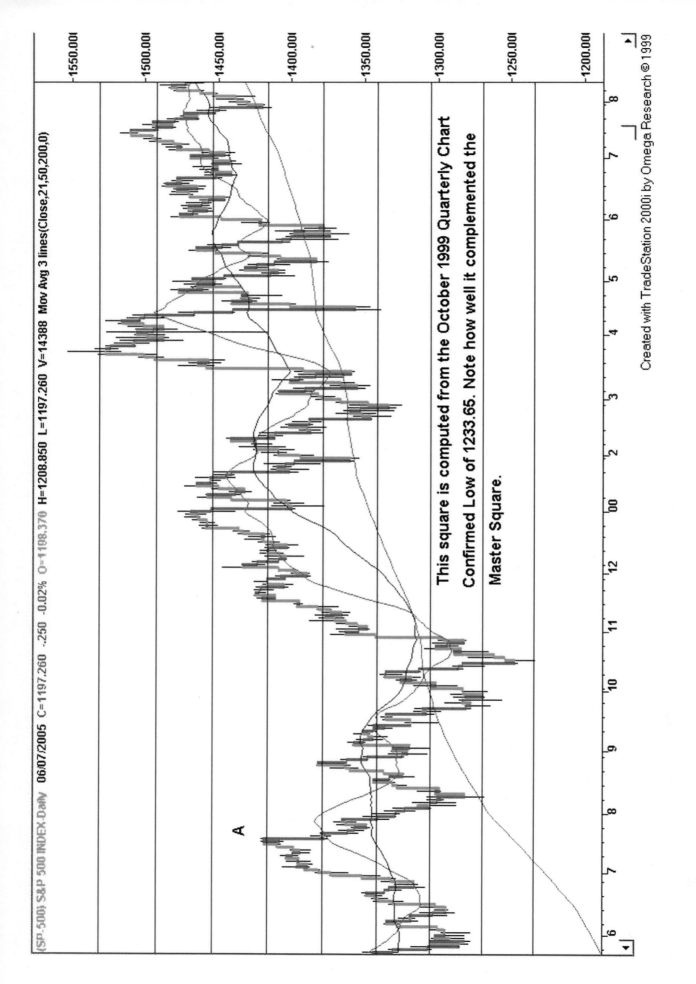

(SP-500) S&P 500 INDEX-Daily   06/07/2005   C=1197.260   -.250   -0.02%   O=1198.370   H=1208.850   L=1197.260   V=14388   Mov Avg 3 lines(Close,21,50,200,0)

1550.00t
1500.00t
1450.00t
1400.00t
1350.00t
1300.00t
1250.00t
1200.00t

A

This square is computed from the October 1999 Quarterly Chart
Confirmed Low of 1233.65. Note how well it complemented the
Master Square.

Created with TradeStation 2000i by Omega Research © 1999

Unlocking the Profits of the New Swing Chart Method — PAGE 180

CHART 81A

These squares are computed from the last important quarterly low in October 1999.

(A) Label (A) shows the high prior to a correction 5 squares down in the 4th quarter low in October 1999. Going backwards from the low to point (A) 'proves' the high. From the October low the market gives a completion move of six squares up. The correction of three drives or swings to a test of the breakout point in November is 360 degrees. Note how the steep correction into April is dead on the square from October.

NOTES ~~~~~~

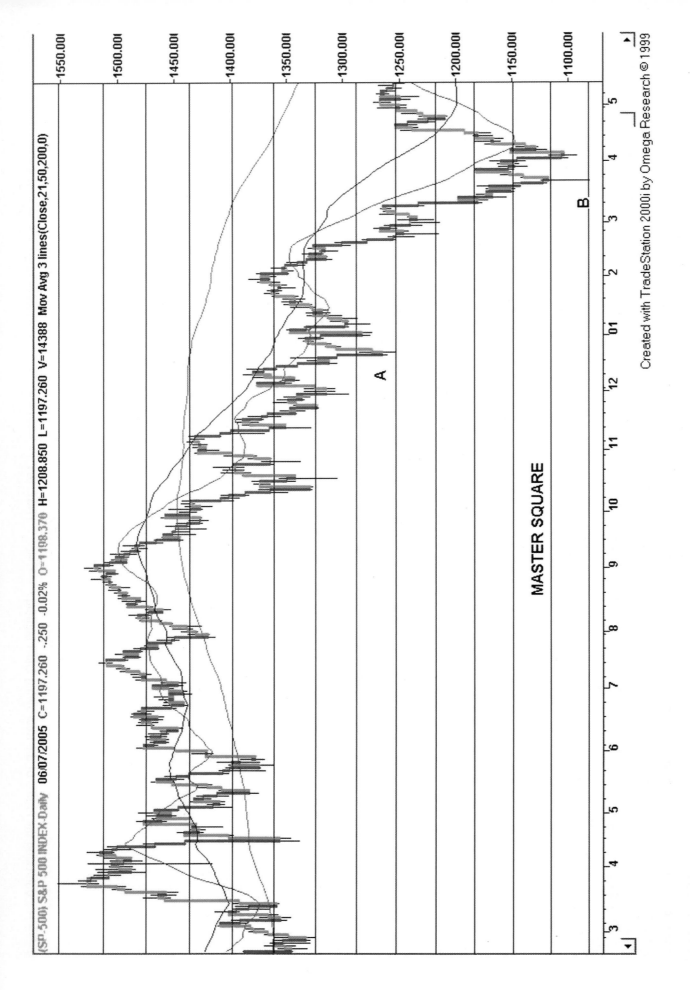

(SP-500) S&P 500 INDEX-Daily 06/07/2005 C=1197.260 -.250 -0.02% O=1198.370 H=1208.850 L=1197.260 V=14388 Mov Avg 3 lines(Close,21,50,200,0)

MASTER SQUARE

A

B

Created with TradeStation 2000i by Omega Research © 1999

— Unlocking the Profits of the New Swing Chart Method —   PAGE 182

CHART 82

The top of the bull market is a dead hit on the master square. What's more it is a 540 degree move of completion. Remember, precise hits and completion moves many times indicate the market is talking. Moreover, this precise hit and 540 degree move into a March time frame occurred in LESS THAN 30 DAYS signifying the idea that a blow off was playing out. The market wasn't talking, it was shouting. Moreover, nearly the whole move is corrected in just 8 days: the 'overbalance' in time and the substantial volatility suggest something important is happening. The double bottom in May is a solid hit on the square. Note the 3 swings to a test pattern. Four squares up or 360 degrees up to a July high is a precise hit. The pullback to the 200 DMA generates a rally to a test of the high which traces out a mirror image 3 swings to a test of the March high. This last move is 270 degrees.

(A) The angular Rule of 4 Breakdown after the top gives a 720 degree (2 revolutions of 360) decline (from the high high) into December, a three month decline. From the March high the decline was 9 months or 270 degrees in time. The dead hit on this square out is followed by a 270 degree bounce, a fractal of the final bounce into the September test. As above, so below.

(B) The move into the low at (B) is a symmetrical 8 squares or 720 degrees down from the bounce into the February top. The complete move from the historic high was 3 revolutions of 360 plus 90 degrees down. Note the last 90 degree overthrow and the tail in March 2001.

NOTES ∿∿∿

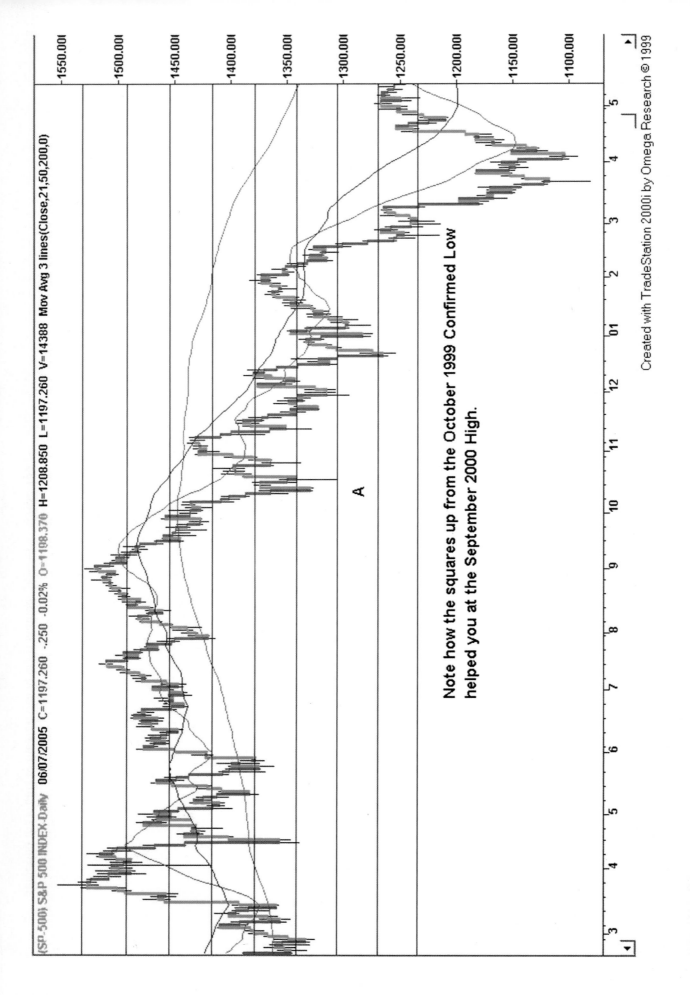

(SP-500) S&P 500 INDEX-Daily   06/07/2005   C=1197.260   -.250 -0.02%   O=1198.370   H=1208.850   L=1197.260   Mov Avg 3 lines(Close,21,50,200,0)

Note how the squares up from the October 1999 Confirmed Low
helped you at the September 2000 High.

A

Created with TradeStation 2000i by Omega Research © 1999

Unlocking the Profits of the New Swing Chart Method   PAGE 184

CHART 82A

Note how the squares from the confirmed low in 1999 helped you catch the return rally test of the top in September 2000.

(A) Label (A) shows a completion move of 540 degrees and offers a chance to take a trade. Label (A) is another case of how an exact hit with a tail defines a good opportunity.

NOTES

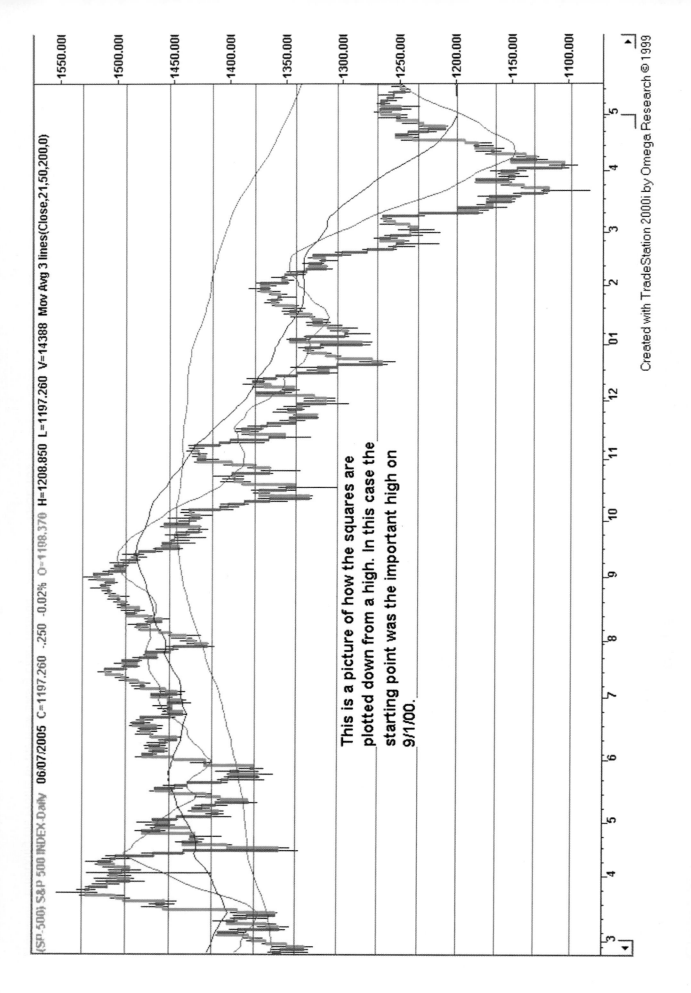

This is a picture of how the squares are plotted down from a high. In this case the starting point was the important high on 9/1/00.

Created with TradeStation 2000i by Omega Research © 1999

Unlocking the Profits of the New Swing Chart Method ——— PAGE 186

CHART 82B

Once you have a test failure (at the September 2000 test) and a significant breakdown you can also start to measure down from a high. From the September high to the 2001 low is 3 revolutions of 360 degrees.

NOTES

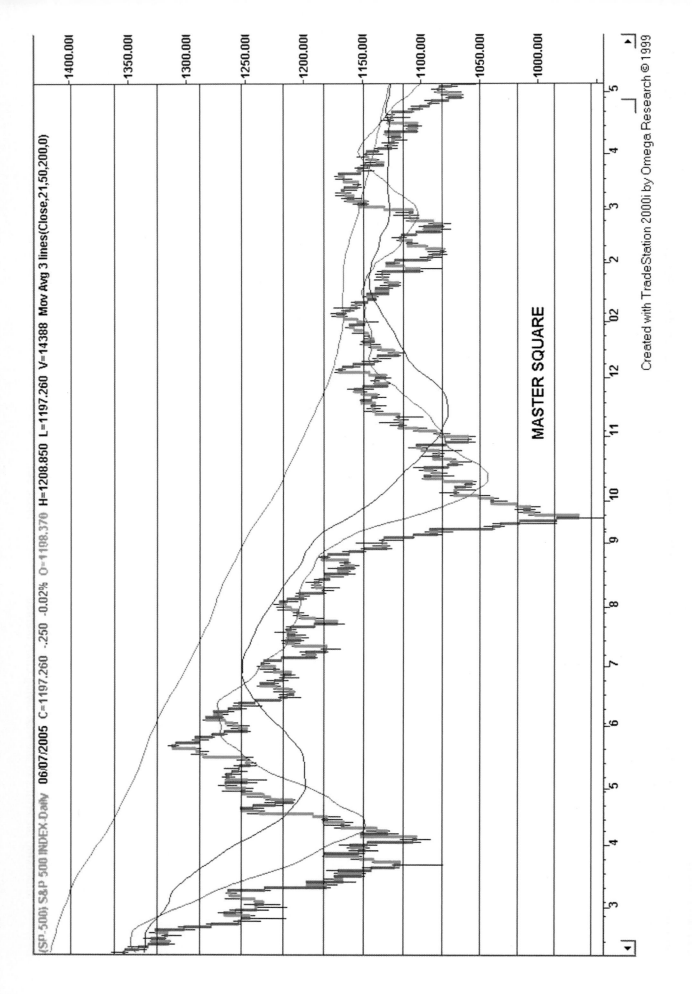

(SP 500) S&P 500 INDEX Daily 06/07/2005 C=1197.260 -.250 -0.02% O=1198.370 H=1208.850 L=1197.260 V=14388 Mov Avg 3 lines(Close,21,50,200,0)

MASTER SQUARE

Created with TradeStation 2000i by Omega Research © 1999

Unlocking the Profits of the New Swing Chart Method —————— PAGE 188

CHART 83

This chart shows how the master square is back in play. You must always take into account and know where the squares from major bear market lows and bull market highs are.

Here there is a direct hit at the low after 9/11. Despite the panic and emotionalism, the waterfall low occurred 360 degrees down or 360 degrees of new ground plowed from the prior swing low in March 2001. The complete decline from the May 2001 high to the September low is just shy of 12 squares.

NOTES

Sometimes it pays to plot the squares up or down from a key Monthly Swing High. This one is plotted from the Key May 2001 High.

(SP-500) S&P 500 INDEX-Daily 06/07/2005 C=1197.260 -.250 -0.02% O=1198.370 H=1208.850 L=1197.260 V=14388 Mov Avg 3 lines(Close,21,50,200,0)

Created with TradeStation 2000i by Omega Research © 1999

CHART 83A

Here the squares are plotted from a monthly high.

(A) Label (A) notes how the month of September encompassed a completion of 6 squares down. This is a fractal of the 540 degree, 6 square move, into the March 2000 top. Likewise, the distance between that top and the September 2001 low was 18 months or 540 degrees in time. Happenstance?

(B) Label (B) shows the rally off the low is 7 squares although you might be looking for 6 up. However, the market has a date with destiny in the way of tagging its 200 DMA, which was 7 squares up.

It is important to note that this rally off the low tags the 360 degree move down from the May high.

NOTES

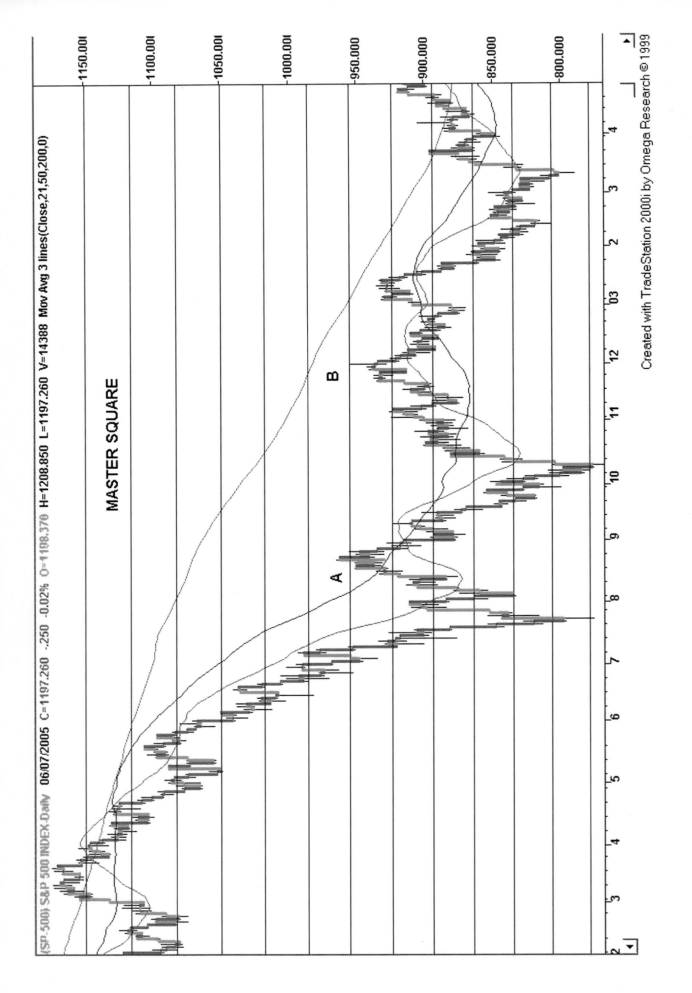

MASTER SQUARE

(SP-500) S&P 500 INDEX-Daily 06/07/2005 C=1197.260 -.250 -0.02% O=1198.370 H=1208.850 L=1197.260 V=14388 Mov Avg 3 lines(Close,21,50,200,0)

Created with TradeStation 2000i by Omega Research © 1999

Unlocking the Profits of the New Swing Chart Method   PAGE 192

CHART 84

The capitulation decline into July 2002 is a dead hit on the master square. The July low was 10x360 degrees up from the 1974 low.

(A) Label (A) shows a 6 square, 540 degree completion move off the low.

(B) Label (B) shows a second 540 degree bounce off the test of the low for a direct hit on a master square. Note the tag of the 200 DMA after the March low, the reflex rally and then the move through the 200 DMA that confirms the Test of a Test pattern.

NOTES

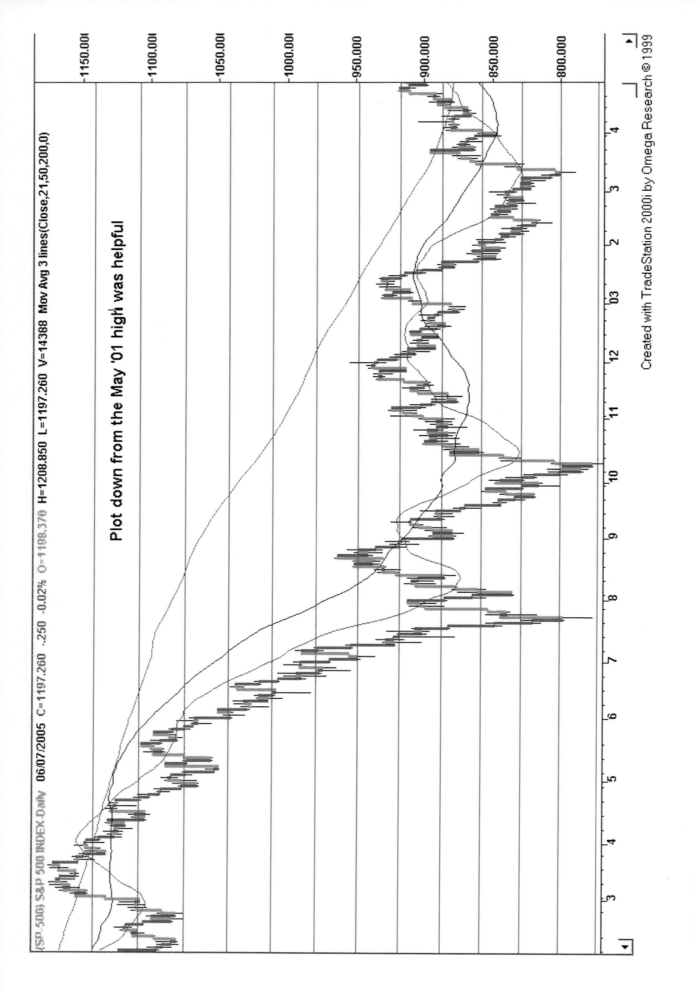

(SP-500) S&P 500 INDEX-Daily 06/07/2005 C=1197.260 -.250 -0.02% O=1198.370 H=1208.850 L=1197.260 Mov Avg 3 lines(Close,21,50,200,0)

Plot down from the May '01 high was helpful

Created with TradeStation 2000i by Omega Research © 1999

Unlocking the Profits of the New Swing Chart Method   PAGE 194

CHART 84A

Plotting squares from the important May 2001 monthly swing high (it was a 'tail' month) proved to be helpful. 14 months or 2x7 months later defined the waterfall bear market low. Remember, seven is the number of panic. The May high in 2002 tagged a square before the free fall began.

Notice the volatility in June 2002 which generated a 180 degree bounce after a 360 degree move down from the May 2002 top. The month of July 2002 encompassed in and of itself six complete squares down for a natural completion square or move.

NOTES

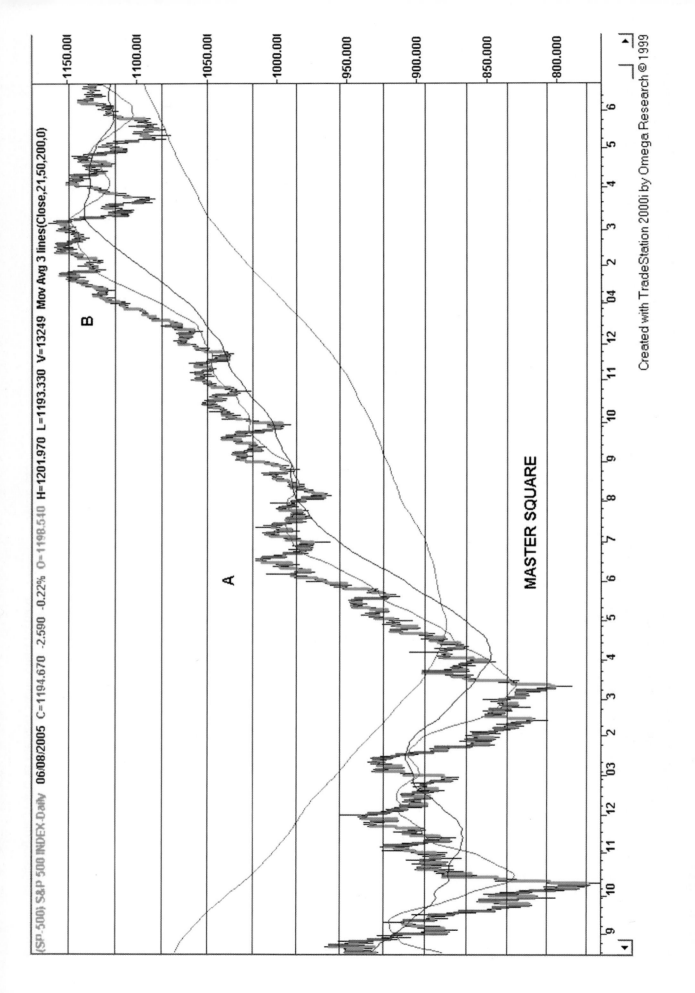

(SP-500) S&P 500 INDEX Daily 06/08/2005 C=1194.670 -2.590 -0.22% O=1198.540 H=1201.970 L=1193.330 V=13249 Mov Avg 3 lines(Close,21,50,200,0)

B

A

MASTER SQUARE

Created with TradeStation 2000i by Omega Research © 1999

CHART 85

Here we are back on the master square coming up from the 2002/2003 tests of the July 2002 capitulation low.

(A) Label (A) shows a dead hit which lasted for three months after a three month move up from March. What is interesting to observe in the message of the market here is that in moving up more than six squares in the advance (the rally off the low was seven squares) and consolidating and holding six squares up the market is talking and suggesting higher prices. Notice how the pullbacks are shy of 180 degrees. (A) is 12 squares of 360 degrees up from the 1974 low. Notice the 360 degree move in time from the July 2002 low up to (A). So, you have a master square being hit at an important natural square or movement in time.

(B) Label (B) shows a 360 degree move up from the breakout after (A). Note the two 180 degree pullbacks that trace out an A-B-C pullback giving a perfect hit of the 200 DMA at a square. You want to be a buyer here.

NOTES

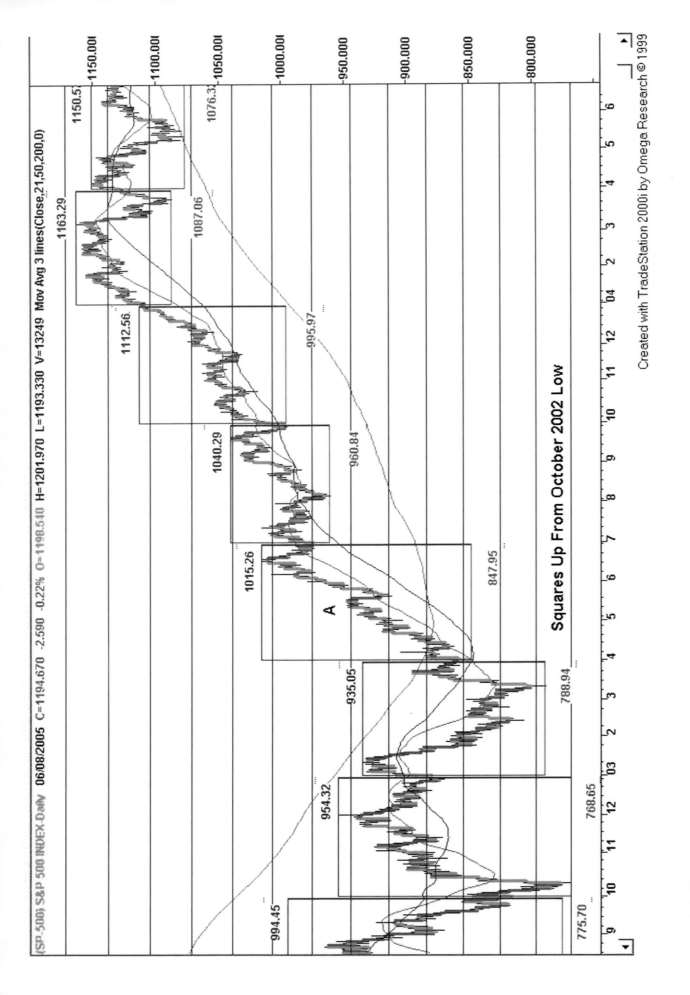

(SP 500) S&P 500 INDEX Daily 06/08/2005 C=1194.670 -2.590 -0.22% O=1198.540 H=1201.970 L=1193.330 V=13249 Mov Avg 3 lines(Close,21,50,200,0)

1150.5

1163.29

1112.56.

1040.29

1015.26

A

935.05

954.32

994.45

775.70

1076.3

1087.06

995.97

960.84

847.95

788.94

768.65

Squares Up From October 2002 Low

Created with TradeStation 2000i by Omega Research © 1999

—— Unlocking the Profits of the New Swing Chart Method ——————— PAGE 198

CHART 85A

Here are the squares up from the 2002 low.

(A) Label (A) equals six squares up from the 2002 low where you get a 90 degree pullback and then the market powers through the important level of six squares up signaling higher. (A) also demonstrates the Principle of Reflexivity after the quarterly chart turns up you get the 90 degree pullback.. You can't make this stuff up. Notice how the advance is roughly 12 squares up from the October 2002 low, or 3 squares of 360 degrees. If 360 degrees is important, then perhaps six squares of 360 degrees fulfills an important cube as well. Hence 1/2 this cube is important, i.e. the 3 squares of 360 degrees.

June 2003 is 8 squares or 720 degrees (2x360) up from the October 2002 low. You would expect a consolidation, at a minimum, at this main cycle point in price.

NOTES

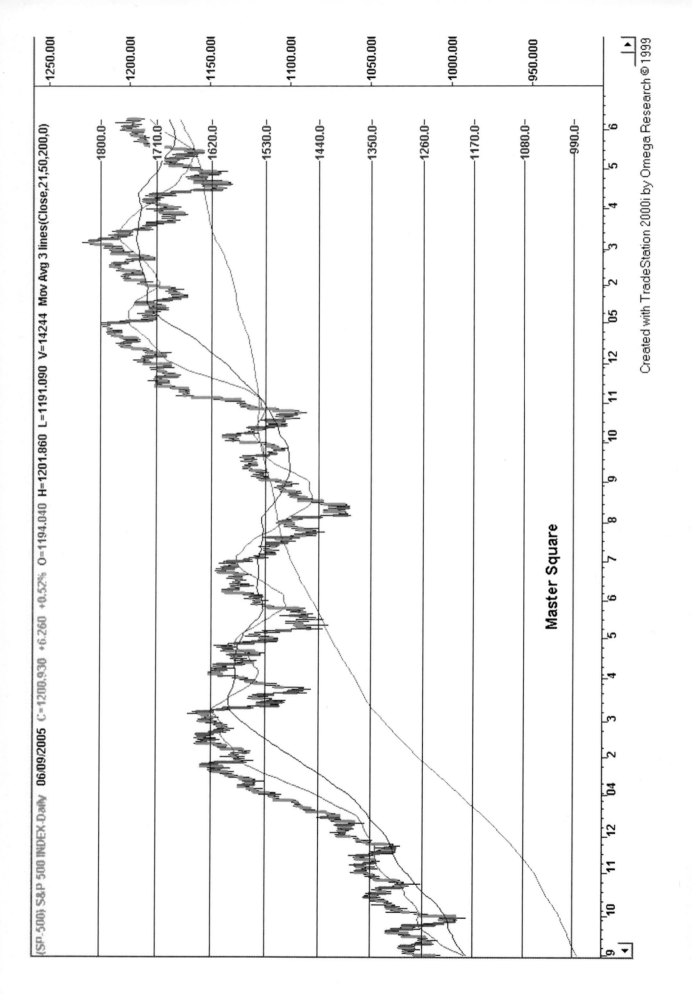

(SP-500) S&P 500 INDEX-Daily 06/09/2005 C=1200.930 +6.260 +0.52% O=1194.040 H=1201.860 L=1191.090 V=14244 Mov Avg 3 lines(Close,21,50,200,0)

1250.00I

1200.00I

1150.00I

1100.00I

1050.00I

1000.00I

950.000

1800.0—

1710.0—

1620.0—

1530.0—

1440.0—

1350.0—

1260.0—

1170.0—

1080.0—

990.0—

Master Square

Created with TradeStation 2000i by Omega Research © 1999

Unlocking the Profits of the New Swing Chart Method   PAGE 200

CHART 86

Note the Principle of Fractals as the January high comes with three mini drives to a high and the August low comes in 3 larger drives to a low. This is a "3 Swings to a Test" pattern. It is a pullback of approximately 50% of the prior range. The 3 drives to the test of 50% of the range is 270 degrees down. Some have 3 drives encompassing 3 squares of 90 degrees. Corrective moves are typically 90, 180, and 270 degrees and are seldom 360 degrees.

The January 2005 high is a perfect hit of a master square suggesting a significant high. Because the move up in March does not even tag a higher square it suggests a test rather than a new leg.

Note the Jackknife back through the January high. The decline in April is 270 degrees and a quarterly turndown, which defines a low, as momentum fails to accelerate to the downside as the 200 DMA is undercut but recaptured relatively quickly. We expect a test of the highs at a minimum.

NOTES

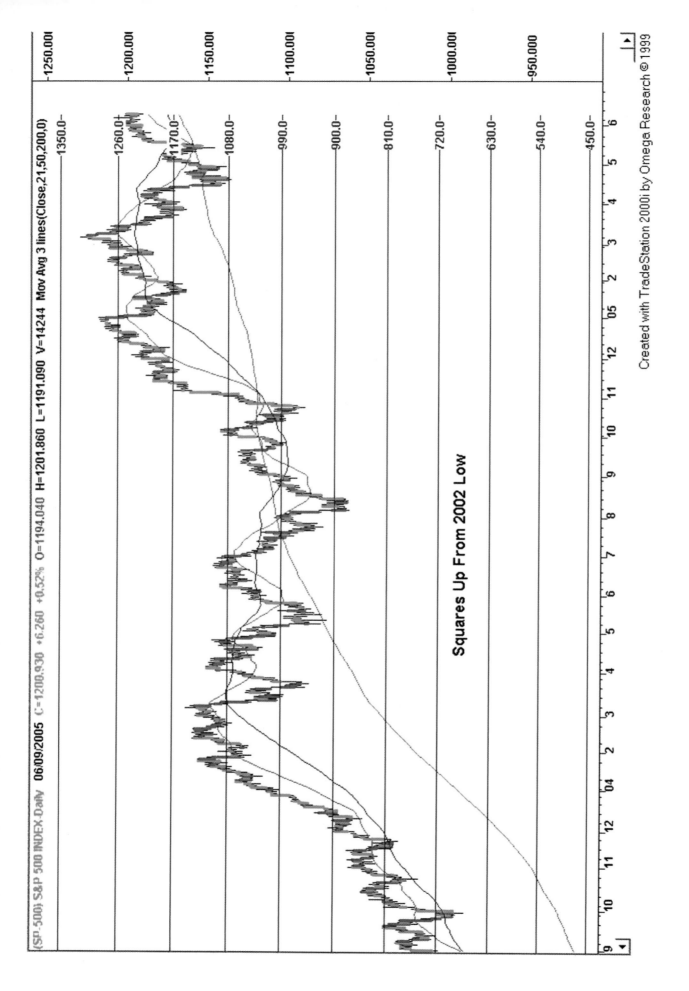

(SP-500) S&P 500 INDEX-Daily 06/09/2005 C=1200.930 +6.260 +0.52% O=1194.040 H=1201.860 L=1191.090 V=14244 Mov Avg 3 lines(Close,21,50,200,0)

Squares Up From 2002 Low

Created with TradeStation 2000i by Omega Research © 1999

Unlocking the Profits of the New Swing Chart Method   PAGE 202

CHART 86A

Note the action at the August 2004 low around a square on the third drive down.

The pullback into the April 2005 low that turns the quarterly chart and shakes out the 200 DMA tags a square perfectly from the bear market low. This pullback also kisses the breakout point from the angular Rule of 4 Breakout from November 2004.

NOTES

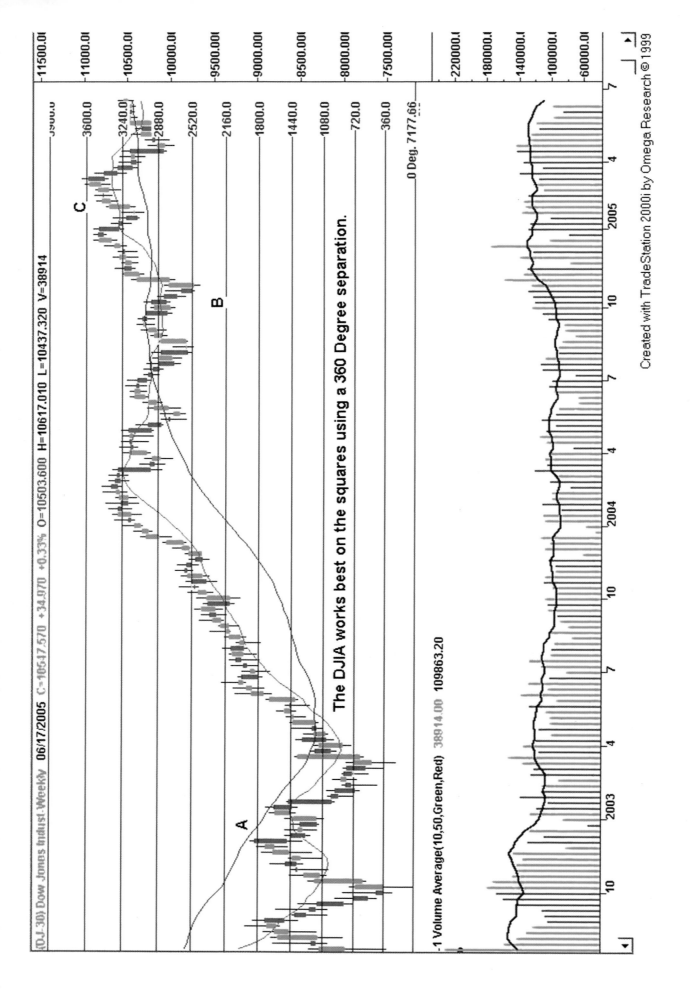

The DJIA works best on the squares using a 360 Degree separation.

Created with TradeStation 2000i by Omega Research © 1999

CHART 86B

90 degree plots on the Dow are meaningless because of the high numbers of the index.

(A) Label (A) is 5x360 degrees up

(B) Label (B) is 3 squares of 360 degrees down.

(C) Label (C) is a dead hit 10 squares of 360 degrees up from the October 2002 low.

NOTES

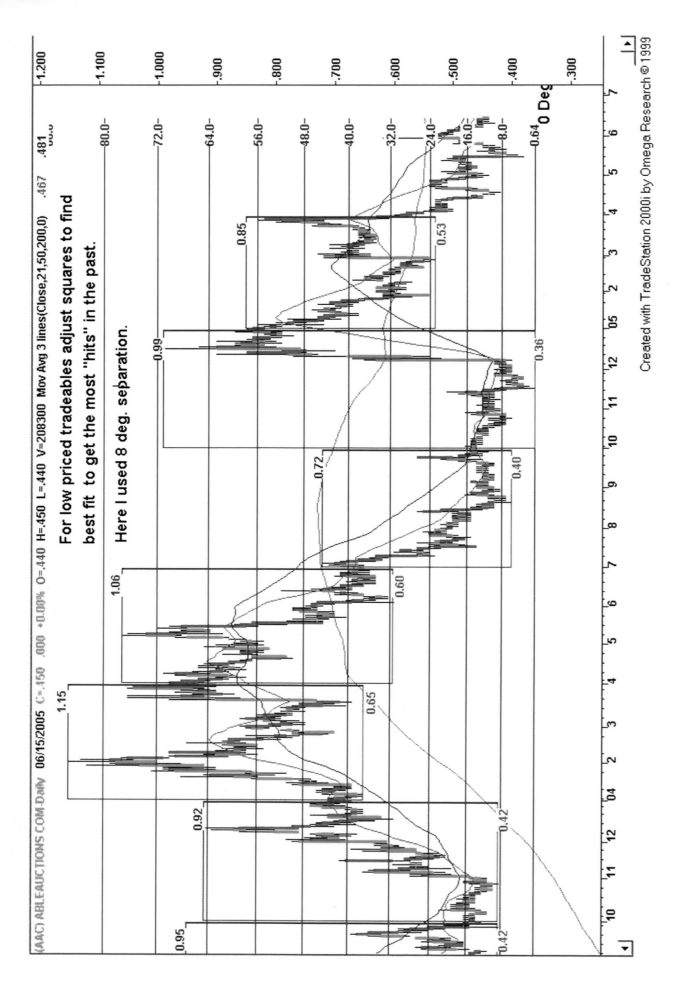

For low priced tradeables adjust squares to find best fit to get the most "hits" in the past.

Here I used 8 deg. separation.

Created with TradeStation 2000i by Omega Research © 1999

CHART 86C

What works best in the past to get the most hits, will usually lead to successful hits in the future. In this case, 8 degrees or 8 cents is capturing a lot of hits.

This is just one picture. You can try several different separations to see what works best.

NOTES

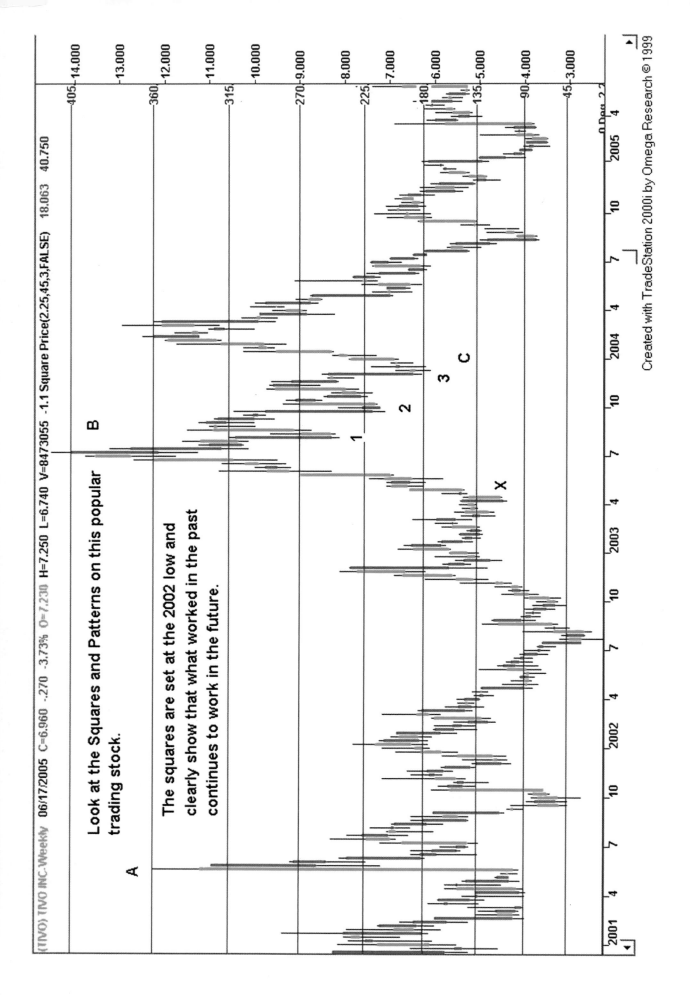

Look at the Squares and Patterns on this popular trading stock.

The squares are set at the 2002 low and clearly show that what worked in the past continues to work in the future.

Created with TradeStation 2000i by Omega Research © 1999

CHART 86D

Here the squares are set 45 degrees apart and work best.

(A) Label (A) 'proves' the geometry and the importance of setting the square at the 2002 low.

(B) Label (B) captures the high 45 degrees above (A). When the stock Jack-Knifes through the old high at (A) a serious decline ensues.

(C) Label (C) shows a 1-2-3 Swing to a Test Pattern which is a test of the last point of acceleration at X.

NOTES

(DJ-30) Dow Jones Indust. Daily 06/13/2005 C=10522.560 +9.960 +0.09% O=10503.600 H=10611.100 L=10437.320 V=19839

The 200 Day Reif AVX on the DJIA made it's all time
high of 5.15% on 7/7/1932.

The price low was on 7/8/1932

7/7/1932

Reif AVX(200) 1.55

-1 Volume Average(50,0,Green,Red) 19839.00 24134.16

Created with TradeStation 2000i by Omega Research © 1999

CHART 87

This method to provide a measure of volatility was developed in 2004 and is still being researched. The appendix explains how it is calculated, and the rationale behind it.

Amazingly, the market bottom in 1932 coincided with a peak in 200 day average volatility. The average daily volatility during this period had an average range of 5.15%.

NOTES

(@COMPQX) NASDAQ COMPOSITE-Daily 06/13/2005 C=2068.960 +5.060 +0.29% O=2059.960 H=2078.260 L=2058.720 V=14256

The 200 day Reif AVX made it's high of 4.22% on 6/21/01.

Reif AVX(200) 1.18

6/21/01

-1 Volume Average(50,0,Green,Red) 14256.00 16696.02

Created with TradeStation 2000i by Omega Research © 1999

Unlocking the Profits of the New Swing Chart Method   ———   PAGE 212

CHART 88

Here is the 200 Day Reif AVX, which peaked 15 months after the NASDAQ topped. The point is you can't generalize with this tool. It fluctuates in both directions. You have to watch the behavior.

The study of past volatility shows how important it is to be risk adverse and how bad volatility can get and that if you are on the wrong side of the market you can lose a lot quickly.

NOTES

We currently use the 50 Day AVX and 50 Day Average Volume to define an accumulation or a distribution day.

Created with TradeStation 2000i by Omega Research © 1999

Unlocking the Profits of the New Swing Chart Method — PAGE 214

CHART 89

This is a chart of what we call Real Accumulation Days (RAD) and Real Distribution Days (RDD).

We don't know if the 50 DMA is the ideal measurement but it is what we have started with and works well. Research is in progress but this method proves more valuable than using an arbitrary measurement of an accumulation day (or distribution day) as price closing above or below the prior days range. This 'real' method relates to what is and has been occurring in the market.

The important things to understand are that multiple or piggyback signals can define a climax in a move as opposed to a continuation of a move. Multiple signals can also define a kickoff move.

NOTES

(@COMPQX) NASDAQ COMPOSITE-Weekly 06/17/2005 C=2068.960 +5.960 +0.29% O=2059.960 H=2078.260 L=2058.720 V=14256

We use a 10 week Reif AVX and a 10 Week MA of Volume to define an accumulation or distribution week.

Reif AVX(10) 2.70

-1 Volume Average(10,0,Green,Red) 14256.00 75359.70

Created with TradeStation 2000i by Omega Research ©1999

CHART 90

Here is a chart of the NASDAQ Composite showing Weekly RAD's and RDD's.

(A) Label (A) shows a weekly RAD at the important March 2003 turn.

(B) Label (B) shows Railroad Track Signals. You have a RDD followed by a RAD. A failure to follow through on the sell signal was bullish and gave rise to a fast move when the sell signal was immediately offset by a buy signal, the weekly RAD. Before Label (C) note the multiple signals that helped define a low.

(C) Label (C) piggyback RAD's signal momentum.

Note the RDD (red bar) at the high (after C) was an outside down reversal week as well which issued a Get-Out-of-Dodge sell signal.

NOTES

(CTX) CENTEX CORP Weekly 06/17/2005 C=66.680 +.430 +0.65% O=66.240 H=66.860 L=65.600 V=808400 -1 Reif Acc/Dist Day(10,10,0)

Having this indicator in your analysis kit can be very helpful, particularly on the Weekly Chart.

Reif AVX(10) 6.60

-1 Volume Average(10,0,Green,Red) 808400.00 7697790.50

Created with TradeStation 2000i by Omega Research © 1999

A B C D E

65.000
55.000
45.000
35.000
25.000
15.000

14.00
12.00
10.00
8.00
6.00

2400000
1800000
1200000
6000000

2000 2001 2002 2003 2004 2005

CHART 91

(A) Label (A) shows a period with two green bars (RAD's).

(B) Label (B) shows multiple red bars without follow through. However, note the false breakout and then the test of the prior green bars.

(C) The red bars without follow through show that it is the behavior that counts. The lack of follow through suggests consolidation rather than a steep decline. Note the Railroad Tracks at the 2001 low.

(D) Once again, Railroad Tracks kick off a nice advance.

(E) Here, the stock is advancing with lower volume which may mean a change in trend may not be too far away in price or time.

NOTES

(STX) SEAGATE TECHNOLO-Weekly   06/17/2005   C=20.530 +.110 +0.54% O=20.300 H=20.790 L=20.300 V=3218300 -1 Reif Acc/Dist Day(10,10,0)

Another Example of the Weekly Follow Through.

Reif AVX(10) 7.99

-1 Volume Average(10,0,Green,Red)   3218300.00   17631040.00

Created with TradeStation 2000i by Omega Research © 1999

CHART 92

The red bar at the low before the breakout generates no follow through.

Note the series of green bars and the follow through that is generated. What more do you need to know to stay with the major trend? Although the red bar at the high didn't get you out at the top, it still allowed you to capture the lion's share of the move. Note the railroad tracks at the April 2005 low and the ensuing Second Mouse green bar.

NOTES

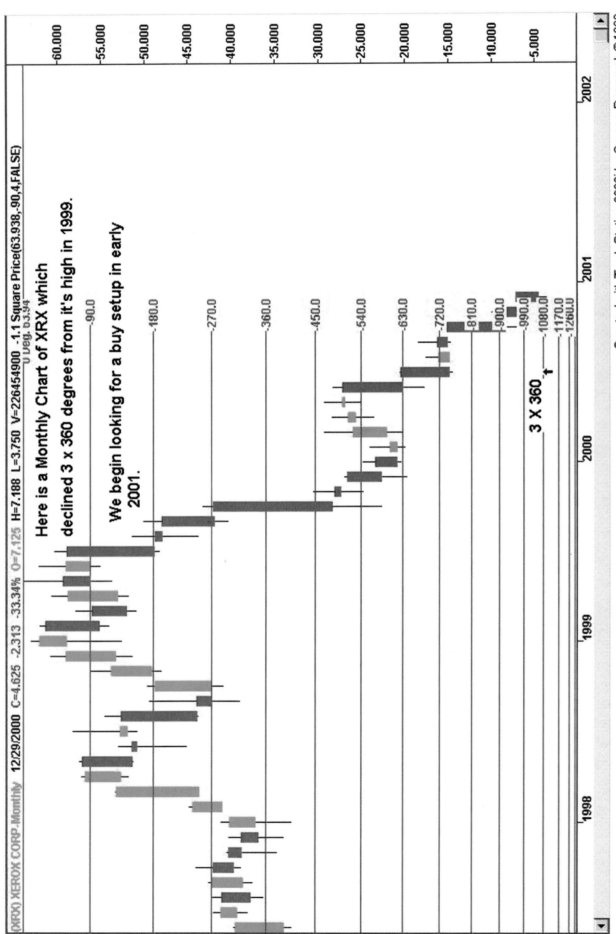

(XRX) XEROX CORP-Monthly 12/29/2000 C=4.625 -2.313 -33.34% O=7.125 H=7.188 L=3.750 V=226454900 -1.1 Square Price(63.938,-90,4,FALSE)
U Deg. 0.3.94

Here is a Monthly Chart of XRX which

declined 3 x 360 degrees from it's high in 1999.

We begin looking for a buy setup in early
2001.

3 X 360

CHART 93

Here is a monthly chart of Xerox.

Using the squares from late 1999 into 2000, you get a decline of 3 cycles of 360 degrees and you'd be looking for a buy set up.

NOTES

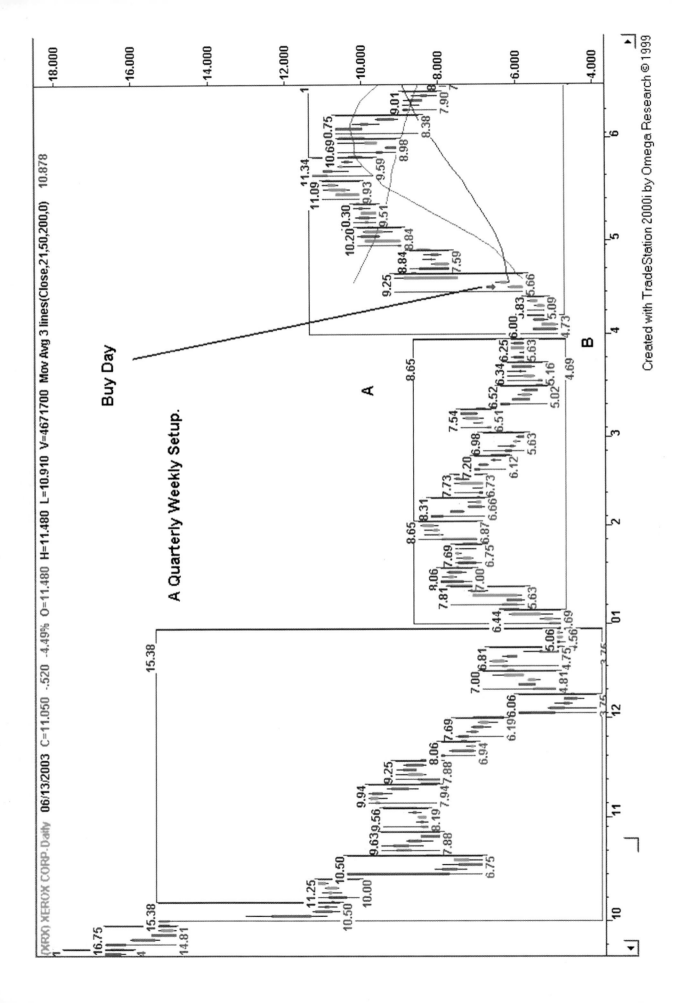

A Quarterly Weekly Setup.

Buy Day

CHART 94

This chart shows how to combine the squares with the True Swing charts to find an entry point.

(A) Label (A) is a down inside quarter and the expectation would be to look for a rally.

(B) Label (B) shows a down inside week. When that signal triggers you get a thrust.

NOTES

(XRX) XEROX CORP Daily 06/08/2001 C=9.008 -.140 -1.53% O=9.055 H=9.094 L=8.383 V=6439100 Mov Avg 3 lines(Close,21,50,200,0) 10.191 8.581

Our price target was the square at 270 degrees up from low. Th outside down week the week of 5/25/01 was a signal to take profits.

The gain was 5.84 to 9.58 or 64% in six weeks.

Created with TradeStation 2000i by Omega Research © 1999

Unlocking the Profits of the New Swing Chart Method ——— PAGE 226

CHART 95

After XRX moves up 180 degrees off the low you'd be looking for 270 degrees or even 360 degrees up from the low. The test of the low in April 2001 is 45 degrees above the low in December 2000.

XRX just missed hitting the square up 270 degrees in May 2001, which suggest a pullback at the very least which is confirmed by the outside down week.

NOTES

(CVX) CHEVRONTEXACO CO-Daily 10/03/2003 C=36.540 +.140 +0.38% O=36.700 H=36.880 L=36.450 V=5109400 Mov Avg 3 lines(Close,21,50,200,0)

At the end of the third quarter 2003, many stocks had Up Inside Quarterly Plots. The table in my CMT paper shows that there is a 65% probability of continuing to go higher. Hence, we look for a Buy setup in early October 2003.

Created with TradeStation 2000i by Omega Research © 1999

CHART 96

As we know a down inside pattern on the quarterly chart has a good probability to generate a rally. Counter-intuitively, up inside quarters have 65% probability of leading to a rally as well.

(A) Label (A) shows an up inside quarter that came off a thrust from a big correction. This is also a Narrow Range 7 quarter. Periods of low volatility are typically followed by a period of high volatility. Notice how the 200 DMA is flattening as well. Once you have the up inside quarter, you want to track the weekly chart to identify an entry point.

The important thing to remember is that the squares are set to the quarterly low once the quarterly low is confirmed. Notice how the quarterly 'flag pattern' is 90 degrees up from the low.

NOTES

(CVX) CHEVRONTEXACO CO-Daily   11/03/2003   C=36.965   -.185   -0.50%   O=37.275   H=37.500   L=36.925   V=6830250   -1.1Weekly Synthetic(12,0,1000101)

BUY 36.80
10/03/03

Stop

35.03

A

B

Unlocking the Profits of the New Swing Chart Method

Created with TradeStation 2000i by Omega Research © 1999

CHART 97

(A) Label (A) shows the end of the third quarter 2003. Notice how there is an outside down week just before, at the end of the quarter. However, the first week of October offsets that outside down week with an outside UP week triggering a buy signal.

Notice this is a low risk trade as the stop is circled at 35.03.

(B) Label (B) shows another test of the low setting up the "Second Mouse" buying opportunity.

NOTES

(CVX) CHEVRONTEXACO CO.Weekly 06/17/2005 C=56.130 -.170 -0.30% O=56.300 H=56.450 L=55.770 V=10243900

Here is what can happen when you buy an Up Inside
Quartely Breakout.

We use 30 degree separations here.

Buy

CHART 98

This chart shows the power of putting the pieces together; the power of the Wheels-of-Price-and-Time, and True-Swing-Chart Theory. This kind of move can happen and you can capture it if you know what you are looking for on the big picture. ChevronTexaco moves up almost 360 degrees before the first significant reaction which was 180 degrees. Notice how Time, Price and Pattern came together, where the BUY is signaled as a low level Cup & Handle pattern is carved out.

NOTES

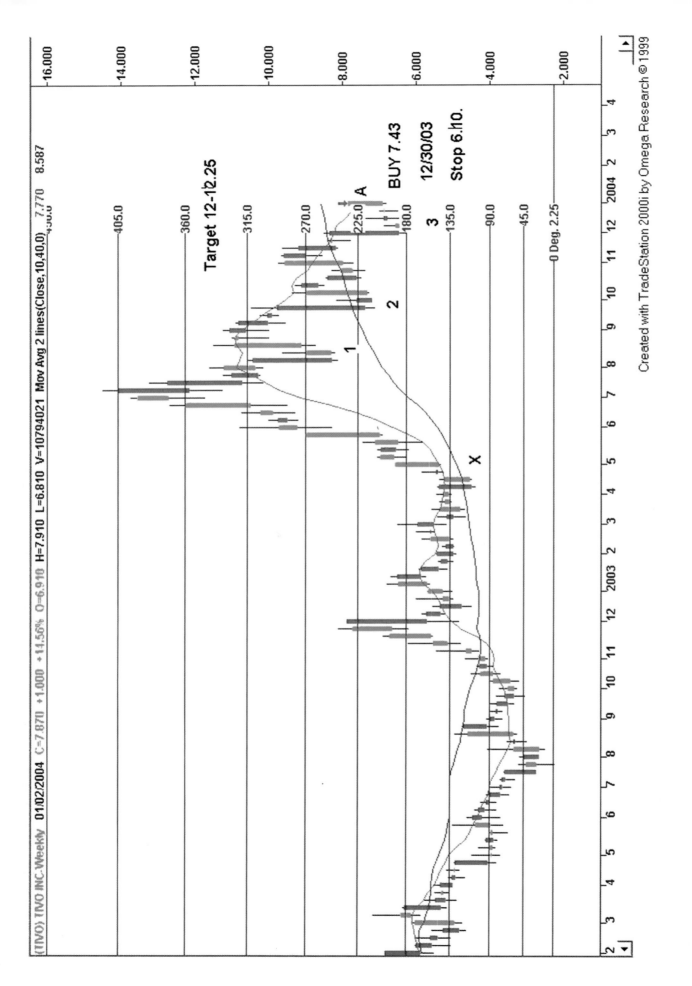

Target 12-12.25

A

BUY 7.43

12/30/03

3

Stop 6.10.

2

1

X

(TIVO) TIVO INC. Weekly 01/02/2004 C=7.870 +1.000 +14.56% O=6.910 H=7.910 L=6.810 V=10794021 Mov Avg 2 lines(Close,10,40,0) 7.770 8.587

Created with TradeStation 2000i by Omega Research © 1999

Unlocking the Profits of the New Swing Chart Method   PAGE 234

CHART 99

This chart shows the power of putting the pieces together; the power of the Wheels-of-Price-and-Time, and True-Swing-Chart Theory. This kind of move can happen and This chart shows how to trade the 1-2-3 Swing-to-a-Test pattern. As you know the market many times plays out in threes: three prices to a high, three drives to a low, three drives to a test, etc. etc. etc.

Here TIVO traces out three drives to test of the last breakout point. Note the down inside weekly set up near (A), which is 180 degrees up from the July 2002 low.

NOTES

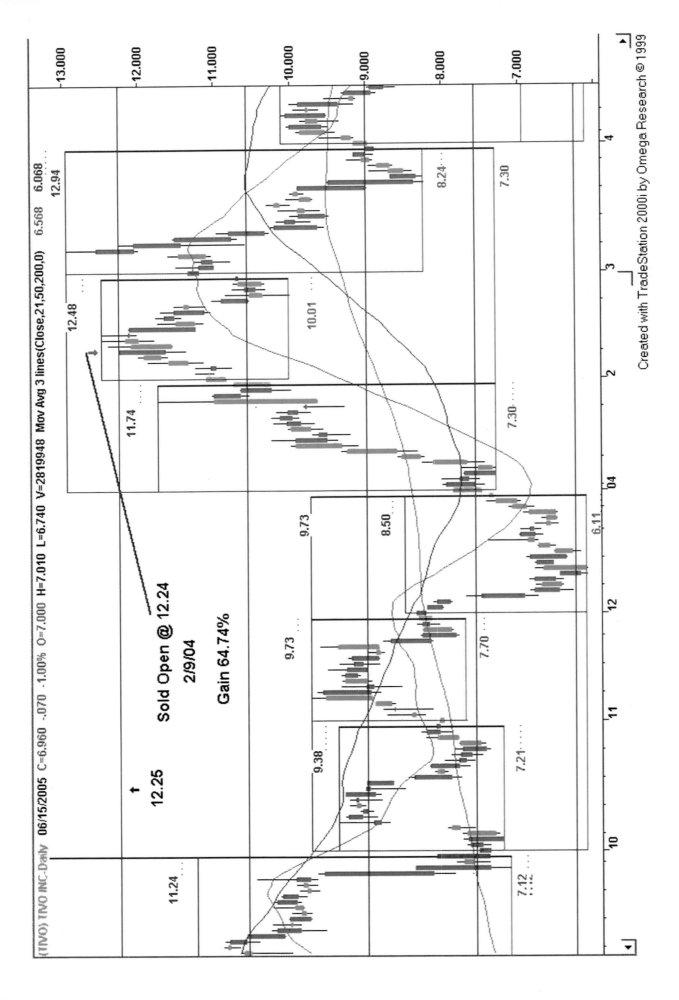

Created with TradeStation 2000i by Omega Research © 1999

| Unlocking the Profits of the New Swing Chart Method | PAGE 236

CHART 100

Here is a daily chart with quarterly and monthly boxes. The separation on the squares is 45 degrees.

When the monthly chart turns up the stock accelerates and you could anticipate a minimum 90 degree move up. Notice the tail at the test of the high for a graceful exit (leaving a Jack-Knife sell signal). 12.25 equals 180 degrees up from low and 90 degrees up from the buy set up. The set up generates a 65% gain in 5 to 6 weeks.

NOTES

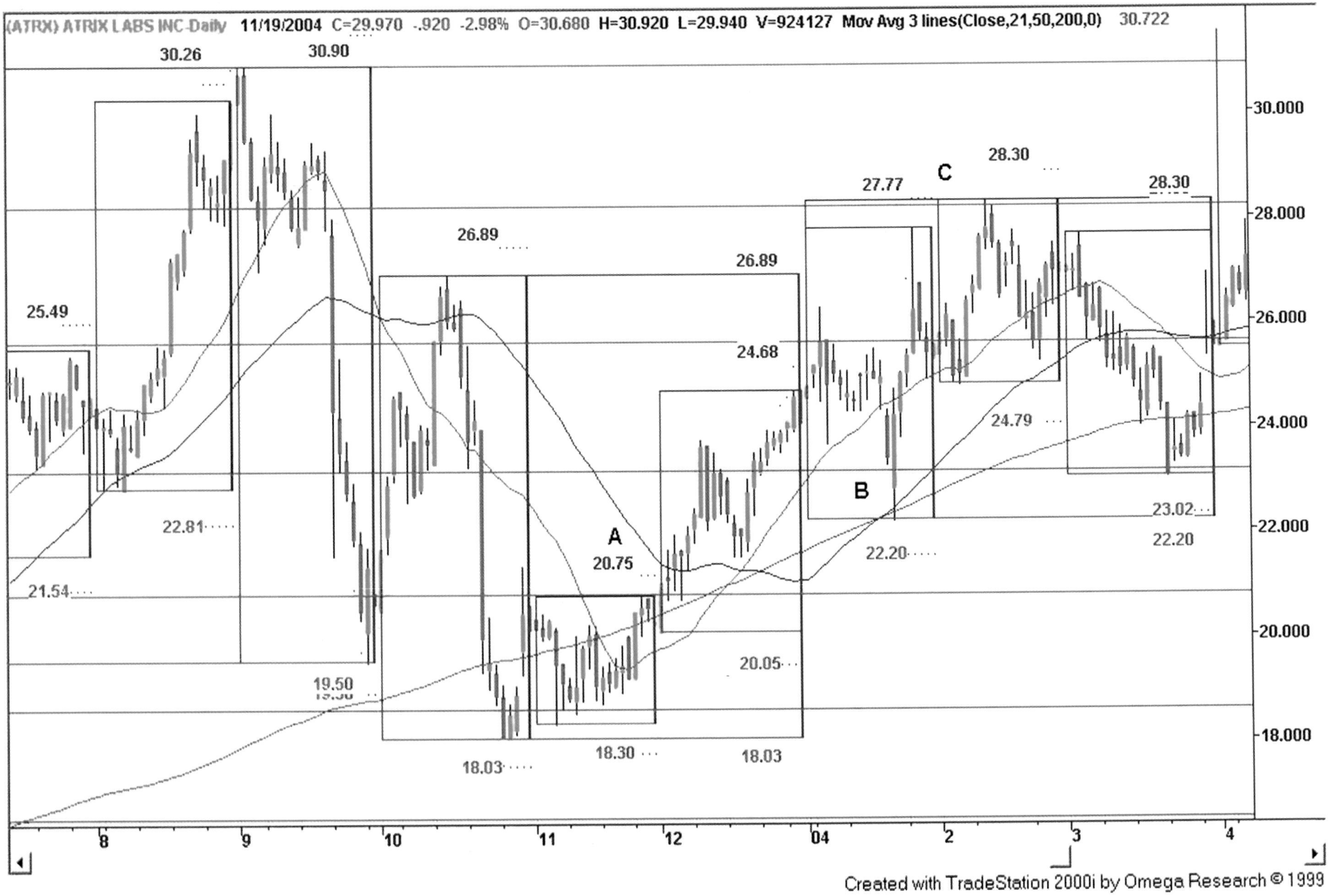
(ATRX) ATRIX LABS INC-Daily 11/19/2004 C=29.970 -.920 -2.98% O=30.680 H=30.920 L=29.940 V=924127 Mov Avg 3 lines(Close,21,50,200,0) 30.722
30.26
30.90
25.49
22.81
21.54
19.50
26.89
18.03
A
20.75
18.30
26.89
24.68
20.05
18.03
27.77
C
28.30
28.30
B
22.20
24.79
23.02
22.20
30.000
28.000
26.000
24.000
22.000
20.000
18.000
8
9
10
11
12
04
2
3
4
Created with TradeStation 2000i by Omega Research © 1999

CHART 101

There were many stocks with down inside months in November 2003.

(A) Label (A) is a down inside month. We know that down inside months have an 82% chance of turning up according to the tables. Hence, you can either buy on the turn up or buy prior to the turn up (anticipating a rally) and adhering to a tight stop.

(B) Label (B) is a 90 degree pullback.

(C) Label (C) shows how the stock tagged the low of the high bar week which was 45 degrees down from the high. That would be a good place to book profits from the turn up in the monthly chart at (A).

NOTES

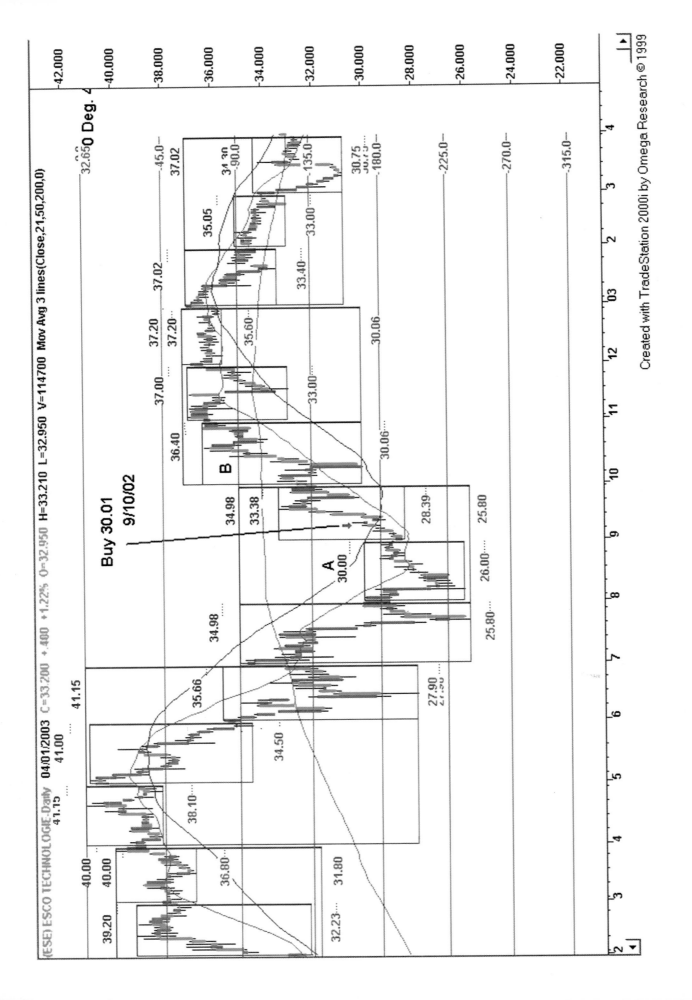

CHART 102

(A) Label (A) shows a down inside month after a +1 -2 down inside quarter and we'd be looking for a buy entry. This chart shows 45 degree separations. Notice how the bottom occurs 225 degrees down from high and that time on the side at the bottom is traced out between 225 and 180 degrees down. A turn-up on the monthly is a logical place to be a buyer. Notice the A-B-C pullback and the Two Feet that are planted subsequent to the thrust after the monthly chart turns up. Note that the Principal of Reflexivity works perfectly here.

(B) The quarterly chart turns up and since the stock had been in a downtrend you want to watch the behavior carefully as the turn up could define a high as the larger trend is still down. 45 degrees down from high, which is $38, is a good target to lock up profits. Notice how the stock fails to tag $38. That is a bearish sign.

NOTES

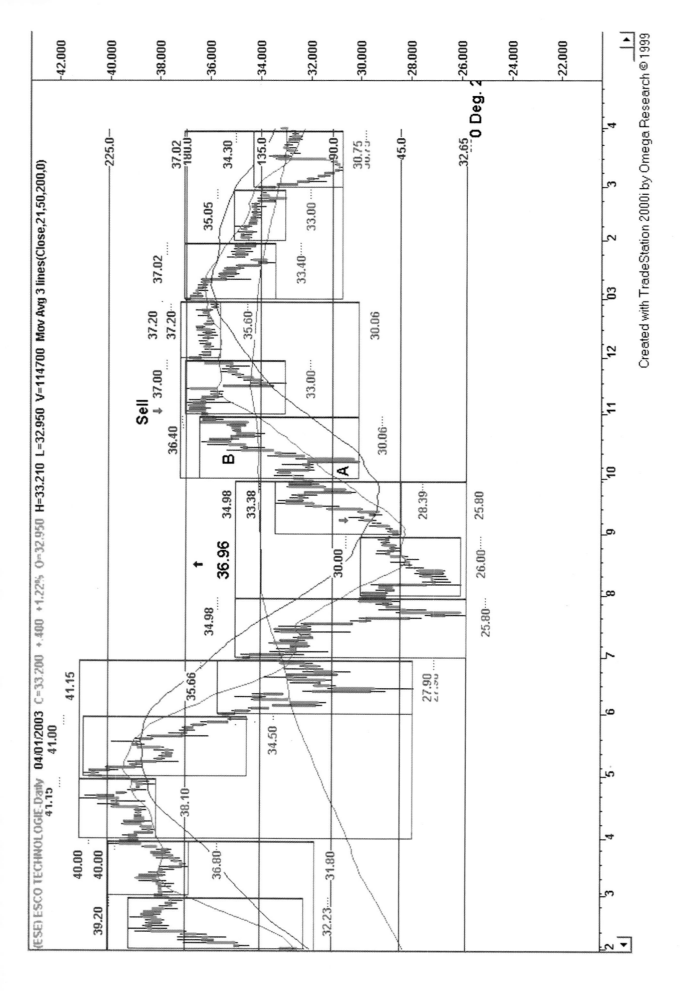

Created with TradeStation 2000i by Omega Research © 1999

CHART 103

(A) The important thing to remember is that when the quarterly chart turns up you must re-zero the squares to the low. 180 degrees up equals $36 (arrow).

(B) After the quarterly turns up, you get a reflex pullback and then a test of the high. The move up was 4 squares of 45 degrees or 180 degrees.

NOTES

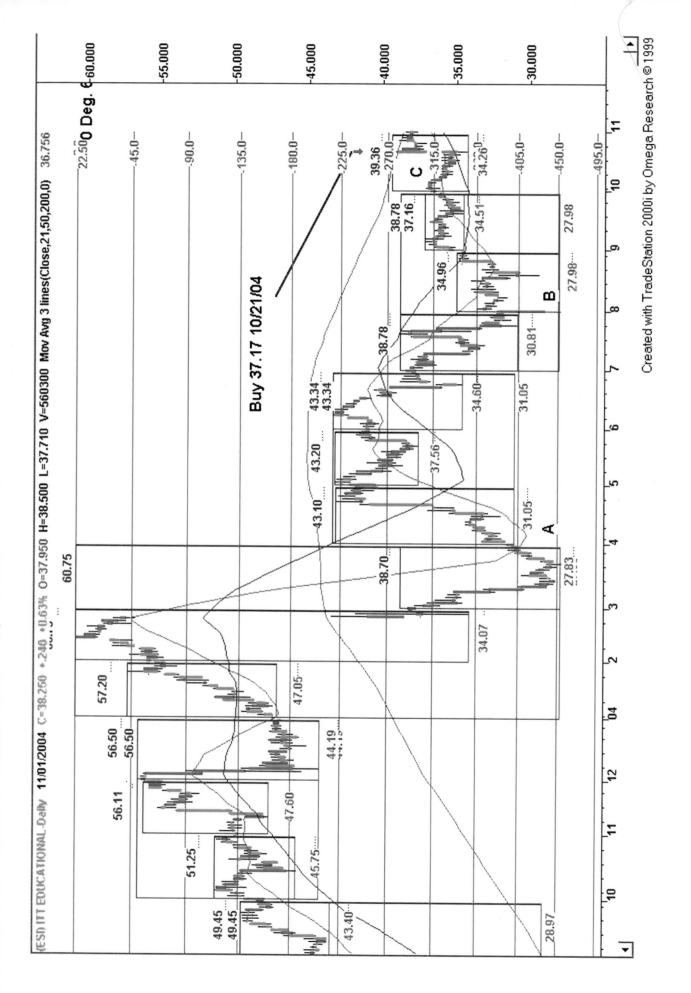

Created with TradeStation 2000i by Omega Research © 1999

CHART 104

These squares are 45 degrees apart.

(A) Label (A) this stock 2-plots on the quarterly chart and crashes. You would think its dead. It's not. It was 450 degrees down into the crash low. You can see in the past that 45 degree increments had validity so you want to use what worked in the past. Notice the symmetry: the gap was 225 degrees and the low was another 225 degrees down; a remarkable example of the Principle of Fractals.

(B) Label (B) marks a double down inside quarter, a good time to look for an entry.

(C) October provides a setup to enter a long position. Note how the monthly chart turns down by a few ticks and then two plots back up, triggering a buy signal. Note how the quarterly chart turns up as well.

NOTES

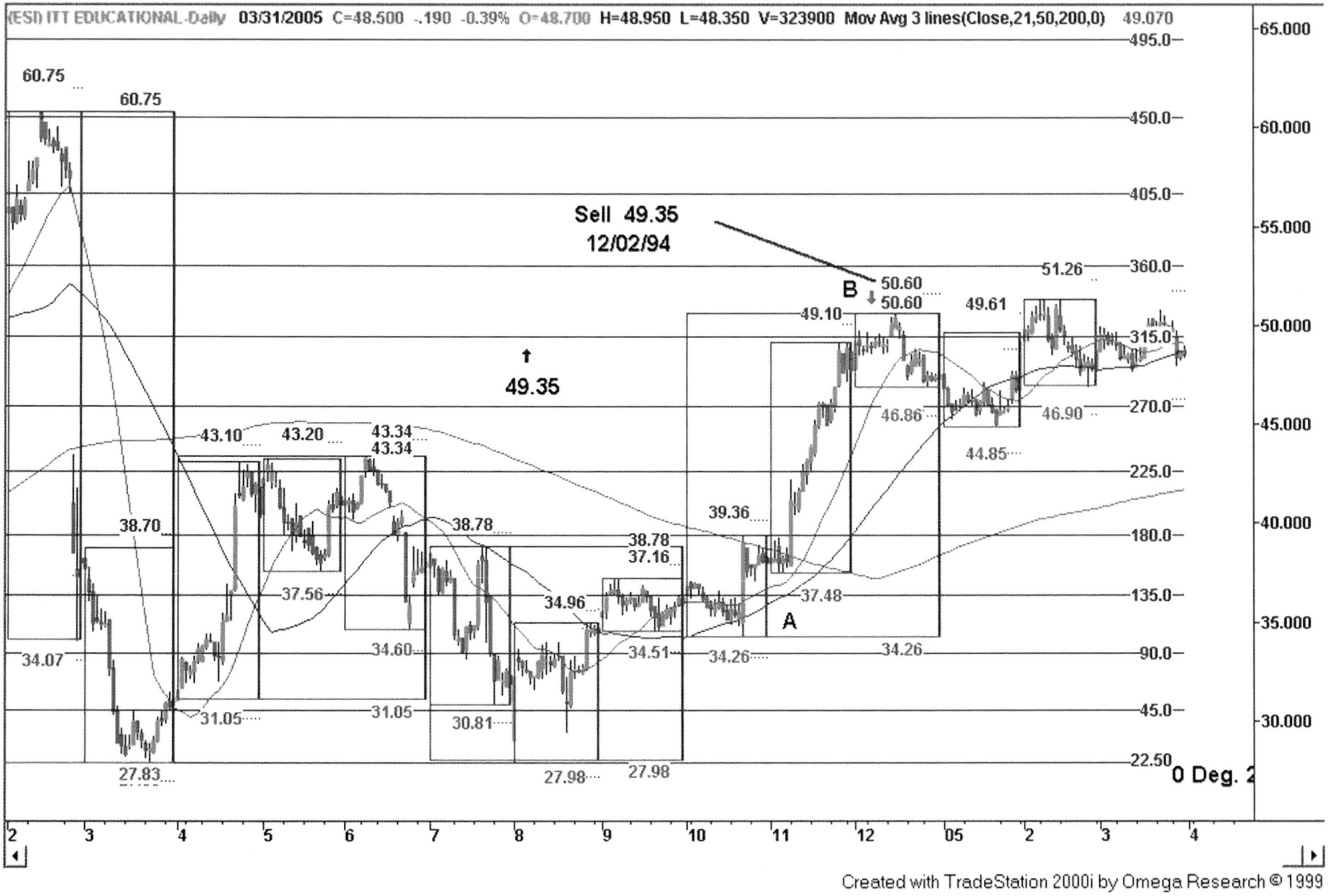
(ESI) ITT EDUCATIONAL-Daily 03/31/2005 C=48.500 -.190 -0.39% O=48.700 H=48.950 L=48.350 V=323900 Mov Avg 3 lines(Close,21,50,200,0) 49.070
Sell 49.35
12/02/94
49.35
B
50.60
50.60
49.10
49.61
51.26
46.86
46.90
44.85
A
37.48
34.26
39.36
38.78
37.16
34.96
34.51
34.26
27.98
27.98
30.81
38.78
43.10
43.20
43.34
43.34
37.56
34.60
31.05
31.05
38.70
60.75
60.75
34.07
27.83
495.0
450.0
405.0
360.0
315.0
270.0
225.0
180.0
135.0
90.0
45.0
22.50
0 Deg. 2
65.000
60.000
55.000
50.000
45.000
40.000
35.000
30.000
2
3
4
5
6
7
8
9
10
11
12
05
2
3
4
Created with TradeStation 2000i by Omega Research © 1999

CHART 105

This chart shows how you get out of the long position from the entry on the prior chart.

(A) Label (A) is the buy point from the prior chart at 37.17. Remember, when the quarterly chart turns up you want to re-zero the squares. Everyone else is probably looking for the gap to be filled. You might be looking for a trade to 360 degrees up but you don't want to look a gift horse in the mouth as this was a crash and burn stock.

(B) Label (B) 3 squares of 45 degrees up from entry is into the middle of the gap and a good place to look to take profits. If you did not sell at (B) after observing how the square is acknowledged you would want to sell a test of (B).

NOTES

(MBT) MOBILE TELESYSTE:Weekly 04/23/2004 C=31.388 -1.237 -3.79% O=32.813 H=34.125 L=30.500 V=6058800 (MBT)

(MBT) MOBILE TELESYSTE -1.1 Square Price(5.938,45,4,FALSE)

C

Sell Turn down In Weekly
32.28 Week of 4/16/04

B

A

Engulf 5-10 Week.

Buy open 21.70
Week of 1/9/04

Bonus Setup.

Created with TradeStation 2000i by Omega Research © 1999

Unlocking the Profits of the New Swing Chart Method   PAGE 248

CHART 106

(A) Label (A) shows how the stock is range trading above and below the 360 level up. The important thing to observe here is that the stock is holding this 360 degree level well. Note the N/R 7 (narrowest range in 7) week at (A), which typically suggest a volatility move in one direction or the other. Additionally, there is an Engulfing 5 setup which occurs when a stock engulfs the body of the prior 5 weeks action. You buy at the open at 21.70 on the open as the stock breaks above the next square 45 degrees up which suggests higher prices as well.

(B) Label (B) many times when a stock breaks out you get what we call a 'tail scare' as the stock tails off and kisses the breakout point.

(C) Label (C) 6 squares up from 360 degrees the stock finds high. After a strong move when the angle of attack gets steeper and steeper you look for any sign of reversal to exit. Note how the last three weeks up was a vertical move which was shortly followed by a large range reversal at a square which gives us our signal to exit.

NOTES

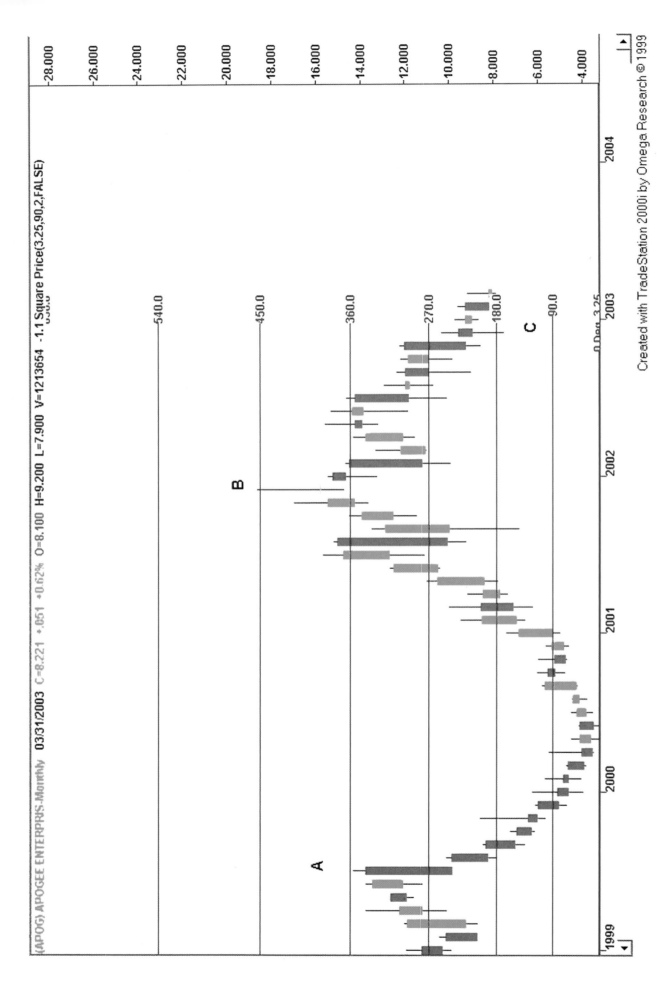

(APOG) APOGEE ENTERPRS.Monthly   03/31/2003   C=8.221 +.051 +0.62% O=8.100 H=9.200 L=7.900 V=1213654 -1.1 Square Price(3.25,90,2,FALSE)

Created with TradeStation 2000i by Omega Research © 1999

Unlocking the Profits of the New Swing Chart Method —— **PAGE 250**

CHART 107

(A) Here we set the squares starting at the 2000 low (note the down inside month at the 2000 low). Running backwards you get a direct hit telling you that 90 degree squares are working. In late 2000 there is a + 1 -2 set up on the monthly chart from which the stock screams up 270 degrees. This is 360 degrees up from low.

(B) Note, the near 270 degree pullback and how the high comes in 90 degrees above the old high.

(C) Label (C) shows a 270 degree pullback which is 180 degrees up from the low.

NOTES ～～～～～～～～～～～～～～～～～～～～～～～～～～～～～～～～～～～

(APOG) APOGEE ENTERPRS.Weekly 03/07/2003 C=8.200 +.030 +0.37% O=8.100 H=8.500 L=8.060 V=227520

Buy Week of 3/14 when
weekly chart turns up.
8.51

Stop below
December low at 7.56.

A

Created with TradeStation 2000i by Omega Research © 1999

CHART 108

This chart shows the set up from point (C) on the prior chart.

(A) Going into March 2003 there are three down inside months. You get a bounce and a test as you most always do, according to the Principle of Tests-as-Two Feet are planted. Notice at (A) there are also two down inside weeks and you look to buy a weekly turn up.

NOTES

(APOG) APOGEE ENTERPRSS-Weekly 07/04/2003 C=8.890 -.020 -0.22% O=8.950 H=9.035 L=8.850 V=313213 -.1 Square Price(3.25,45,2,FALSE)

Sell 10.90 or better.

+28.1% in 8 weeks.

10.91

A

B

270.0

225.0

180.0

12.000

11.000

10.000

9.000

8.000

Created with TradeStation 2000i by Omega Research © 1999

Unlocking the Profits of the New Swing Chart Method   PAGE 254

CHART 109

In low priced stocks 90 degree moves are big. These are 45 degree squares.

(A) Label (A) $10.90 equals 90 degrees up from low.

(B) Label (B) shows two down inside weeks and the stock may be ready to go again.

NOTES

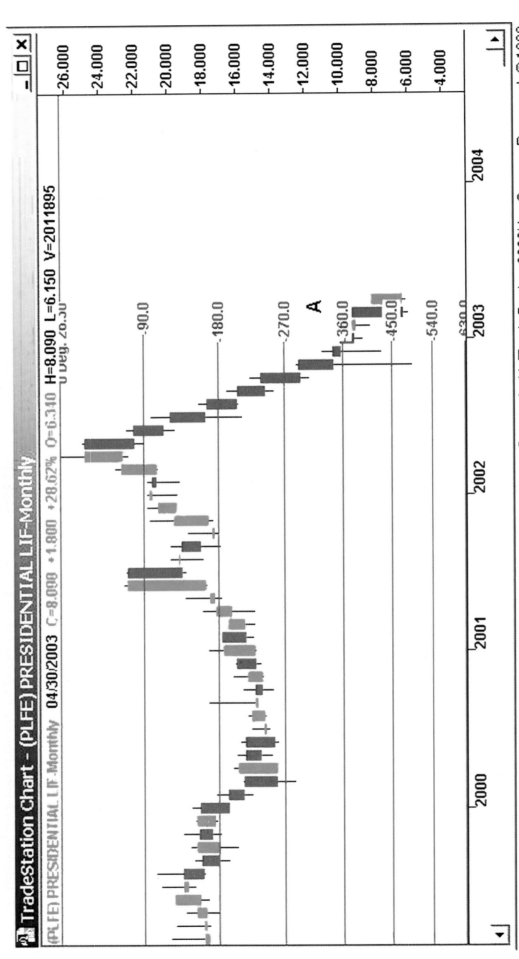

Created with TradeStation 2000i by Omega Research © 1999

CHART 110

(A) Label (A) at this point there are 5 down inside months. The stock hasn't plotted for 5 months.

NOTES

(PL[F]) PRESIDENTIAL LIF-Weekly 04/18/2003 C=7.120 +.720 +11.25% O=6.610 H=7.360 L=6.400 V=332701

Buy week of 4/18/03 at 7.23

Stop 5.76 (Nov low).

A

Created with TradeStation 2000i by Omega Research © 1999

Unlocking the Profits of the New Swing Chart Method   PAGE 258

CHART 111

Here is a weekly picture of the 5 down inside months.

(A) Label (A) shows two down inside weeks suggesting a turn up. There is also a down inside quarter. You look to buy a weekly turn up from the set up as the wheels of time and price are wound up. You go long at $7.23.

NOTES

(PLFE) PRESIDENTIAL LIF-Weekly 07/04/2003 C=14.110 -.170 -1.19% O=14.340 H=14.340 L=13.870 V=100577 Mov Avg 2 lines(Close,10,40,0) 12.075

Take partial profits
at 11.59. +60% in
5 weeks.. ↓

A

11.59

-1 Volume Average(10,50,Green,Red) 100577.00 714044.69

Created with TradeStation 2000i by Omega Research © 1999

Unlocking the Profits of the New Swing Chart Method — PAGE 260

CHART 112

This chart shows how to get out of the trade from the prior chart.

Remember that you want to re-zero to the November low once the quarterly chart turns up. We said that 90 degree moves are big moves for low priced stocks, so you should at least take partial profits at $11.59. Although, the stock achieves a 180 degree move up that's just the reality of the game. The object is to make money not to pick tops or bottoms. Note how the weekly chart made 10 higher lows in its move up into (A). You could have used a stop below the prior weekly low as your second exit, up near 14.00.

NOTES

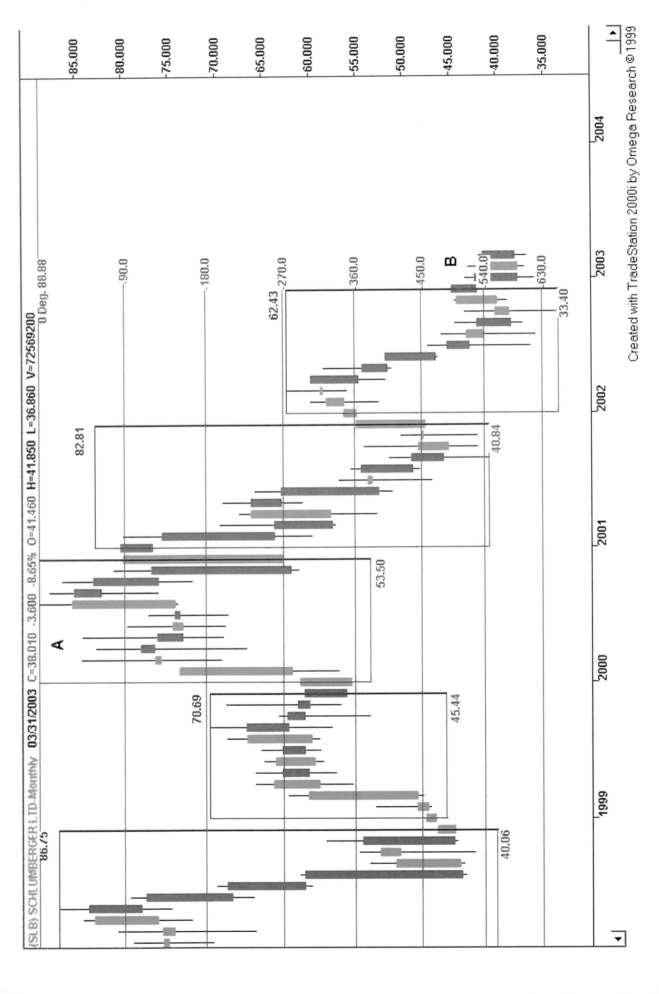

(SLB) SCHLUMBERGER LTD-Monthly 03/31/2003 C=38.010 -3.600 -8.65% O=41.460 H=41.850 L=36.860 V=72569200

0 Deg. 88.88

Created with TradeStation 2000i by Omega Research©1999

CHART 113

(A) Label (A) the move from high to the 2001 low is 540 degrees. The following bounce is 270 degrees.

(B) Label (B) shows a 360 degree move down, which is 90 degrees below the prior low. Note the two down inside months at this juncture.

NOTES

(SLB) SCHLUMBERGER LTD-Weekly 04/18/2003 C=38.880 +.810 +2.13% O=36.080 H=39.120 L=36.080 V=10302900 Mov Avg 2 lines(Close,10,40,0)

Buy week of 4/18/03

at 38.93

A

Stop 35.61 (Jan low)

-1 Volume Average(10,50,Green,Red)   10302900.00   16511901.00

Created with TradeStation 2000i by Omega Research © 1999

Unlocking the Profits of the New Swing Chart Method   PAGE 264

CHART 114

Here is a weekly picture of the double down inside month from the prior chart.

(A) Label (A) shows a test of the January low and a 2-plot week. This is a good buy signal.

NOTES

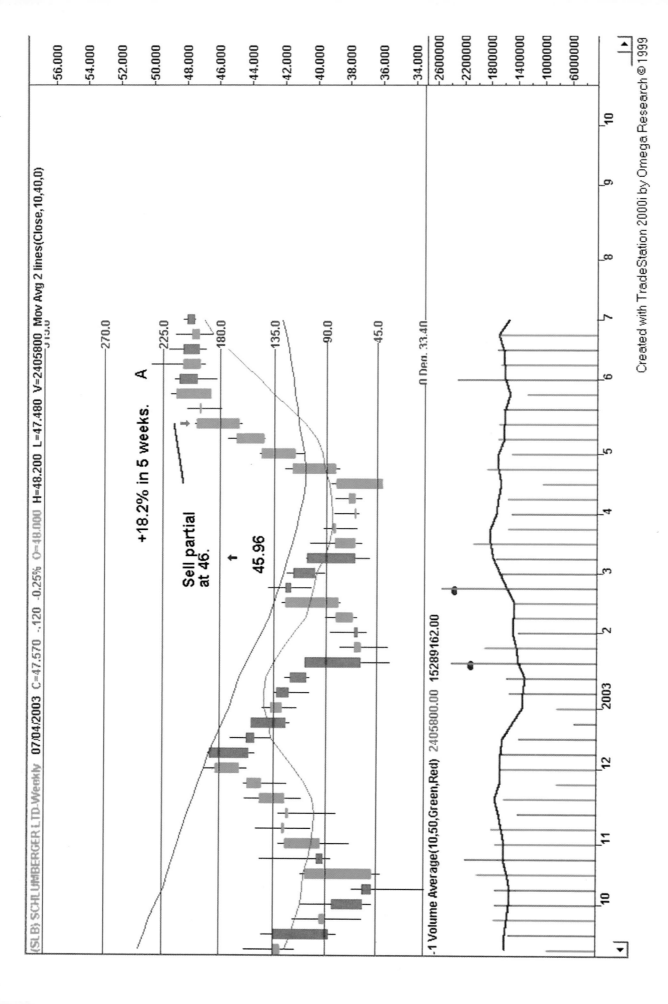

(SLB) SCHLUMBERGER LTD-Weekly   07/04/2003   C=47.570   -.120   -0.25%   O=48.000   H=48.200   L=47.480   V=2405800   Mov Avg 2 lines(Close,10,40,0)

A

+18.2% in 5 weeks.

Sell partial
at 46.

45.96

-1 Volume Average(10,50,Green,Red)   2405800.00   15289162.00

Created with TradeStation 2000i by Omega Research © 1999

CHART 115

When the quarterly chart turns back up you want to re-zero to the quarterly low in October. Recent price action shows that 45 degree squares are working so you use them. Notice how the first move up in November 2002 is 180 degrees. A good place to take partial profits is at old highs.

(A) Label (A) shows how 180 degrees up stalled the stock. This was at a test of the 2002 high, and would have been a good place to exit the balance of the trade.

NOTES

(C-I1601) Light Crude Oil-Monthly 09/30/2005 C=64.750 -4.180 -6.06% O=68.950 H=69.590 L=62.540 V=2342862 -1.1 Square Price(10,90,3,FALSE) 75.035

The is the Master Square on Crude Oil which starts at the price of 10.00

9/05 is 60 months
from 9/00 High

On the Square of Nine Wheel, 71 is the price opposite
to the date 8/30, so we had a square out that day

when the price hit 70.85

High 9/00

990.0

900.0

810.0

720.0

630.0

540.0

450.0

360.0

270.0

180.0

90.0

0 Deg. 10.00

55.64
39.99
37.79
33.64
32.70
32.20
27.14
26.89
26.73
25.07
23.69
20.98
20.82
18.05
17.85
17.50
17.07
16.69
16.60
13.88
11.30
10.34

80.000
70.000
60.000
50.000
40.000
30.000
20.000
10.000

95 96 97 98 99 00 01 02 03 04 05 06

Created with TradeStation 2000i by Omega Research © 1999

CHART 116 - NOTES

(C11601) Light Crude Oil-Daily 09/19/2005 C=67.390 +4.390 +6.97% O=64.590 H=67.590 L=64.590 V=0 Mov Avg 3 lines(Close,21,50,200,0) 65.995 63.155

This is a daily chart with monthly and quarterly boxes.

The squares are plotted using 30 degree separations.
The advance from the Dec. '04 low to the recent high was a near

perfect 360 degree advance.

We start the squares up from the December, 2004 low which was a +1,-2 on the
Monthly Swing Chart. Also note the near perfect "X" pattern in

April/May 2005

The correction from the 8/30 high was
an exact 90 degree pullback from the high.
The bounce so far has been 5.00 up.

Created with TradeStation 2000i by Omega Research © 1999

Unlocking the Profits of the New Swing Chart Method   PAGE 270

CHART 117 - NOTES

(#PD) PRE PAID LEGAL S-Daily 09/16/2005 C=38.270 -.950 -2.42% O=39.220 H=39.220 L=38.270 V=212000 Mov Avg 3 lines(Close,21,50,200,0) 40.421

The squares are plotted up from the 22.25 low in the
third quarter (July) of 2004.

Let's see what you have learned.

Created with TradeStation 2000i by Omega Research © 1999

CHART 118 - NOTES

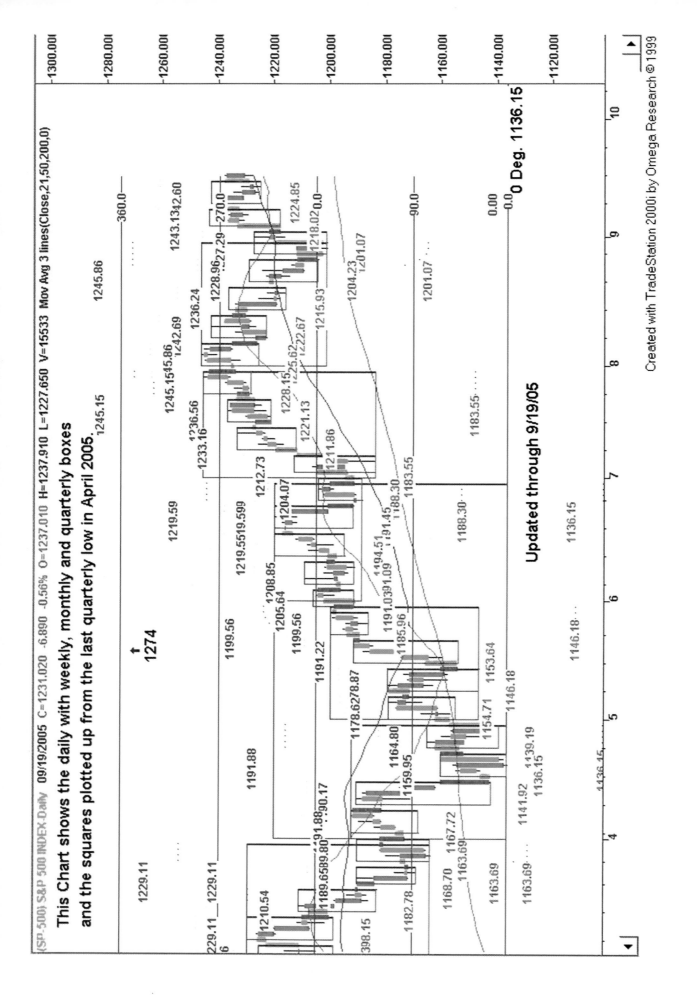

This Chart shows the daily with weekly, monthly and quarterly boxes and the squares plotted up from the last quarterly low in April 2005.

Updated through 9/19/05

0 Deg. 1136.15

Created with TradeStation 2000i by Omega Research © 1999

CHART 119 - NOTES

Appendix A

THE REIF SWING CHART METHOD

By David C. Reif
Copyright © 1993, All Rights Reserved

INTRODUCTION

The purpose of this paper is to provide the analyst with a precisely defined method for plotting a swing chart. This method plots the 5 minute, hourly, daily, weekly, monthly quarterly, and yearly time frames in exactly the same way without exceptions. The author will show how any price action is plotted, so that all the key highs and lows are identified. It will be show how the plots of various time periods are related to each other using the "wheel concept" of cyclical analysis. It will be shown that one of the most useful observations is the study of price behavior after the various swing charts turn up or down.

BACKGROUND

W. D. Gann was one of the first market analysts to develop various types of swing charts. In his book, *How to Make Profits In Commodities*, Gann described the use of a 2 day, 3 day, and a 7 calendar day chart. In his *Stock Market Course*, he developed an entire trading method on a swing chart approach called the Overnight Chart. In addition, in his books *45 Years on Wall Street* and *New Stock Trend Indicator*, he described two types of 3 day charts: a trading day version and a calendar day version. The author has found it very difficult to use all of these charts, because there are times when the price action is so volatile that it becomes quite difficult to know how to plot it. Moreover, Gann did not provide us with the method he used to tie the analysis of all these charts together so that a consensus forecast could be made.

There have been other methods that provide the analyst with precisely defined pivot points. Arthur Merrill, in *Filtered Waves*, described an excellent method to measure swings in the market. He used a percentage reversal that would filter out any reversal less than the percentage selected. For example, if the analyst only wanted to see swings greater than 10%, the chart would remain up until a 10% or more decline, from the highest high reached up to that point, occurred. Once a decline of 10% occurred, the last high was defined. The next low would not be defined until the market moved up 10% from the lowest point reached. In 1979, Merrill published *M & W Patterns*, which provided excellent research on the probabilities of any given 5 point wave (M or W) to project future price action. The author has had trouble with this approach wondering if a 9.7% correction was not significant, while a 10.1% correction was significant. Despite this concern, I have found this approach to be quite helpful in defining key pivots in market action.

Jerry Favors, of *Jerry Favors Analysis*, is probably the modern day expert on the Gann swing charts. In his presentation before the Market Technicians Association monthly meeting in November, 1990, he described an Inside 5, a Daily Trendline, and a Three Day Chart. Favors keeps numerous swing charts, each having its own rules for plotting and analysis.

Another approach was developed by John R. Hill in his book, *Stock and Commodity Market Trend Trading by Advanced Technical Analysis*. Hill describes a method to determine a pivot point with a swing being the movement from one pivot point to the next. In his book, a top pivot point is defined as the highest point reached in a swing prior to the penetration of the low of the top day. A bottom pivot point is the lowest point reached in a swing prior to the penetration of the high of the low day. The main problem I have found with this approach is determining what to do when a long bar period presents itself in the price structure.

In 1986, after studying all of the above methods in great detail, the author decided to try and develop a single plotting method that was precisely defined and that could be used on any time frame, be it a 5 minute chart or a yearly chart. In addition, I wanted the chart to show the periods that were not plotted, including "inside periods" and "multiple plot" periods. I also wanted to be able to study a daily, weekly, monthly and quarterly chart of a stock or commodity and compare each chart's picture at key historical turning points. This effort led to the following plotting rules.

NOTES ～～～～～～～～～～～～～～～～～～～～～～～～～～～

THE REIF SWING CHART DEFINED

The following instructions apply <u>to any time period</u>, and to any stock, commodity, or index. The following describes how the daily swing chart is plotted.

Let us assume that we have the following daily price information on Pork Bellies:

DATE	OPEN	HIGH	LOW	CLOSE	CHANGE
10/2	6510	6605	6510	6550	+30
10/3	6575	6650 ↑	6560 ↑	6560	+55
10/4	6610	6675 ↑	6540 ↓	6545	-60
10/5 *	6650	6630 ↓	6550 ↑	6575	+30
10/6	6540	6675 ↑	6510 ↓	6645	+70
10/9	6675	6750 ↑	6650 ↑	6705	+60
10/10	6700	6745 ↓	6630 ↓	6630	-75

To plot the swing chart of the above price action, you need a starting point. In this example, the data for 10/2 is the starting point. On 10/3 we have a higher high and a higher low (if you use a red and green fine line pen, it is easier to follow and visualize). Puts the arrows on the data series, and for 10/3 place a green up arrow beside 6650 and 6560. If the low had been equal to the 10/2 low, the arrow would still be pointed up as <u>the chart stays up until a lower low than the prior period's low is made</u>. On 10/4 the price action is higher than 10/3 at the opening but later in the day the price trades lower than 10/3's low. This action turns the chart down and there are two plots placed that day. First, take the chart up to the high made on 10/4 and then take the chart down to the low price reached on 10/4. Place a green square on the high price reached on 10/4, and mark the high price reached on the chart. The 10/4 high is called a confirmed high (see Chart #1). Note: The closing price is not plotted on a swing chart, only the highs and the lows are plotted. Another piece of important information is recorded on the plot after the close on 10/4. The price that had to be penetrated to turn the chart down was 6550. *prior low* A tick mark is placed on the plot at that exact price as shown in Chart #1 at A. On 10/5, with the last plot being down, there is a higher low and a lower high. This day is not plotted but is noted on the chart with the date as in the plotted example (Chart #1). This is down inside day. On 10/6 the price opens down and goes lower than 10/4 and then turns up exceeding the price of the 10/5 high. Place a square around the low of 6510 (which is now confirmed low) with a red pen along with the red down arrow. The plot is then taken up to the high of 10/6, and this is another two plot day. Again place a tick mark on the plot at 6630. *prev high*

On 10/9 the high and the low are higher so the chart is plotted up to the high of that day, along with the green up arrows. On 10/10 there is a lower high and a lower low, and the moment the prior day's low of 6650 is penetrated we place a square around the highest high reached in green and take the chart down to the low reached. This action created a confirmed high of 6750 on 10/9. We knew that the chart turned down the moment that a low lower than 6650 was made. It was not until after the close that we know how far down to take the plot. The same action is taken when the prior day's high is penetrated and we know that the chart is up, but we don't know how far to plot it until the market closes. Below in Chart #1 is shown the plot of the above action. Note: The prices of the highs and the lows have a square around them on the data records and the prices are noted on the chart. Note the reversal days of 10/4 and 10/6 and how the arrows show the price action, and also that the date of the inside day is shown although there is no plot for the day 10/5.

Use arrows on the chart to show the reversals on 10/4 and 10/6. 10/5 is written between the spaces in red to denote the inside day. An asterisk is placed next to the price action in the data to show this day was an inside day.

There are times when you use the open and close to ascertain whether the high or the low came first on a day. It is also possible to have a 3 or more plot day. In these cases it might require a source of hourly data or a call to your broker to get the swing highs or lows during the day.

Assume that we have trading day 10/11 as follows:

DATE	OPEN	HIGH	LOW	CLOSE	CHANGE
10/11	6605 ↓	6775 ↑	6430 ↓	6430	-200

This day presents a problem for us. We had taken the chart down after the close on the 10/10 to 6630. On 10/11 the price opened lower so we know that we have to take the chart down to at least 6605, yet during the day, the prior day's high of 6745 was exceeded on the upside thereby turning the chart up. Obviously later during the day the market reversed and took out the low of 6605, a confirmed low made the same day, and closed down limit. In a case such as this

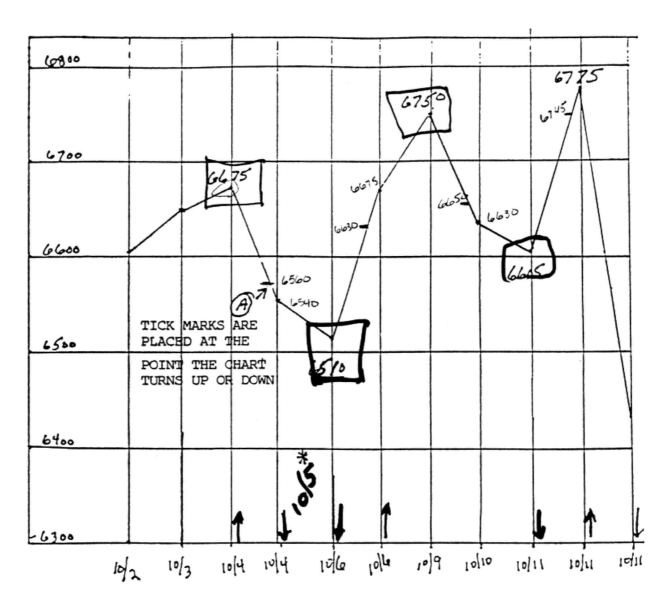

Chart 1 - Daily Swing Chart on Porkbellies

you have to assume the initial low was the open, take the chart down to 6605, a confirmed low, then up to the high of 6775, a confirmed high, and then down to the low of 6430. This is a 3 plot day which is very rare, but it does happen. Had we known the low made after the open with a source of hourly data, this low would have been the first low plotted on 10/11.

These plotting rules are designed so that there can be no misunderstanding of what to do with any price action. Below are examples of situations that occur quite frequently and how they should be handled. A series of bar charts days are shown in a row and then how the swing chart would be plotted.

In Example #1 the swing is plotted higher each day until day #4, which is an 'inside' day (the high is less or equal to day 3 and the low is higher than or equal to day 3) consequently day 4 is an 'inside' day and is noted on your chart as a 'no plot' day as described above. Now comes the tricky part. On day 5, you have a price action that has a higher high than day 4 and the high is lower than or equal to day 3. Day 5 also has a lower low than day 4, but the low is equal to or higher than the low of day 3. In other words, you have an 'outside' day of day 4, but 'inside' of day 3. In this example you must bring the swing chart down from the day 3 high to the day 5 low because the high on day 5 occurred first. This is most likely since the day 5 opening was higher than the day 4 close and since the chart was already plotted up to day 3's high, and day 5's high was less than or equal to day 3, the chart could not be taken up or plotted higher; however, the moment day 4's low was penetrated the chart turned down and a square was placed around the high of day 3 on your data file in green and posted to your chart as a confirmed high. You did not know how low to take the chart down until after the close.

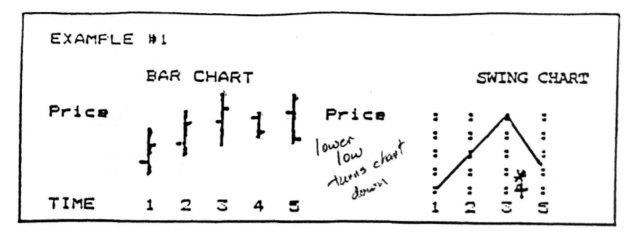

Example #1

Now what would the swing chart look like if day 5 action showed a lower opening price and a higher closing? In this case the low probably occurred first and the high second. If this happened, you would bring the chart down first to the low of day 5 since the day 4 low was penetrated, turning the chart down, and then take it up to the high price of day 5 and thereby plot day 5's price action twice. The bar chart and the swing chart of this example are shown below in Example #2. This action creates a confirmed high on day 3 and a confirmed low on day 5.

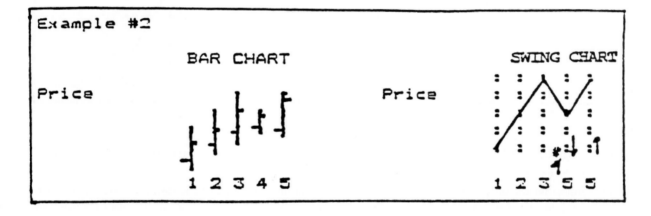

Example #2

The same type of logic is used for a down trend. Two examples with associated plots are shown below.

NOTES

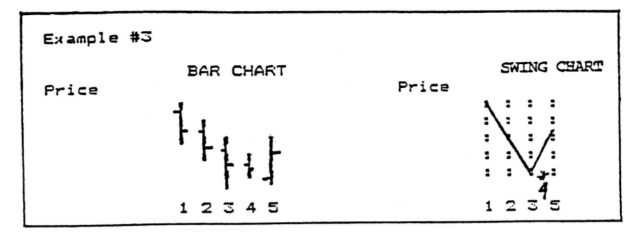

Example #3

Note: The open and close on day 5 indicate that the low occurred first. Since the swing chart was already down you could not plot lower. When the high of day 4 was exceeded, the chart turned up creating a confirmed low on day 3. You don't know how high to plot until the close of day 5. The low of the plot is established the moment that day 4's high was penetrated.

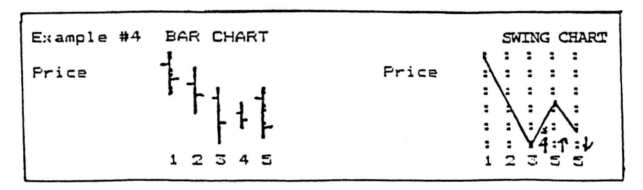

Example #4

In this case the high occurred first on day 5 as shown by observing the opening price, and day 5 is plotted twice. This action creates a confirmed low on day 3 and a confirmed high on day 5.

There will be times that the only way to determine what happened first, the high or the low, is by the observation of the day's opening price and the prior day's close or via a source of hourly data. It is important to have this information when you are actually trading the market and now doing historical work. It is quite easy to instruct your broker to give you the sequence of events. For example, you know that the day following an inside day is very important. You would ask your broker to watch this market and tell you if the high or low penetration occurred first.

The best way to learn how to plot a swing chart is to practice. At the end of each day you must ask yourself "what can happen tomorrow that will change my plot?"

Let's look at another example using weekly data on the D-Mark.

DATE	OPEN	HIGH	LOW	CLOSE
1/07	5510	5560	5460	5550
1/14	5555	5650↑	5510↑	5640
1/21	5625	5700↑	5405↓	5420
1/28	*inside 5455	5675↓	5455↑	5625
2/05	* 5610	5650↓	5420↓	5475
2/12	* 5495	5595↓	5495↑	5555
2/19	5540	5650↑	5450↓	5625

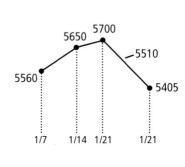

In the above example, the week of 1/21 was a reversal week with two plots. The swing chart was taken to the high of 5700 and then the moment that the prior week's low of 5510 was penetrated you placed a square around the high and turned the plot down. This action created a confirmed high at 5700. You knew that it was down, but until the close on Friday you did not know how low to take the plot. It turned out that you plotted it down to 5405 after Friday's close on 1/21. Since the plotting rules state that the only way you can take the chart back up is by penetrating the prior time period's high you could not take it up for some time. You can see that there were lower highs in the weeks of 1/28, 2/05, and 2/12. Consequently, you could not take the swing chart up during that period, nor could you take it down because it did not trade lower than the swing low plot at 5405. Therefore, all three weeks are no plot weeks, and dates noted on your chart but not plotted. It was only when the high of 5595 was penetrated during the week of 2/19 that you turned the chart up. The moment that 5595 was penetrated you knew that the chart had turned up and a square was placed around the 5405 low on your data record. This action created a confirmed low at 5405. You did not know how high to take the plot until the close Friday.

A good rule to follow once the swing chart turns up or down is to ask the following question the moment that it changes direction: What is the action required to turn it back in the other direction? Since you know what the prior time period's low price (or last confirmed low) was prior to the turn-up, you can easily make a note to remind you of the reversal price to turn the plot back down. It is my hope that this example will keep you from getting confused. Practice will be the only way to learn this thoroughly and correctly. An insert has been provided that summarizes the rules and definitions.

The above instructions are designed to teach anyone to plot price action by hand. In 1990, the author, working with an experienced programmer, Ed Kasanjian, was able to develop a proprietary program that plots swing charts.(1) This program uses color coding to describe the price action. For example, the plot is green until the down reversal price is hit, at which point the plot turns red. Inside periods show up as a side-ways yellow line. Two or 3 plot periods show the action in white. The charts presented in the remainder of this paper will use the charts from this program, although the color features will not be visible. This program allows shifting from a daily, weekly, monthly, quarterly or yearly bar chart to its equivalent swing chart in seconds.

THE PLOT ADVANTAGES

During 1991 after viewing hundreds of charts in various time frames using my new program, it become apparent that the yellow bars (inside periods) were very important precursors of future price action, particularly, in the monthly, quarterly and yearly charts. I have a daily file on the DJIA that starts in September, 1928, and continues up to the present day. It was also apparent that 2 and 3 plot periods were key to future price behavior. When working with Ed Kasanjian on the best way to plot the swing chart with a computer, I decided that the best way to view the swing highs and lows on the screen was to use a zero balance plot. Larry Williams was one of the first analysts to use the zero balance concept and it has been used for many years by Curtis Hesler of Professional Timing Service. The method varies depending upon how you select your pivot points. The theory of zero-balance is best understood by a thorough study of reference 7. For the purposes of this paper, I will provide the formula needed to compute it. The first requirement to compute this indicator is a method to define key highs and lows in the market. In my opinion, my swing chart plotting rules provide an excellent method to define pivot points. Once 6 pivot points have been established, you can compute two points out into the future using the following formula.

$$P8 = P6 + P5 - P3$$

For example, when the swing chart turns down, it creates a high pivot which immediately becomes a new point 6. Counting back from that point provides the values for points 5 and 3. In this way, as prices move from high to low and back to high, you develop a corresponding zero-balance plot of the price action that is two steps out in front of the actual price action. Consequently, when I call up a swing chart of a stock or index on the computer screen, the last eleven swings are shown on the upper left of the screen with the zero balance points computed next to the corresponding pivot point. In addition, the next two zero balance points are computed out into the future. Once the swing chart turns up or down, a plus or minus sign is added to the last confirmed high or low, therein telling you immediately if the price action is comparatively weak or strong relative to the zero balance points. The three step rule and last ditch setup, described in Reference 7 also work very well on the swing charts as will be shown later in this paper.

SWING CHART EXAMPLES: THE YEARLY DJIA 1929-1992

Chart #2 is the yearly swing chart of the DJIA from 1929 to 1992. The chart is much more impressive if viewed in color, however, I have noted the key set ups and yellow bars (inside years). The key multiple plot years are also noted. Note that there are only four down inside periods in the last 63 years. The 1938 low of 97.50 was not broken until April, 1942, and then the new low was only 4.9% lower than 92.7. The years 1939, 1940 and 1941 were no plot years, signifying a lengthy trading range. When the yearly chart turned up on January 4, 1943, it created the first higher low on this chart since July, 1932. The chart continued to make higher highs and higher lows until 1946 when another lengthy consolidation began. The years 1947 and 1948 were up inside (no plot) years. The two plot back up in 1949 signified the resumption of the bull market. There were down inside years in 1967, 1975 and 1979. All of these were followed by a turn up in the chart. Consequently, you can see that of the four down inside periods, 3 turned up afterwards while one made a slightly lower low before beginning the uptrend. This is one of the key behaviors I have discovered using swing charts. Down inside periods are a major clue when looking for a trend reversal. Interestingly enough, the up inside plots on the yearly proved to be consolidations, before a continued up move in the market. The years 1947, 1948, 1984 and 1988 were of this type, and only the back to back plot years of 1947 and 1948 led to a turn down in the chart.

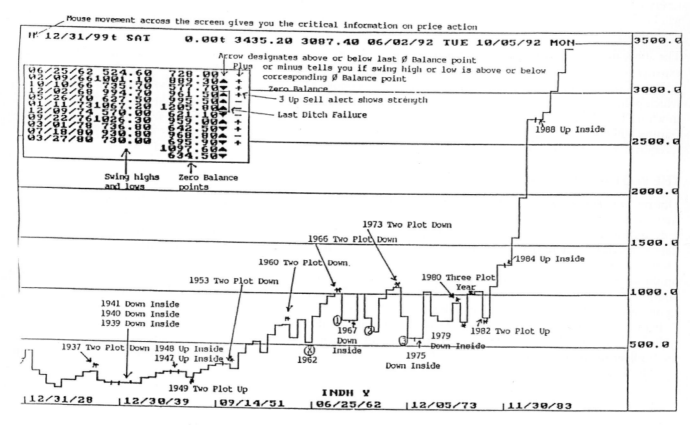

Chart 2 - Yearly Swing Chart of DJIA, 1929 to 1992

Tables #1 and #2 provide summaries of the up inside and down inside behavior of the DJIA for the past 63 years on the yearly, quarterly, monthly and weekly swing charts.

As can be seen by studying Table #1, it could be valuable to know at the end of a given quarter that you just completed an up inside period. The history shows that the odds of the chart breaking the prior quarters intra day low is 62.5%. Other than for the up inside results on the yearly chart, the evidence shows that an up inside period has a better than 62.5% chance of trading lower and turning the chart down. In the case of the down inside results, there is an even higher probability for the charts to turn up after a down inside period. This can be valuable information to the trader, depending upon his overall view of the market.

Table 1 - Dow Jones Industials Up Inside Behavior

PERIOD	TOTAL CASES	# RESOLVED DOWN	# RESOLVED UP	PERCENTAGE DOWN
YEARLY	3	1	2	33.3%
QUARTERLY	8	5	3	62.5%
MONTHLY	27	18	9	66.7%
WEEKLY	169	108	61	63.9%

Table 2 - Dow Jones Industials Down Inside Behavior

PERIOD	TOTAL CASES	# RESOLVED DOWN	# RESOLVED UP	PERCENTAGE UP
YEARLY	4	1	3	75.0%
QUARTERLY	15	5	10	66.7%
MONTHLY	52	13	39	75.0%
WEEKLY	142	48	94	66.2%

After computing the above results on the DJIA, I then decided to do the same study on 59 of my stocks with the longest histories. The minimum file length was 5 years, with many files going back 20 years. The yearly chart was not studied due to the lack of enough long files. Tables #3 and #4 show the results of this study.

Table 3 - 59 Stock Data Base Up Inside Behavior

PERIOD	TOTAL CASES	# RESOLVED DOWN	# RESOLVED UP	PERCENTAGE DOWN
QUARTERLY	95	33	62	34.7%
MONTHLY	247	122	125	49.4%
WEEKLY	617	416	201	67.4%

Table 4 - 59 Stock Data Base Down Inside Behavior

PERIOD	TOTAL CASES	# RESOLVED DOWN	# RESOLVED UP	PERCENTAGE UP
QUARTERLY	115	15	100	87.0%
MONTHLY	283	51	232	82.0%
WEEKLY	482	179	303	62.9%

This study once again showed that inside activity can be a significant bit of information to the analyst. The results on the down inside quarterly and monthly charts show that more than 8 out of 10 cases resolve themselves by turning the chart up. If at the end of a given month, a stock has a down inside plot, you have excellent odds (82%) that a prior month's high will be exceeded before the recent low is taken out.

Another advantage of the swing chart plot is the ability to see chart patterns very clearly. In addition to the familiar head and shoulders pattern, double and triple tops and bottoms are easy to see. I have observed a pattern that has shown up as a major top or bottom formation. I call it the "X" pattern. Chart #1 shows this pattern starting with the low marked "X" in 1962. The next 3 lows are all higher than "X" and low #2 is lower than low #1, and #3 is lower than #2. When the chart turns up after this type of set up, the odds are quite high that a significant advance will occur. The degree of the chart increases its significance. A yearly "X" buy pattern is much more bullish than a daily one.

Another pattern I have found to be useful is what I call the "Y" pattern (it has nothing to do with the shape of the letter y). This pattern is most often found on the weekly swing chart and is basically a rapid turning of the weekly chart over a period of 3 to 5 weeks. A recent example is the period 12/16/92 to 12/30/92 in the S & P 500 price action. Chart #3 is a plot of the action that shows this set up. The week of 12/18/92 was a two plot week as the chart turned down, made low and turned back up on the 18th. Prices rallied slightly higher the week of the 24th. During the week of the 31st, the chart turned down on Monday and made a low, turned back up on Tuesday to make a new high, and reversed down again on Wednesday to create a 3 plot week. When prices turn down for the 3rd time, a significant decline normally follows. In this case the S & P declined from 442.65 to 425.88 in only 8 trading days. Note that the zero balance plot was also signaling a last ditch rally on the final advance to 442.65.

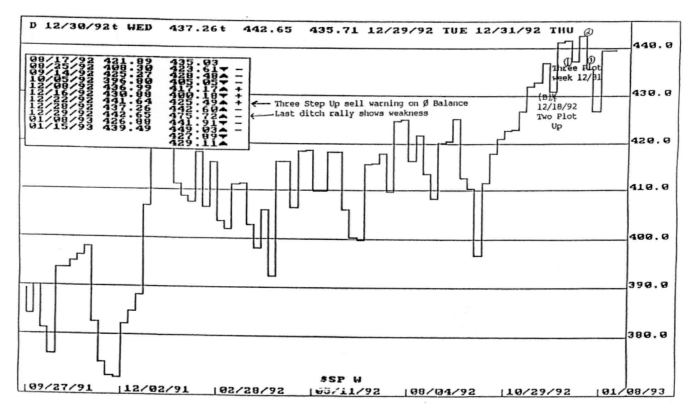

Chart 3 - Weekly Swing Chart of the S&P 500 Index

I have found that zero balance can be quite helpful even on the yearly swing charts. Chart #1 shows an example of a 3 step sell signal in 1968 that showed strength alerting you to expect the next upswing to go to new highs. This occurred like clock work in January, 1973. When the yearly chart turned down at 883.39 on May 21, 1973, the expectation should have been for a severe bear market to develop. The next 18 months proved this expectation of be correct.

Another big advantage of the swing charts is the ability to check the price action on all of the time periods at the same time. I call this the "wheels of time" concept of cycle analysis. If you study a yearly and quarterly chart of a stock and find them both up you may find that a major reaction on the daily and weekly chart is only setting up a higher low on the monthly or quarterly chart. I have found that it is quite common for a stock or index to trace out on ABC correction on the weekly or monthly chart turning many analysts bearish. In reality, all that is happening is a turn down in the chart of next higher degree—in this case the monthly or quarterly which could now be set up to create a higher low. In his books and courses, W. D. Gann stated that in a very strong advance on a daily chart, prices will not react for more than two or three days before turning back up on the second or third day.

This behavior is easily seen on the daily swing chart. Chart #4 is a daily swing chart of the S & P 500 Index. From the October, 1992 low, you can count the number of reaction days, and it wasn't until mid-December that an ABC correction lasted long enough to turn the weekly chart down. This daily chart is interesting for several reasons. The chart covers the period from the October, 1992 low, through January 22, 1993. I have labeled each reaction after the low with the number of days the swing chart was down. As you can see, Gann was correct in his statement about 3 day reactions. I have labeled an "X" pattern in circles to show that this pattern shows up on daily charts as well as on charts of higher degree. In this case, the pattern turned the weekly down to create a higher low. This is shown on Chart #3 at B. Similarly, when the weekly goes into an extended correction, you must check the condition of the monthly and quarterly charts to determine if they have a chance of turning up or down. Basically, if the market is bullish, the corrections in the

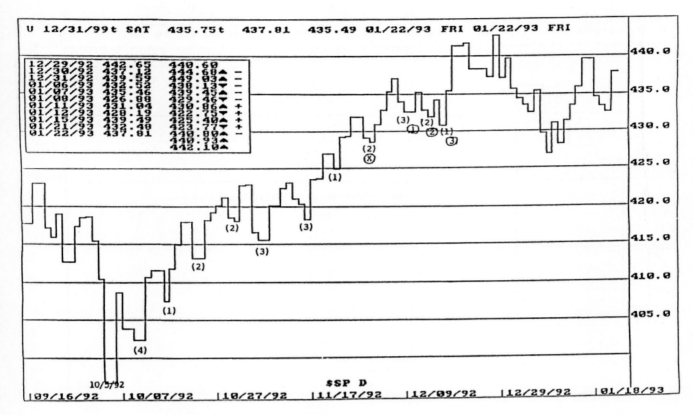

Chart 4 - Daily Swing Chart of the S&P 500 Index

weekly will cease once the monthly has turned down, giving it a chance to create a higher low. If the market is bearish, the turn up in the charts will quickly create highs and proceed to go lower.

In the August, 1992, issue of "Technical Analysis of Stocks and Commodities" magazine, I published an article on the Gann Quarterly Chart. I pointed out one of the most important characteristics of this chart was the simple fact that a large number of DJIA lows were made within 15 calendar days after the chart turned down. At the time the article was published, 14 out of 47 turndowns in the chart made a significant low within 15 calendar days. This means that in 30% of the cases, the analyst should be looking for reasons to find a low once the quarterly chart turns down. 51% of the 47 cases made their low within 60 calendar days.

The chart recently turned down once again on October 2, 1992. As of January 25, 1993, the low on the DJIA was only one trading day later on October 5, 1992; and although the chart is still down, it will turn up in the first quarter of 1993 on any penetration of 3364.90 intra day. If this occurs, it will create the sixth higher low on this chart since 1981.

NOTES ∼∼∼

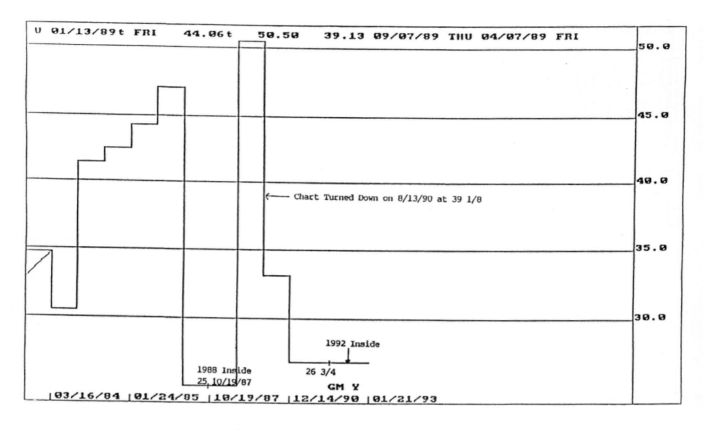

U 01/13/89t FRI   44.06t   50.50   39.13 09/07/89 THU 04/07/89 FRI

← Chart Turned Down on 8/13/90 at 39 1/8

1992 Inside

1988 Inside
25, 10/19/87

26 3/4

GM Y

|03/16/84 |01/24/85 |10/19/87 |12/14/90 |01/21/93

Chart 5 - GM Yearly Swing Chart

AN INDIVIDUAL STOCK ANALYSIS

I will now show a complete example of how I use the swing charts in my analysis of a stock to determine if it is set up for a trade. I will use GM for this purpose. Since we know that a turn down in the quarterly chart of DJIA has a 30% probability of making a low within 15 calendar days, the turn down of the DJIA quarterly on October 2, 1992, was a good time to check the positions of the DJIA stocks and GM in particular.

I start with the yearly chart. Chart #5 is the yearly swing chart of GM. I have noted the key information that you need to know about this stock's price action on the chart. As of October 5, 1992, the yearly chart had been down since August 13, 1990, when it penetrated 1989's low of 39 1/8. There was a yellow down inside bar working as 1992 was coming to an end, and in October the key 1991 low was 26 3/4. As of that time, the 1992 high was 44 3/8. The most important piece of information is that 26 3/4 low in 1991 was within the parameters of a double bottom. Since the yearly chart did not turn up in 1992, and prices were now approaching 30 again, it was a good time to proceed to the quarterly chart to see if it provided us with more significant information as to the stock's prospects.

Chart #6 is the Quarterly Chart. The key points that are readily visible when this chart is put up on the screen are as follows: (1) There are 4 up inside periods since 1984, and 3 of 4 preceded a turndown in the chart. (2) There is only one down inside quarter and it led to a significant advance. These results are in line with the expected results shown in Tables 3 and 4. (3) The latest quarterly turndown occurred in August 20, 1992, when the price broke 36. This tells us that if GM is bullish, a low should appear within 60 calendar days. This time window ends on October 19, 1992, exactly. We also know that if the price makes a low between 30 3/8 and 26 3/4 a head and shoulders bottom will appear on the chart. If price turns up in this range, an M4 pattern will be completed which according to Merrills book *M & W Wave Patterns* has a 73.3% buy rating on stocks with this pattern. When the price penetrated 30 3/8, the chance for the more bullish M8 pattern was lost. If the price dropped below 26 3/4, it would give an M3 pattern, which can also be short term bullish. The information we have gleaned from a study of this chart is potentially bullish, so the next step is to look at the monthly chart.

Chart #7 is the Monthly Chart of GM. Since this is being written in hindsight, I cannot remove the price action that has occurred since October. I have labeled the up and down inside action, and once again the results show their value.

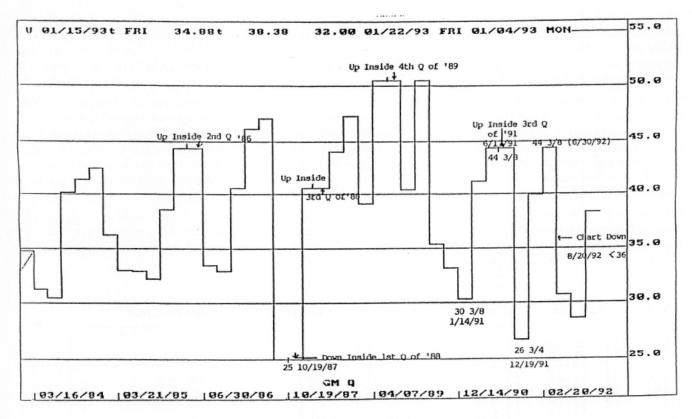

Chart 6 - GM Quarterly Swing Chart

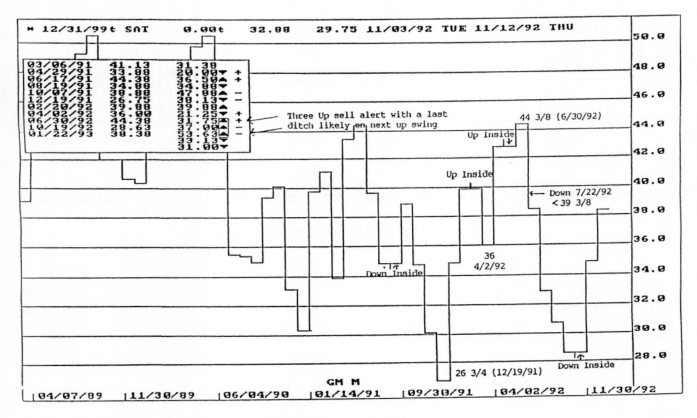

Chart 7 - GM Monthly Swing Chart

The zero balance box in the upper left hand corner of the chart shows that the 3 step up pattern that occurred in June, 1992, showed strength and that after the next low comes in, a good rally should occur. This chart in early October was giving us 2 possible "M" patterns. If the low came in above 26 ¾, we would have an M14 which has an excellent record for performance in stocks. If the 26 ¾ low was broken, an M9 pattern would be completed. The M14 is more bullish so we begin to root for GM to hold above 26 ¾.

We now shift to the weekly chart #8, and once again, I have labeled the up and down inside periods. The first thing we notice in early October is that there is a bullish 3 downstep zero balance setup. Since prices were below 33, the corresponding zero balance point, we had a warning that after a rally, a new low could occur on the next swing down. We therefore decide to wait for further developments. Sure enough, the weekly chart turned back up on October 13, and made a new high the same day. We decide that the next turndown in the chart will be the time to take a hard look at the daily. We don't have to wait long, because on October 19, 1992, exactly 60 calendar days from the day the quarterly chart turned down, the weekly turned down by penetrating the prior week's low at 28 7/8.

I do not use M & W patterns on the weekly chart at this time, but this is part of my ongoing research into this type of chart. Before moving to the daily chart on Monday the 19th, we need to know what price will turn the weekly back up. Looking at the weekly bar chart, we see that a penetration of the prior week's high of 31 5/8 will turn the chart back up, and that this price is the prior swing high on the weekly swing chart.

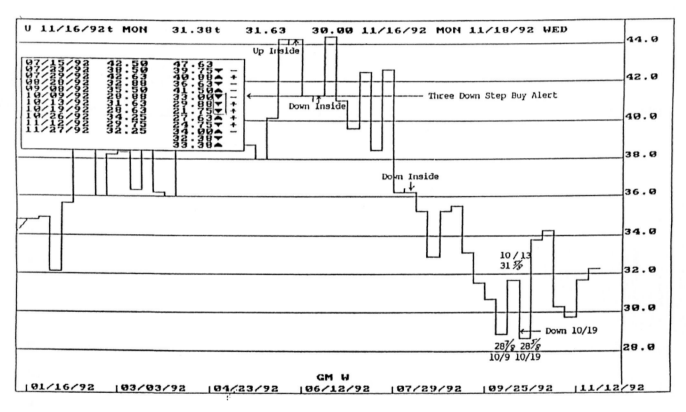

Chart 8 - GM Weekly Swing Chart

Chart #9 is the Daily Swing Chart. As you can see, it is a much busier chart. I use these charts to draw trendlines for the most part because with this method, the weekly chart is the most important. On the Daily Chart, there is a two month 5 point trendline, that once penetrated, should provide some upside fireworks. I do not pay much attention to inside periods on the daily chart because the swings are too small to worry about. It is clear after October 19, that a rally above 31 would break above this trendline. We also know that if the price exceeds 31 5/8 during the current week, a two plot back up will occur and this would be the third reversal in the weekly chart in only 10 trading days. This is a possible "Y" pattern buy setup that frequently forms near key lows. This type of action normally leads to a nice advance. The minimum I would expect is a 33% to 50% retracement from the 28 5/8 low to the 44 3/8 high on the monthly chart. This would give a minimum target of 33 7/8, which would be high enough to turn the key monthly swing chart back up.

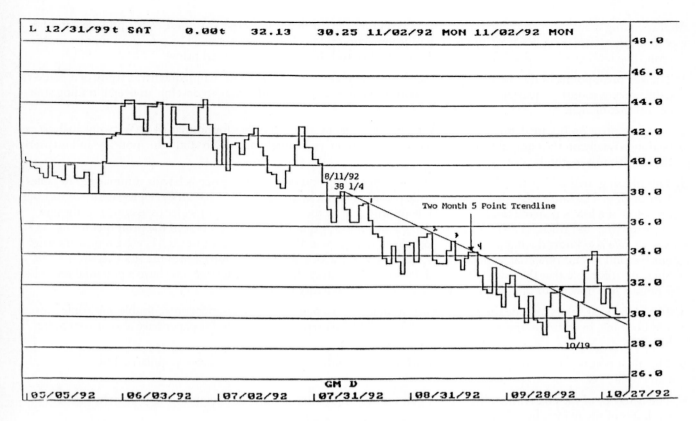

8/11/92
38 1/4

Two Month 5 Point Trendline

10/19

GM D

05/05/92   06/03/92   07/02/92   07/31/92   08/31/92   09/28/92   10/27/92

Chart 9 - GM Daily Swing Chart

In a case like this I would normally place a buy stop at the 31 ¾ level for the balance of that week, just in case prices did turn back up. This exact scenario occurred on October 22, as the price gapped open from a prior day close of 31 and proceeded to close that day at 32 7/8. This frequently happens when a two plot week occurs. The stop on this trade initially should be below the 10/19 low at 28 5/8. At the current time, the stock has traded as high as 38 3/8, turning the key monthly and quarterly charts back up.

This set up had some nice things going for it. We knew that (1) A down inside year was very close to completion. (2) An inverted head and shoulders formation was developing on the monthly and weekly charts, (3) Beginning January 1, 1993, the quarterly chart could turn up by penetration of the 4th quarter high of 34 7/8, giving us a higher low on this chart. As of January 25, 1993, the stop should be brought up to breakeven, as the monthly, quarterly, and weekly charts are all up. Since the entire year of 1992 was down inside, we now have a high probability that the yearly chart will turn up in 1993 by exceeding 44 3/8. If this occurs, it will make this a very nice trade indeed.

All of the above analysis is based on the swing charts, without the benefit of using other indicators. Obviously, with numerous programs available, I would have checked the point and figure charts, and the position of the 50 day, 200 day, 13 week, and 39 week moving averages.

THE PLOT'S DISADVANTAGES

The main disadvantage I have found using the swing charts is the lack of a volume display. Consequently, it must be used in conjunction with other types of bar chart analysis that show volume.

Another problem is the possibility that trendlines might be distorted due to the considerable number of two plot periods. This has not been as much of a problem as I once thought it was; however, it is always a good idea to print out a bar chart to check the trendlines' validity.

SUMMARY AND CONCLUSIONS

In this paper, the author has presented a method to plot swing price action on any market for any time period. The method is precisely defined and has no exceptions. Consequently, there is no price movement that can occur in a market that is not represented on the swing chart plot.

After spending many years studying the price action on these charts, it became clear that these charts provided another way to measure a market's behavior and that significant technical knowledge was obtained by plotting a market in this fashion. The key benefits derived from using this method of technical analysis are listed below.

1. The key pivot points in the market are precisely defined on any time frame chart. Consequently, a study of a market's daily, weekly, monthly, quarterly and yearly charts provides the analyst with a way to develop an overall trading strategy on that market.

2. Since the pivot points are defined by a market's own movement, the author has found that M & W swing analysis can be done visually on the computer screen. I have found it to be particularly helpful to study the monthly and quarterly charts with this method.

3. This plotting method has revealed the valuable statistics on up and down inside price behavior summarized in tables 1 through 4. The knowledge that a down inside period on a stocks quarterly chart has an 87% probability of turning up before the low is penetrated can be valuable information to the analyst. For example, let us assume it is the end of the quarter and stock XYZ has just completed a down inside quarter. The lowest plot in the prior quarter on XYZ was 38. We also know the high of the just completed quarter was 48. If the current price is 41, we can now measure our risk and reward potential. A purchase of the stock at 41 with a stop at 37 8/8 measures the risk exactly at 3 1/8. Since it is probable that the price will exceed 48 sometime during the next quarter, we now have a potential reward of 7 points. It is now up to the analyst to decide if this is a satisfactory situation.

4. The swing chart plots provide the analyst with the ability to recognize easily flags, pennants, double and triple tops and bottoms. In addition, the discovery of the "Y" and "X" patterns described in this paper have also proven quite helpful.

5. The pivot points generated by the method work very well with the zero balance concept popularized by Larry Williams.

6. The behavior of the charts when they turn up or down can give the analyst considerable insight into the strength or weakness of the market being analyzed

BIBLIOGRAPHY

1. Blair, Scott A., "Jerry Favors On Interpreting The Gann Swing Charts," *MTA Newsletter*, January, 1991.

2. Favors, Jerry, "Jerry Favors Analysis," 7238 Durness Drive, Worthington, Ohio.

3. Gann, W. D., *How To Make Profits In Commodities*, Lambert-Gann Publishing, Pomeroy, Washington, 1976.

4. Gann, W. D., *Stock Market Course*, Lambert-Gann Publishing, Pomeroy, Washington.

5. Gann, W. D., *45 Years In Wall Street*, Lambert-Gann Publishing, Pomeroy, Washington.

6. Gann, W. D., *New Stock Trend Indicator*, Lambert-Gann Publishing, Pomeroy, Washington.

7. Hesler, Curtis, J., *The Three Signals of Dynamic Price Movement*, Professional Timing Service.

8. Hill, John R., *Stock & Commodity Market Trend Trading by Advanced Technical Analysis*, Commodity Research Institute LTD, Henderson, NC, 1977.

9. Merrill, Arthur A., *Filtered Waves: Basic Theory*, Analysis Press, Box 228, Chappaqua, NY 10504, 1977.

10. Merrill, Arthur A., *M & W Wave Patterns*, Analysis Press, Box 228, Chappaqua, NY 10514, 1979.

11. Reif, David C., "The Gann Quarterly Revisited," *Technical Analysis of Stocks & Commodities*, August, 1992.

Footnotes:

(1) All of the swing charts in this paper were created by a proprietary program developed by Mr. Ed Kasanjian of Kasanjian Research, P.O. Box 4608, Blue Jay, California 92317 (909-337-0816).

REIF SWING CHART PLOTTING RULES

1. A Period can represent any time period from a 5 minute bar chart up to a yearly bar chart. The data file must include the open, high, low and close for the period.

2. A Confirmed High is the highest price traded from the time the plot turned up until it turns down.

3. A Confirmed Low is the lowest price traded from the time the plot turned down until it turns up.

4. The Swing Chart is plotted from a confirmed high (low) to a confirmed low (high) in an alternating fashion. It is not possible to have two confirmed highs (lows) in a row, without a confirmed low (high) in between them.

5. When the chart is up, it can only turn down by penetrating the prior periods low, or a confirmed low that was created during that same period.

6. When the chart is down, it can only turn up by penetrating the prior period's high or a confirmed high that was created that same period.

7. An "up inside" no plot period is created when the chart is up, and the current period's low is higher than or equal to the prior period's low. In addition, the current period's high must be less than or equal to the prior period's high, or the highest price plotted in the current upswing.

8. A "down inside" no plot period is created when the chart is down and the current period's high is less than or equal to the prior period's high. In addition, the current period's low must be greater than the prior period's low or the lowest price plotted in the current downswing.

9. The period following an "inside" period can be quite tricky. Please refer to examples #1 through #4 for guidance.

10. A two or more plot period can and does occur quite frequently. If the chart is down and price goes lower than the prior period's low or the lowest low plotted in the current downtrend before reversing and taking out the prior period's high, then the chart is plotted lower first, then taken up. This action creates a confirmed low the second it turns up. If prices remain above the confirmed low for the remainder of the period, then this is a two plot period. On the other hand, if prices reverse again by penetrating the confirmed low of that same period, then a confirmed high is created. This action is a 3 plot period with a confirmed low followed by a confirmed high, both occurring in the same period.

The same action can occur when you go into the current period in an uptrend. If the chart is up and prices trade higher than the period or the highest price plotted in the current uptrend before reversing and taking out the prior period's low, then the chart is plotted higher first then taken down. This action creates a confirmed high the second the chart turns down. It prices remain below the confirmed high for the remainder of the period, this is a two plot period. On the other hand, if price then reverses back up and penetrates the confirmed high just created, you have a three plot period with a confirmed high followed by a confirmed low, both occurring during the same period.

	MO / YR	RESOLVED	CLOSE INSIDE MONTH	% CHANGE NEXT CONFIRMED H/L	
				UP	DOWN
1	4/29	UP	319.30	3.66	
2	12/29	UP	248.50	19.64	
3	8/30	UP	240.40	2.83	
4	1/31	UP	168.90	16.64	
5	8/33	UP	102.40	5.18	
6	6/34	DOWN	95.80		11.69
7	9/34	UP	92.50	17.08	
8	5/36	UP	152.60	22.15	
9	12/37	UP	121.60	11.02	
10	5/38	UP	107.80	35.71	
11	2/39	UP	147.30	3.67	
12	12/39	UP	150.00	2.20	
13	3/40	UP	147.50	3.12	
14	3/41	UP	122.70	2.10	
15	1/42	DOWN	109.40		15.26
16	5/42	UP	100.90	45.09	
17	12/43	UP	135.90	2.21	
18	3/46	UP	199.60	6.91	
19	11/46	UP	169.80	8.95	
20	12/48	UP	177.30	2.93	
21	4/49	DOWN	174.10		7.75
22	3/52	DOWN	269.50		5.49
23	5/53	DOWN	272.30		4.22
24	6/56	UP	492.80	6.19	
25	3/57	UP	474.80.	10.17	
26	12/57	UP	435.70	5.53	
27	3/58	UP	446.80	34.67	
28	10/59	UP	646.00	6.43	
29	8/60	DOWN	626.00		9.87
30	10/61	UP	703.90	5.31	
31	2/62	UP	708.10	2.68	
32	7/62	UP	597.90	4.03	
33	7/65	UP	881.70	10.01	
34	9/66	DOWN	774.20		4.97
35	3/69	UP	935.50	4.21	
36	8/69	UP	836.70	1.11	
37	6/70	UP	683.50	40.18	
38	6/74	DOWN	802.40		28.56
39	6/77	DOWN	916.30		19.59

40	12/77	DOWN	831.20		11.36
41	12/78	UP	805.00	9.89	
42	6/79	UP	842.00	7.47	
43	4/80	UP	817.10	19.01	
44	10/81	UP	852.60	5.38	
45	4/84	UP	1170.80	2.02	
46	5/87	UP	2291.60	19.86	
47	12/87	UP	1938.80	8.88	
48	9/88	UP	2112.90	3.89	
49	11/89	UP	2706.30	4.72	
50	2/90	UP	2627.30	15.11	
51	7/92	DOWN	3391.30		8.96
52	9/92	DOWN	3271.70		5.63
53	7/94	UP	3764.50	5.53	
54	12/94	UP	3834.40	37.35	
55	8/96	UP	5616.21	27.46	
56	11/97	UP	7823.12	4.94	
57	7/00	UP	10521.98	9.47	
58	10/01	UP	9075.14	14	
59	2/02	UP	10106.13	6.16	
60	8/02	DOWN	8663.50		17.15
61	4/04	DOWN	10225.57		3.95
62	2/05	UP	10766.23	2.42	
63	5/05	UP	10467.48	?	
	TOTAL	UP = 48	77%		
		DOWN = 14	23%		
			AVE	11.36	11.03
			MEDIAN	6.31	9.42

	MO / YR	RESOLVED	CLOSE INSIDE MONTH	% CHANGE NEXT CONFIRMED H/L	
				UP	DOWN
1	3/31	DOWN	172.40		30.45
2	8/38	DOWN	139.30		8.18
3	12/38	DOWN	154.40		11.85
4	10/39	DOWN	151.90		4.61
5	9/41	DOWN	126.80		26.89
6	8/42	UP	106.30	37.72	
7	11/47	DOWN	179.50		8.58
8	5/55	UP	424.90	11.01	
9	12/55	UP	488.40	0.51	
10	7/61	UP	705.40	3.98	
11	12/61	DOWN	731.10		6.05
12	3/65	UP	889.10	6.26	
13	6/68	DOWN	897.80		3.84
14	5/71	DOWN	907.80		8.03
15	6/72	DOWN	929.00		3.11
16	9/72	DOWN	953.30		3.80
17	2/79	UP	808.80	9.37	
18	7/83	DOWN	1199.20		3.93
19	9/84	DOWN	1206.70		4.02
20	10/86	UP	1877.80	29.32	
21	3/89	UP	2293.60	22.48	
22	7/91	DOWN	3024.80		6.23
23	9/91	DOWN	3016.80		3.03
24	2/92	UP	3267.71	1.55	
25	6/93	DOWN	3516.10		2.07
26	2/94	DOWN	3832.00		8.12
27	6/96	DOWN	5654.63		8.57
28	12/98	UP	9181.43	22.47	
29	5/00	DOWN	10522.23		3.43
30	7/03	UP	9233.80	16.91	
31	2/99	UP	9306.58	20.82	
	TOTAL	UP = 12	39%		
		DOWN = 19	61%		
			AVE	15.20	8.15
			MEDIAN	13.96	6.05

Appendix C - DJIA QUARTERLY DOWN INSIDE

	QTR / YR	RESOLVED	CLOSE INSIDE QTR	% CHANGE NEXT CONFIRMED H/L	
				UP	DOWN
1	1/30	UP	286.10	3.91	
2	3/31	DOWN	172.40		76.45
3	3/40	UP	132.60	4.68	
4	1/49	DOWN	177.10		9.32
5	1/58	UP	446.80	54.03	
6	2/60	DOWN	640.60		11.93
7	3/62	UP	579.00	63.18	
8	3/70	UP	760.70	25.95	
9	2/74	DOWN	802.40		28.96
10	1/79	UP	862.20	4.95	
11	2/80	UP	867.90	18.79	
12	4/81	DOWN	875.00		12.00
13	1/88	UP	1988.10	52.12	
14	3/00	DOWN	10650.92		10.13
15	4/01	UP	10021.50	7.06	
16	1/03	UP	7992.13	35.07	
	AVE			26.97	24.80
	MEDIAN			22.37	11.97
	16 CASES	6 DOWN	37.50%		
		10 UP	62.50%		

Appendix C - DJIA QUARTERLY UP INSIDE

	QTR / YR	RESOLVED	CLOSE INSIDE QTR	% CHANGE NEXT CONFIRMED H/L	
				UP	DOWN
1	4/32	DOWN	60.30		17.58
2	4/39	DOWN	150.00		26.40
3	4/47	DOWN	181.20		9.44
4	1/52	DOWN	269.50		5.49
5	3/56	DOWN	475.30		3.13
6	4/59	UP	679.40	1.30	
7	2/76	UP	1002.80	2.34	
8	4/84	UP	1211.60	126.70	
9	3/92	DOWN	3271.70		5.63
10	4/94	UP	3834.40	52.12	
	AVE			45.62	11.28
	MEDIAN			27.23	7.54
	10 TOTAL	4 UP	40%		
		6 DOWN	60%		

Case #	Date Chart Turned Down	Price Turn Down	Date of Low	Price Low	Turn Down to Low % Decline	CAL Days Turn Down to Low	Date Prior High	CAL Days High to Low	% Decline High to Low
1	10/03/29	332.20	11/13/29	195.40	41.20	41	09/03/29	71	49.39
2	06/12/30	241.80	07/08/32	40.60	83.20	757	04/16/30	814	86.34
3	02/16/33	55.60	02/27/33	49.70	10.61	11	09/08/32	172	38.94
4	10/19/33	84.50	10/20/33	83.60	1.07	1	07/18/33	93	24.34
5	05/07/34	96.30	07/26/34	84.60	12.15	80	02/05/34	171	24.40
6	04/30/36	141.60	04/30/36	141.50	0.07	0	04/06/36	24	13.24
7	04/08/37	177.00	06/17/37	163.30	7.74	70	03/10/37	99	16.51
8	09/07/37	163.30	03/31/38	97.50	40.29	205	08/16/37	227	48.66
9	01/23/39	142.60	04/11/39	120.00	15.85	67	11/10/38	141	24.48
10	01/15/40	144.90	06/10/40	110.40	23.81	147	09/13/39	271	30.03
11	01/20/41	127.80	05/01/41	114.80	10.17	97	11/08/40	174	17.29
12	10/09/41	122.50	04/28/42	92.70	24.33	231	07/22/41	280	29.29
13	11/08/43	133.90	11/30/43	128.90	3.73	22	07/15/43	138	11.95
14	07/23/46	198.50	10/30/46	160.50	19.14	99	05/29/46	154	24.79
15	04/14/47	170.10	05/19/47	161.40	5.11	35	02/10/47	98	12.76
16	01/20/48	175.20	02/11/48	164.10	6.33	22	07/25/47	201	12.57
17	09/27/48	176.00	06/14/49	160.60	8.75	260	06/14/48	365	17.43
18	07/11/50	205.90	07/13/50	195.40	5.10	2	06/12/50	29	14.75
19	04/24/52	257.40	05/01/52	254.70	1.05	7	09/14/51	230	8.22
20	10/15/52	267.10	10/23/52	262.00	1.91	8	08/11/52	73	6.93
21	04/01/53	277.60	09/15/53	254.40	8.36	167	01/05/53	253	13.79
22	10/10/55	445.70	10/11/55	433.20	2.80	1	09/23/55	18	11.57
23	10/01/56	474.20	11/29/56	460.40	2.91	59	04/09/56	234	12.20
24	02/11/57	460.40	02/12/57	453.10	1.59	1	01/04/57	39	13.60
25	08/26/57	473.10	10/22/57	416.20	12.03	57	07/16/57	41	20.44
26	01/29/60	624.60	10/25/60	564.20	9.67	270	01/06/60	293	17.92
27	01/18/62	693.10	06/25/62	524.60	24.31	158	11/15/61	222	29.23
28	06/14/65	865.10	06/29/65	832.70	3.75	15	05/14/65	46	11.86
29	03/03/66	924.40	10/10/66	735.70	20.41	221	02/09/66	243	26.51
30	11/03/67	853.20	03/22/68	817.60	4.17	140	09/26/67	178	14.08
31	01/07/69	932.90	02/25/69	895.40	4.02	49	12/02/68	85	9.98
32	06/12/69	895.40	05/26/70	627.50	29.92	348	05/14/69	377	35.63
33	07/29/71	866.30	11/23/71	790.70	8.73	178	04/28/71	209	17.41
34	07/13/72	917.40	07/18/72	900.10	1.89	5	05/30/72	49	8.11
35	03/23/73	917.10	08/22/73	845.50	7.80	152	01/11/73	223	20.77
36	11/20/73	845.50	12/09/74	570.00	32.58	384	10/29/73	406	42.86
37	10/01/75	785.80	10/01/75	780.80	0.64	0	07/15/75	78	12.19
38	10/06/76	954.10	11/10/76	917.90	3.79	35	09/22/76	49	10.56
39	03/30/77	917.90	03/01/78	736.80	19.73	336	01/03/77	422	26.89

Case #	Date Chart Turned Down	Price Turn Down	Date of Low	Price Low	Turn Down to Low % Decline	CAL Days Turn Down to Low	Date Prior High	CAL Days High to Low	% Decline High to Low
40	10/30/78	800.90	11/14/78	779.10	2.72	15	09/11/78	64	15.06
41	10/19/79	818.00	11/08/79	792.20	3.15	20	10/05/79	34	12.45
42	03/17/80	792.20	03/27/80	730.00	7.85	10	02/13/80	43	20.50
43	07/02/81	956.70	08/09/82	770.00	19.51	403	04/27/81	469	25.32
44	02/01/84	1208.70	07/25/84	1078.30	10.79	175	11/30/83	238	16.86
45	10/15/87	2391.30	10/20/87	1616.20	32.41	5	08/25/87	56	41.16
46	08/17/90	2627.70	10/11/90	2344.30	10.78	55	07/17/90	86	22.48
47	12/11/91	2836.30	12/11/91	2832.30	0.14	0	11/01/91	40	8.40
48	10/02/92	3200.90	10/05/92	3087.40	3.55	3	06/02/92	125	10.12
49	04/04/94	3544.10	04/04/94	3520.80	0.66	0	01/31/94	63	12.04
50	07/15/96	5327.74	07/16/96	5170.11	2.96	1	05/23/96	74	11.36
51	04/14/97	6318.96	04/14/97	6315.84	0.05	0	03/11/97	34	11.77
52	10/27/97	7556.23	10/28/97	6936.45	8.20	1	08/07/97	82	16.83
53	08/04/98	8524.55	09/01/98	7379.70	13.43	28	07/17/98	46	21.59
54	10/15/99	10055.20	10/18/99	9884.20	1.70	3	08/25/99	54	13.52
55	02/24/00	9884.20	10/18/00	9571.40	3.16	237	01/14/00	278	19.63
56	03/21/01	9571.40	03/22/01	9047.56	5.47	1	01/04/01	77	19.39
57	09/17/01	9303.05	09/21/01	7926.93	14.79	4	05/21/01	123	30.69
58	06/07/02	9443.32	10/10/02	7177.66	23.99	125	03/08/02	216	33.10
59	05/10/04	9975.86	10/25/04	9660.18	3.16	168	02/19/04	249	10.51
60	04/14/05	10317.10	?	?	?	?	03/07/05	?	?
AVE					11.68	101.56		165.10	21.03
MEDIAN					7.80	41.00		125.00	17.29

Note 1 : Turn Down to Low CAL Days					Note 2 : High to Low CAL Days				
	0-5 Days = 17	28.81%				0-90 Days = 25	42.37%		
	0-30 Days= 25	42.37%				0-125 Days= 29	49.15%		
	0-60 Days= 31	52.54%							

Wheel of Price and Time

45 DEGREES
MAY 6

0 DEGREES
MAR 21

315 DEGREES
FEB 4

90 DEGREES
JUNE 21

270 DEGREES
DEC 21

135 DEGREES
AUG 8

180 DEGREES
SEPT 23

225 DEGREES
NOV 7

15° — 30° — 60° — 75° — 105° — 120° — 150° — 165° — 195° — 218° — 240° — 255° — 285° — 300° — 330° — 345°

4/6 — 4/20 — 5/21 — 6/5 — 7/7 — 7/23 — 8/23 — 9/8 — 10/8 — 10/23 — 11/22 — 12/7 — 1/6 — 1/20 — 2/19 — 3/6

Unlocking the Profits of the New Swing Chart Method

Appendix E

THE MATHEMATICS OF THE PRINCIPAL OF SQUARES

(The Gann Square of Nine)

If you look at the square of nine, you will note that the numbers going down at a 45° angle from the center are, 9, 25, 49, 81 etc. Hence each revolution of 360° starting at 1 in the center comes up to one of the above numbers. If you take the square root of each of the numbers above, you will see that the square roots are separated by 2. The square roots are 3, 5, 7, 9 etc. As a result, we now know how to convert price movements into degrees of a circle. Each revolution of 360 degrees is represented by 2, so 1 degree is equal to 2/360 or 0.0056 added to or subtracted from the square root of the number we are converting.

Let us assume that a stock has a monthly swing chart low of 25 and we want to see where the important squares going up or down are located. Let us also assume we want to know the price increments every 45 degrees up and down up to 360 degrees. To start, take the square root of 25 which equals 5. We know that 360° equals 2 added or subtracted from 5, so 360 degrees down will be 5- 2 = 3. 3 squared is equal to 9. 360 degrees up would be 5 + 2 = 7. 7 squared is 49. You can easily see these relationships on the *Gann Square of Nine Wheel*.

To get 45 degree increments, we divide 360 / 45 to get 8 increments. 2 / 8 = 0.25 which is the increment for each 45 degrees up or down. Case A shows the squares going up 360° and Case B shows the squares going down 360°.

CASE A

0°	= 25
45°	= (5.25)² = 27.56
90°	= (5.50)² = 30.25
135°	= (5.75)² = 33.06
180°	= (6.00)² = 36.00
225°	= (6.25)² = 39.06
270°	= (6.50)² = 42.25
315°	= (6.75)² = 45.56
360°	= (7.00)² = 49

CASE B

0°	= 25
-45°	= (4.75)² = 22.56
-90°	= (4.50)² = 20.25
-135°	= (4.25)² = 18.06
-180°	= (6.00)² = 16.00
-225°	= (3.75)² = 14.06
-270°	= (3.5)² = 12.25
-315°	= (3.25)² = 10.56
-360°	= (3.00)² = 9

Hence, we can now take any swing chart high or low and determine the key principal of square relationships going up or down from that price. I normally use the last quarterly swing chart high or low to begin looking to see what worked in the past. If you get several key hits going back in time from the price low or high, you can expect it to work just as well in the future.

For low priced tradeables like the EURO, unleaded gas, and low priced stocks, I have found that multiples of 3 degrees or 10 degrees work best. For high priced items like the DJIA, I have found 360 degree or 180 degree increments work best.

Appendix F - MASTER SQUARE

START 74 LOW = 62.28 ON 10/3/74					*INDICATES COMPLETED CIRCLE			
	° Degrees			° Degrees			° Degrees	
	0	62.28	6*	2160	395.68	12*	4320	1017.08
	90	70.42		2250	415.82		4410	1049.23
	180	79.06		2340	436.47		4500	1081.87
	270	88.21		2430	457.61		4590	1115.01
1*	360	97.85	7*	2520	479.25	13*	4680	1148.65
	450	107.99		2610	501.39		4770	1182.79
	540	118.63		2700	524.03		4860	1217.44
	630	129.77		2790	547.18		4950	1252.58
2*	720	141.41	8*	2880	570.82	14*	5040	1288.22
	810	153.56		2970	594.96		5130	1324.36
	900	166.2		3060	619.6		5220	1361
	990	179.33		3150	644.74		5310	1398.14
3*	1080	192.98	9*	3240	670.38	15*	5400	1435.79
	1170	207.12		3330	696.53		5490	1473.93
	1260	221.76		3420	723.17		5580	1512.57
	1350	236.91		3510	750.31		5670	1551.71
4*	1440	252.55	10*	3600	777.95	16*	5760	1591.35
	1530	268.69		3690	806.09			
	1620	285.33		3780	834.73			
	1710	302.47		3870	863.88			
5*	1800	320.15	11*	3960	893.52			
	1890	338.26		4050	923.66			
	1980	356.9		4140	954.3			
	2070	376.04		4230	985.44			

Appendix F - SIGNIFICANT HITS ON MASTER SQUARE

CASE #	DATE	INTRADAY HIGH/LOW OR CLOSE	MASTER SQUARE	SQUARE TO CLOSE % DIFFERENCE	HIGH OR LOW
1	11/29/68	108.37	107.99	0.35	HIGH
2	05/26/70	69.29	70.42	(1.60)	LOW
3	01/11/73	120.24	118.63	1.36	HIGH
4	10/03/74	62.28	DECADE LOW		LOW
5	09/21/76	107.83	107.99	(0.15)	HIGH
6	03/06/78	86.9	88.21	(1.49)	LOW
7	09/12/98	106.99	107.99	(0.93)	HIGH
8	02/13/80	118.44	118.63	(0.16)	HIGH
9	03/27/80	98.22	97.85	0.38	LOW
10	11/28/80	140.52	141.41	(0.63)	HIGH
11 *	07/17/85	196.07	192.98	1.60	HIGH
12	09/26/85	179.45	179.33	0.07	LOW
13	07/02/86	253.2	252.55	0.26	HIGH
14	08/27/86	254.24	252.55	0.67	HIGH

15	12/03/86	254.87	252.55	0.92	HIGH
16	03/26/87	302.72	302.47	0.08	HIGH
17	04/07/87	303.65	302.47	0.39	HIGH
18	08/25/87	337.89	338.26	(0.11)	HIGH
19	10/20/87	216.45	221.76	(2.39)	LOW
20	12/04/87	221.24	221.76	(0.23)	LOW
21	03/09/88	270.76	268.69	0.77	HIGH
22	05/19/88	248.85	252.55	(1.49)	LOW
23	10/24/88	283.95	285.33	(0.49)	HIGH
24	10/10/89	360.44	356.9	0.99	HIGH
25	01/03/90	360.59	356.9	1.03	HIGH
26	01/30/90	319.83	320.15	0.10	LOW
27	09/03/91	397.62	395.68	0.49	HIGH
28	01/15/92	421.18	415.82	1.29	HIGH
29	04/08/92	392.41	395.68	(0.83)	LOW
30	10/05/92	396.8	395.68	0.28	LOW
31	01/31/94	482.85	479.25	0.75	HIGH
32	04/04/94	435.86	436.47	(0.14)	LOW
33	08/07/97	964.17	954.3	1.03	HIGH
34	08/18/97	893.34	893.52	(0.02)	LOW
35	10/07/97	983.12	985.44	(0.24)	HIGH
36	10/28/97	855.27	863.88	(1.00)	LOW
37	12/05/97	986.25	985.14	0.11	HIGH
38	07/20/98	1190.58	1182.79	0.66	HIGH
39	10/08/98	923.32	923.66	(0.04)	LOW
40	04/13/99	1362.35	1361	0.10	HIGH
41	01/03/00	1478	1473.93	0.28	HIGH
42	02/28/00	1325	1324.36	0.05	LOW
43	03/24/00	1552.85	1551.71	0.07	HIGH
44	05/24/00	1361.1	1361	0.01	LOW
45	07/17/00	1517.3	1512.57	0.31	HIGH
46	11/06/00	1438.45	1435.79	0.19	HIGH
47	03/22/01	1081.2	1081.87	(0.06)	LOW
48	09/21/01	944.75	954.3	(1.00)	LOW
49	01/30/02	1081.65	1081.87	(0.02)	LOW
50	07/24/02	775.7	777.95	(0.29)	LOW
51	08/22/02	965	954.3	1.12	HIGH
52	10/10/02	768.75	777.95	(1.18)	LOW
53	12/02/02	954.32	954.3	0.00	HIGH
54	06/17/03	1015.26	1017.08	(0.18)	HIGH
55	01/26/04	1155.38	1148.65	0.59	HIGH
56	05/12/04	1076.32	1081.87	(0.51)	LOW
57	06/24/04	1146.34	1148.65	0.20	HIGH
58	01/03/05	1217.9	1217.44	0.04	HIGH

NOTES:	1) CASES LESS THAN (+/-) .25% = 23 OR 39.7%
	2) CASES LESS THAN (+/-) .50% = 31 OR 53.4%
	3) CASES LESS THAN (+/-) 1.00% = 44 OR 75.9%

Appendix G

THE REIF AVX & ACCUMULATION/DISTRIBUTION DAYS & WEEKS DEFINED

In 2002 I noticed that *Investors Business Daily* began using different percentages to define a follow through day. For many years, the paper used a 1% gain or loss on the NASDAQ index on higher volume to define an accumulation or distribution day. In 2002, they were using a 1.75% gain or loss to define an accumulation or follow through day. After thinking about this problem for some time, I decided to create the following indicator, and I called it the Reif AVX.

The Reif AVX is computed by taking the true range for today (or this week) and dividing this range by yesterdays or last weeks close. We use the absolute value and then take a 50 day (10 week) average of this percentage. I then combined this with a 50 day (10 week) average volume to give us the definition of an accumulation or distribution day or week. Hence an accumulation day (RAD), or distribution day (RDD) is a day when the percentage change is greater than the 50 day AVX and the volume is greater than the 50 day average volume, if the percentage gain was up it was accumulation and if down it was distribution, on the weekly chart we use a 10 week AVX and a 10 week MA of volume. Please note that our definition is different than IBD's because we only require volume to be greater than the average and it may or may not be greater than the prior day or week.

NOTES ~~~~~~

TRADING RESOURCES

Hit and Run Trading: *The Short-Term Stock Traders' Bible - Updated*
by Jeff Cooper

Discover winning methods for daytrading and swing trading from the man who wrote the bible on short-term trading. Jammed packed with a full arsenal of new tools and strategies to help short-term traders compete and survive in this fast-paced, volatile arena.

$100.00 Item #BC110x3156887

Hit and Run Trading II: *Capturing Explosive Short-Term Moves in Stocks - Updated*
by Jeff Cooper

Following up on his original collection of trading methods in *Hit & Run Trading*, is Jeff Cooper's second and equally exceptional book, *Hit & Run Trading Volume II*. Start increasing your profits using Coopers updated personal techniques and easy-to-master setups today!

$100.00 Item #BC110x3156887

Intra-Day Trading Strategies: *Proven Steps to Trading Profits - DVD*
by Jeff Cooper

The famous *Hit & Run Trading* author and TheStreet.com columnist unveils personal weapons for winning in short-term markets. Jeff goes beyond anything he's written, sharing his coveted intra-day strategies with you, one-on-one. He'll teach you ... - How to read intra-day charts for maximum profits - 3 principles he routinely uses to profit - Time-tested techniques for spotting unique trading set-ups - The best set-ups for volatile markets - How to pick the right entry price, place protective stops, how to prosper in tumultuous markets - and so much more. "The wealth of different patterns presented is awesome - and very usable. A truly great workshop for active traders."

$129.00 Item #BC110x1674510

A W.D. Gann Treasure Discovered: *Simple Trading Plans for Stocks & Commodities*
by Robert Krausz

This modern-day classic features a treasure-trove of proven, viable trading plans suitable for every type of trader. Based on the proven methods of trading legend W.D. Gann, this thorough work has been updated to be relevant for today's most active traders – and even includes powerful new swing trading techniques. Each plan featured provides well-defined entry & exit rules, risk management assessments and profit objectives. And, the charts and support materials are large and clear, so you can easily grasp the essence of each plan, and incorporate them into your own trading. A companion videodisc workshop is also included that clarifies each concept in detail, so you can understand exactly when, and how, to implement them. Having a solid, reliable trading plan is the only sure way to achieve consistent trading success. Now, Gann master Robert Krausz reveals numerous trading plans and trading techniques that have been proven to be profitable in all different market climates, and which have endured for decades. It's the definitive guide to Gann trading methods for today's trader.
UPDATED - COMES COMPLETE WITH VIDEODISC!

$199.00 Item #BC110x3744123

To order any book listed
Call 1-800-272-2855 ext. BC110

New Frontiers in Fibonacci Trading: *Charting Techniques, Strategies & Simple Applications*
by Michael Jardine

Traders caught at the crossroads of traditional, proven, trading techniques - and new online tools and methods - have struggled to find a way of blending the two together into a unified trading system. Now, the marriage of the methods is complete, and brought into sharp focus in *New Frontiers in Fibonacci Trading*. This groundbreaking new work combines the foundations of Fibonacci trading with classic charting techniques, modern applications, and cutting edge online analysis tools.

$59.95 Item #BC110x1739885

12 Simple Technical Indicators That Really Work - *DVD*
by Mark Larson

Discover how the right technical indicators will help you get in and out of the markets - with profits in tow. Join market educator Mark Larson, author of *Technical Charting for Profits*, as he shares his 12 favorite indicators and details how he picked them, how he tested them, and how they work together to give traders the kind of success he's enjoyed for nearly a decade. Learn why certain indicators work during certain markets, 2 indicators with a 90% accuracy record, choosing the most effective moving averages, and more. With Mark's thorough new workshop, and online support manual, you'll soon see why "Your profits are within your chart." Comes with Online Support Manual.

$99.00 Item #BC110x3384832

Charting Made Easy
by John J. Murphy

Renowned market technician John Murphy presents basic principals of technical analysis in easy-to-understand term.

He covers...

- All types of chart analysis
- "Need to know" concepts, including trendlines, moving averages, price gaps, reversal patterns, volume & open interest spreads, and more!
- Price forecasting and market timing applications
- A full resource guide of technical analysis aide
- How to use the industry's top tools to obtain a better understanding of what charts can do-and how they can help you grab your portion of today's trading profits.

$19.95 Item #BC110x11353

Moving Averages Simplified
by Clif Droke

Successful traders know that using Moving Averages can result in more profitable trades -if applied properly. But, what are Moving Averages? When -and how- should they be used? Now, noted trader Clif Droke takes the mystery out of Moving Averages by explaining them in detail, describing how they can be employed to zero in on buy/sell signals that result in more profitable trades- more often.

$29.95 Item #BC110x12169

**To order any book listed
Call 1-800-272-2855 ext. BC110**

Swing Trading Simplified
by Larry D. Spears

Learn the basics - or refine your skills - with this fast-reading swing trading primer. With a foreword by the popular "MrSwing.com" - this new guide from Larry Spears makes the powerful swing trading concepts more accessible and easier to implement than ever. Find out how to implement your own profitable program without being glued to your monitor. Simply pick your position, enter a close, and a protective stop, and go back to your day - it's that easy! Add or restore vitality to any investment program - using the simplified techniques found in *Swing Trading Simplified*.

$29.95 Item #BC110x1674501

Technical Analysis Simplified
by Clif Droke

Here's a concise, easy-reading manual for learning and implementing this invaluable investment tool. The author, a well-known technician and editor of several technical analysis newsletters, distills the most essential elements of technical analysis into a brief, easy-to-read volume.

$29.95 Item #BC110x11087

Targeting Profitable Entry & Exit Points - *DVD*
by Alan Farley

Learn what tools "Master Swing Trader" Alan Farley uses to enter and exit trades and how he maximizes his profits this way. You will be on track to master the skills necessary to know when to get in, when to get out and when to stand aside. Included in this tape are:

- his powerful swing management tools
- how to use a failure target and implement price sensitive execution
- how to adjust your methods to changing market conditions

Farley shows you how to combine Bollinger bands, fibonacci and candlesticks to isolate trades with favorable risk/reward profiles and more.

$64.95 Item #BC110x3384831

▲ ▲ ▲ ▲ ▲ ▲

**To order any book listed
Call 1-800-272-2855 ext. BC110**

Free 2 Week Trial Offer for U.S. Residents From Investor's Business Daily:

INVESTOR'S BUSINESS DAILY will provide you with the facts, figures, and objective news analysis you need to succeed.

Investor's Business Daily is formatted for a quick and concise read to help you make informed and profitable decisions.

To take advantage of this free 2 week trial offer, e-mail us at customerservice@traderslibrary.com or visit our website at www.traderslibrary.com where you find other free offers as well.

You can also reach us by calling 1-800-272-2855 or fax us at 410-964-0027.